D1011440

YOU ARE NOT FORGOTTEN

THE STORY OF A LOST WWII PILOT
AND A TWENTY-FIRST-CENTURY SOLDIER'S MISSION
TO BRING HIM HOME

Bryan Bender

W GUINEA CAMPAIGN ★ WORLD WAR II ★ UNITED STATES MARINE COR
BAUL ★ FIGHTER PILOTS ★ F4U CORSAIR ★ BOUGAINVILLE COAS
EW GUINEA CAMPAIGN ★ UNITED STATES MARINE CORPS ★ JPAC
HTER PILOTS ★ F4U CORSAIR ★ BOUGAINVILLE COAST ★ NEW GUIN
MPAIGN ★ WORLD WAR II ★ UNITED STATES MARINE CORPS ★ RABAU
F4U CORSAIR ★ BOUGAINVILLE COAST ★ NEW GUINEA CAMPAIGN
RLD WAR II ★ UNITED STATES ARMY ★ RABAUL ★ FIGHTER PILOT
F4U CORSAIR ★ BOUGAINVILLE COAST ★ NEW GUINEA ★ WORLD WA
A ★ UNITED STATES MARINE CORPS ★ KIOWA ★ FIGHTER PILOTS ★ F4
RSAIR ★ BOUGAINVILLE COAST ★ NEW GUINEA CAMPAIGN ★ WOR
R II ★ UNITED STATES MARINE CORPS ★ IRAQ ★ FIGHTER PILOTS
A ★ F4U CORSAIR   W GUINEA CAMPAIC

you are not forgotten

WORLD WAR II ★   S ★ FIGHTER PILO
J CORSAIR ★ JPAC ★ BOUGAINVILLE COAST ★ NEW GUINEA CAMPAIGN
RLD WAR II ★ UNITED STATES ARMY ★ RABAUL ★ FIGHTER PILO
F4U CORSAIR ★ AFGHANISTAN ★ NEW GUINEA CAMPAIGN ★ WORL
R II ★ UNITED STATES MARINE CORPS ★ RABAUL ★ FIGHTER PILOTS
J CORSAIR ★ BOUGAINVILLE COAST ★ NEW GUINEA CAMPAIGN
RLD WAR II ★ UNITED STATES MARINE CORPS ★ RABAUL ★ FIGHT
OTS ★ F4U CORSAIR ★ JPAC ★ KIOWA★ NEW GUINEA CAMPAIC
WORLD WAR II ★ MIA ★ UNITED STATES ARMY ★ AFGHANISTA
BAUL ★ F4U CORSAIR ★ BOUGAINVILLE COAST ★ WORLD WAR II
UNITED STATES MARINE CORPS ★ FIGHTER PILOTS ★ F4U CORSAIR
UGAINVILLE COAST ★ AFGHANISTAN ★ WORLD WAR II ★ UNITI
ATES MARINE CORPS ★ RABAUL ★ FIGHTER PILOTS ★ F4U CORSA
AFGHANISTAN ★ NEW GUINEA CAMPAIGN ★ MIA ★ WORLD WAR
ITED STATES ARMY ★ FIGHTER PILOTS ★ F4U CORSAIR ★ RABA
BOUGAINVILLE COAST ★ NEW GUINEA CAMPAIGN ★ WORLD W
★ IRAQ ★ JPAC ★ RABAUL ★ MIA ★ FIGHTER PILOTS ★ F4U CORSA
BOUGAINVILLE COAST ★ WORLD WAR II ★ UNITED STATES MARI

 Doubleday *New York London Toronto Sydney Auckland*

All rights reserved. Published in the United States by Doubleday,
a division of Random House, Inc., New York, and in Canada by
Random House of Canada Limited, Toronto.

www.doubleday.com

DOUBLEDAY and the portrayal of an anchor with a dolphin are
registered trademarks of Random House, Inc.

Book design by Maria Carella
Jacket design by Michael J. Windsor
Jacket photogrraph © Travel Image UIG/Getty Images

Library of Congress Cataloging-in-Publication Data
Bender, Bryan.
You are not forgotten : the story of a lost WWII pilot and a twenty-first-century
soldier's mission to bring him home / Bryan Bender. — First edition.
pages cm
1. World War, 1939–1945—Repatriation of war dead—United States. 2. World War,
1939–1945—Missing in action—Papua New Guinea. 3. Iraq War, 2003–2011—
Aerial operations, American. 4. Eyster, George Senseny, V, 1973– 5. McCown,
Marion Ryan, Jr., 1917–1944. 6. Air pilots, Military—United States—Biography.
7. United States. Army—Officers—Biography. 8. United States. Marine Corps—
Officers—Biography. 9. Joint POW/MIA Accounting Command (U.S.) I. Title.
D810.D4B46 2013
940.54'26585092—dc23   2012036354

ISBN 978-0-385-53517-5

MANUFACTURED IN THE UNITED STATES OF AMERICA

1   3   5   7   9   10   8   6   4   2

First Edition

To Maria Cristina, whose love and support has no ending

And to the "one percent," and their families,
who volunteer to serve on our behalf

CONTENTS

YOU ARE NOT FORGOTTEN

*It is not the oath that makes us believe the man,
but the man the oath.*

AESCHYLUS

High on a slope in New Guinea
the Grumman Hellcat
lodges among bright vines
as thick as arms. In 1943,
the clenched hand of a pilot
glided it here
where no one has ever been.

In the cockpit, the helmeted
skeleton sits
upright, held
by dry sinews at neck
and shoulder, and webbing
that straps the pelvic cross
to the cracked
leather of the seat, and the breastbone
to the canvas cover
of the parachute.

Or say that the shrapnel
missed him, he flew
back to the carrier, and every
morning takes the train, his pale
hands on his black case, and sits
upright, held
by the firm webbing.

DONALD HALL, "The Man in the Dead Machine"

PROLOGUE

On an autumn afternoon in 2009, two old friends, both approaching ninety, stood a little taller than usual beneath the glass-paned spire of the National Museum of the Marine Corps. Richard "Cosmo" Marsh and Eugene "Vic" Smith slowly lifted their eyes toward one of the restored fighter planes hanging from the ceiling. It was a Corsair, just like the ones they had flown in the South Pacific. Both men were now frail after lifetimes of living, loving, working, and raising large families. But they still burned with the inner fire sparked more than six decades earlier while fending off swarms of Japanese Zeros in a hailstorm of burning metal and lead. The pair of fliers—two of just six surviving members of the forty "Hell's Angels" who set sail for war in September 1943—made this pilgrimage to the gleaming new museum in Quantico, Virginia, to complete one final mission.

Cosmo, who had left Yale University to join the Marine Corps after Pearl Harbor, had earned his nickname for his "cosmopolitan" background. Nearly as wispy as he had been as a twenty-two-year-old lieutenant, he still worked part-time in the Washington, D.C., law firm he co-founded after the war and where he had penned the squadron's newsletter, kept up the Christmas card list, and planned the reunions—the last one held in California in 2000. On one wall in front of his desk hung a nearly life-sized black-and-white photograph of the Hell's Angels, taken in the Solomon Islands in December 1943, all of them young and vigorous and looking invincible as they prepared to enter the jaws of the enemy.

His companion Vic Smith was still the perennially grinning Ohio farm boy who signed up for flight training as a student at Ohio State in the aftermath of the surprise Japanese attack. Though his once-taut muscles had atrophied, he still exuded the pep and wide-eyed exuberance that had made him a squadron favorite. Smitty, as many called him, had flown home after the war in a Stearman biplane, landing on a grass field near his rural boyhood home, where he still lived and helped run his machinery and warehousing business—that is, when he wasn't traveling to San Diego to visit his grandkids and sail in his beloved schooner. Back in 1987, Vic and his wife had sailed across the South Pacific, returning to the scene of some of those ferocious battles.

Vic and Cosmo had cemented an especially strong bond when they seemed destined to die at Rabaul like so many of their comrades but their fates intertwined to save them both. By late January 1944, the Hell's Angels had already suffered many losses. They had been assigned another mission to escort B-25s on a bombing run over the Japanese stronghold on the tip of New Britain Island when Vic's Corsair was hit by debris from a nearby Allied plane that was riddled with anti-aircraft fire. He had to ditch in the dreaded channel, and none of his fellow pilots saw where he went down. To avoid being spotted by the Japanese, he waited until nightfall to deploy his lifeboat, floating for hours with only the aid of his life preserver. Night turned to day with no sign of the hoped-for flying boats, or Dumbos, that served as rescue planes. Tuckered out, Vic finally fell asleep under more stars than he had ever seen. He was dreaming of hunting raccoons with his uncle back in Ohio when he was startled awake by the barking of sea lions surrounding his small inflatable raft. He had been resourceful, but he was also lucky. December and January were the only months when the current in St. George's Channel traveled northwest to southwest, away from Rabaul and the Japanese torturers. All day and through the night, he drifted nearly fifty miles, until he could make out the landmark of New Ireland.

Back at their base in the Solomon Islands, Cosmo took off on another bomber escort. Approaching the target, he experienced engine trouble and also splashed into the channel near Rabaul. This time, his wingman saw where he went down and swooped in to get a better look at the surroundings, taking readings off the nearby mountains. One of the Dumbos was swiftly dispatched to search for him. Along the flight path the crew spotted Vic, still floating in his life raft from the previous day.

The crew landed and swiftly pulled Vic in before continuing on to Cosmo's reported position. When it was Cosmo's turn to be pulled through the gun ports to safety, Vic greeted his surprised—and doubly relieved—friend with a broad smile. For the rest of his long life Vic liked to quip that the best thing that ever happened to him was that his friend Cosmo had crashed off Rabaul. If he hadn't, he probably never would have been found. He showed his appreciation by making trips to Washington, D.C., every few years to visit his friend in the Maryland suburbs and bought him gifts, such as a winter jacket with the Marine Corps seal on the back.

More than six decades after the war, their journey this day to Quantico, the "Crossroads of the Marine Corps," was for a singular purpose. Cosmo and Vic had come to bestow a special honor on the comrades who went "up the line" with them but weren't so lucky—the ones deprived of the full life that they had embraced with the vigor of men who had watched their friends die and had come perilously close to losing it all themselves. The toll that first tour had taken on their rookie squadron was painfully evident by the two group photographs—the one hanging in Cosmo's office, taken just before they went into combat, the other aboard the USS *Guam*, just after that first tour in the South Pacific. The first had all forty pilots, the other just twenty-three. In their brotherhood of fighter pilots, where the cold simplicity of mathematical odds had reigned supreme, Vic and Cosmo knew the Hell's Angels who never returned lost in the grandest poker game of all. But in a real way, they also felt those who hadn't returned had played their last hand so that the rest of them didn't have to. For every one of the cots that were swiftly removed from their tents when one of their fellow Hell's Angels hadn't returned from a mission, Vic and Cosmo knew their own odds improved. Their comrades had died for the country, yes, but in a very real way they had also died for them.

As their skipper had written to the distraught mother of one of them, "We live for each other a great deal out here, much more than they do at home, I fear—and sometimes we also die for each other."

Now, before they joined their lost comrades, Vic and Cosmo

needed to make sure they were remembered. They came to Quantico to purchase bricks etched with their names at the Marine Corps museum's Semper Fidelis Memorial Park.

There would be one for Newton "Zombie" Blount, the former boxing champion who had been killed in action right after they arrived in the combat zone. Another was for Harvey Carter, the daredevil pilot with the mustache who seemed invincible before he disappeared after a dogfight with a Zero. Nearby would be engraved the name of Roger Brindos, the debonair card shark, who tragically died in captivity when the Japanese POW camp where he was imprisoned was hit by Allied bombs. Vic had owed Brindos four hundred dollars in poker losses when he went down—money he duly sent home to his widow, Patricia. Another spot was reserved for Robert Marshall, whom they remembered as a quiet kid from Louisiana with a toothy grin and gentle southern manner, who had crashed into nearby Simpson Harbor and died either in the crash or from his injuries in a Japanese POW camp. No one really knew for sure. His body had never been recovered, either. In all, there were the names of sixteen Hell's Angels who were either killed or missing.

One memorial stone they donated, labeled 12203, was placed along the plaza in front of the museum. It was etched with "Captain Marion Ryan McCown Jr."

Vic could still picture "Pop" McCown, or, as others in the squadron called him, Mac. How in his genteel manner, a corncob pipe often perched on his lip, he watched over the younger pilots, lifted their spirits with much-needed words of encouragement, and always tried to see the silver lining in what were mostly miserable conditions. McCown was a more experienced pilot who helped give fresh-faced lieutenants like Vic and Cosmo confidence that they would get through this. They flew with Pop McCown on several combat missions and to search for signs of their comrades who had been shot down or crashed. All three of them—Vic, Cosmo, and Pop McCown—were among the swarms of Corsairs that went looking for the iconic Gregory "Pappy" Boyington when word reached the camp that he was missing over Rabaul.

Vic and Cosmo never had a chance to say good-bye before McCown was gone, too. They had heard so many stories of what might have been his fate that day when dozens of the enemy appeared out of the blue, but the mystery was never solved. Ryan McCown was just one of the countless names of those who were missing in action from the war.

The brick etched with his name was Vic and Cosmo's way of bidding him a final farewell and saying thank you. It was also a way, perhaps, for future generations to remember what he had done. They didn't know it that fall day in 2009, but Vic and Cosmo weren't the only ones who had not forgotten Ryan.

PART ONE

The human soul can always use a new tradition.

Sometimes we require them.

Pat Conroy, *The Lords of Discipline*

CHAPTER ONE

THE LEGACY

Almost from the day he was born, July 2, 1974, George Senseny Eyster V thought everyone's dad wore Army green to work. The first time he held him in his arms, in the maternity ward of the base hospital at Fort Carson, Colorado, George's father was wearing the uniform of a second lieutenant and the maroon beret of the Army Airborne Corps. The backdrops for George's baby pictures were the trappings of Army life: as an infant donning "Big George's" drab-green Army cap, or as a toddler grinning on his father's lap in the passenger seat of an Army jeep.

His mother, meanwhile, was the epitome of an Army wife. The former Ann Pate, with her southern charm and beauty-queen good looks, was the daughter of a retired Army Air Corps pilot who had been serving in the Pacific during World War II when she was born. She spent the first year of her life being taught to kiss a framed photograph of her poppa. George's father had been captivated by her when he met her as an ROTC cadet at Florida State University. They were soon married in the base chapel at Patrick Air Force Base on December 28, 1971. Ann, who had a son, Scott, and a daughter, Teri, from a previous marriage, quickly took to her new role, hosting coffees for other Army wives, coordinating sewing demonstrations, and organizing the unit Christmas party when her husband was a young company commander.

"Little George" was born just a few months after a historic shift in the American armed forces: the end of the military draft. Growing up an Army brat in the all-volunteer military meant coming of age in a largely closed society that only occasionally interacted with the outside world. The military was the Eyster family's life, which meant moving every few years to a different assignment, where there were sometimes as many old faces from previous posts as new ones. By the time George was eight, in 1981, the family had moved from Fort Carson to Stuttgart, Germany, to Fort Bragg, North Carolina. Most of the kids George went to school with, and nearly all his friends and neighbors, also had parents in the Army. In addition to photographs of him blowing out birthday candles, the family scrapbooks were filled with shots of George standing awkwardly in front of the Brandenburg Gate and the Berlin Wall, landmarks of the Cold War that he was learning was his father's duty to prevent from becoming a full-blown one.

When George was ten, he began to more fully understand what being a soldier meant. His father was flying helicopters in the Eighty-second Airborne Division at Fort Bragg and came home one day that fall to tell him he would be going away for a while. It was October 1983, and President Ronald Reagan was ordering American combat troops to the Caribbean island of Grenada, where a military coup backed by the Cuban and Soviet governments threatened American citizens living there. The family's tearful good-bye as Big George— Major George S. Eyster IV—went off to Operation Urgent Fury was a formative experience for Little George. The fighting only lasted several days and ended with an American victory over the military government. But nineteen U.S. soldiers were killed and 116 wounded. George would never forget the anxiety on his mother's face as she awaited her husband's return.

But it was not until the following spring, when George was almost eleven and finishing fifth grade, that he realized that the faint sound of the bugler playing reveille each dawn was also for him, when he first heard the family ghosts mustering him to the march. It was a Saturday morning in early May 1984. His father was stationed at Fort Leavenworth, Kansas, where they were living on a tree-lined street of simple brick homes on the sprawling frontier base along the banks of the Missouri River. George was flipping the dial on the living room TV looking for a cartoon. His parents were busy in the kitchen preparing to host a Kentucky Derby party later that day. George was barely paying attention to the changing channels when he heard the television narrator, his voice recorded over grainy combat footage, call out to him.

"GEORGE EYSTER."

At first, he didn't understand what he was watching. He stood there transfixed, unable to move, his right hand motionless on the dial, as the sounds from the television set filled the room. With the crackle of automatic weapons fire, the program quickly trained on an anguished-looking soldier, shirtless and slumped over, as he lay dying on the jungle floor, felled by a sniper's bullet to the neck.

"Mom!" George broke into tears as he ran from the room. "I think Grandpa's on TV."

———

George never knew Grandpa George, once described as a lean, laconic man of few words who resembled film actor Gary Cooper in a military uniform (which was always freshly pressed, even in the jungle, so the story went). Lieutenant Colonel George S. Eyster III was killed in combat in Vietnam seven years before George was born. But George felt as if he knew him. The void his grandfather left behind was palpable. It defined his own father's identity and before long George's, too. Grandma Harriet, a tall, regal-looking southern lady with a warm disposition, spoke adoringly of her late husband whenever her favored grandson came to visit. Grandpa George's lingering presence could be felt at Thanksgiving dinner, on birthdays, and at other family celebrations. At times his loss brought a deep sadness to Harriet's sparkling blue eyes, but her feelings were usually well hidden. Instead, her face would grow bright when she spoke of the profession he had chosen.

More than a decade after Grandpa George's death, when the quagmire that became Vietnam was a dark stain for so many, Harriet still exhibited little bitterness about what it had cost her and her four children.

"George wanted to be a military man, he was trained for it, and we have always been proud of what he did," she told a newspaper reporter in 1977. If she had any anger at all, it was that the United States had walked away from the war, allowing the South Vietnamese capital of Saigon to fall to the North Vietnam Communists. "I don't pretend to know the political subtleties," she said, "but we could not help asking ourselves what all the loss of life was for. Yet I hate to say George's life was wasted."

Theirs, too, was a storybook Army love affair. Grandpa George and the former Harriet LaRoche both grew up in Army families. They met in high school at Fort Leavenworth and were married in the West Point chapel on June 6, 1945, Grandpa wearing his starched white cadet uniform. Harriet's father, who was serving in World War II as the chief military surgeon in the Pacific, couldn't make the ceremony. Harriet's bridegroom did not get a chance to fight in World War II, but he served in the Philippines and then on the staff of General Douglas MacArthur in postwar Japan, where Big George had been. He later led an infantry company in the Korean War. He had been one of the Army's most accomplished battalion commanders when he was cut down early in the Vietnam War.

The fact that a photographer and a war correspondent were standing just feet away when he was shot made his loss even more acute. His wife, children, and grandchildren were in effect forced to watch his violent death. Three weeks after the family first heard the news, three images of his final moments were flashed on national television. An obituary by the Associated Press published in dozens of newspapers across the country further immortalized him.

"He was the son of a general," it began, "a West Pointer and a battalion commander. But Lieutenant Colonel George Eyster was to die like a rifleman."

Harriet received twenty-two hundred letters from strangers offering condolences. After reading her husband's obituary in the *Orlando Sentinel*, she felt compelled to thank the war correspondent who chronicled his death.

"You gave his children a legacy that no one else could have by writing in such a manner that his courage and heroism will live with them and be an inspiration to them forever," she wrote.

Harriet eventually remarried—to a retired Army general of course. But she kept the memory of her first husband very much alive. She did so, in part, by making it known, not always so subtly, that his children could best honor him by living up to his example of selfless service. She was supremely proud when both of their sons followed in his footsteps and their two daughters married military officers. She clearly wanted her favored grandson, George V, to follow suit. But there was time for that.

Big George, who was away at preparatory school when he heard the tragic news from his mother, spoke little about how his father's death affected him. Whenever Little George asked him about Grandpa George, his father volunteered few insights into the man or his influence on him—other than to assure Little George that his father had been far more of a disciplinarian than he was. Only years later would George learn how his father struggled to live up to the ideal that Grandpa George set as a leader of men and how the pressure of it all steered him away from West Point and almost from becoming an Army officer altogether. Big George, too, had ultimately answered the call, earning an ROTC scholarship at Florida State University and graduating in 1971 with the real prospect that he, too, might be sent to the jungles of Vietnam.

But while Big George refrained from lionizing Grandpa George, Grandma Harriet retold stories of his bravery and heroism at every opportunity. Little George ate them up in those early years, rereading his grandfather's obituary countless times, both because he was captivated by the man and in an effort to better understand his own father. A year after he first saw the images of his dying grandfather flash across the TV, a newly published book about the battle further added to the mystique. In the book the men who had been with him that fateful day reported that before he died, Grandpa George voiced his begrudging respect for his enemy.

"Before I go," Lieutenant Colonel Eyster whispered as he gasped for breath on the jungle floor, "I'd like to talk to the guy who controls those incredible men in the tunnels." He never got the chance. After being evacuated to a field hospital, he died on January 14, 1966, at the age of forty-two.

There was a lot to live up to if you were named George Senseny Eyster. But as Little George soon learned, there was more—much more. In fact, most of his male forebears, going back seven generations, had been soldiers, serving in nearly every major conflict in the nation's history. His was a martial legacy—some might say a burden—stretching back more than two centuries to before American independence. It was a paternity that made him eligible for that most exclusive of military fraternities: the Society of the Cincinnati.

The Society of the Cincinnati is located at Anderson House, a stately fifty-room mansion on Embassy Row in Washington, D.C. Distinguishing it from the ornate diplomatic posts along Massachusetts Avenue is the statue of General George Washington standing sentry underneath the flags of the United States and France. The society was established in 1783 at the close of the American War of Independence by officers who served in the Continental Army and their French counterparts who came to their aid. Among its founders were such illustrious patriots as Lieutenant Colonel Alexander Hamilton and Major General Henry Knox. The fraternal order, which took its name from the Roman citizen-soldier Cincinnatus, is essentially the nation's oldest veterans' group—and its most exclusive.

Originally, membership was only for military officers who could trace their parentage directly back to one of the 5,795 eligible officers who served in the Continental Army during the American Revolution. Now in its third century, the society reserves membership for those with the same lineage, but they do not have to serve in the military. With the exception of the South Carolina chapter, each of the original Revolutionary officers can only be represented by one relative at a time, keeping the society exceedingly small; currently, there are roughly thirty-eight hundred members, including several hundred from the French branch. One of those Continental Army officers was George Eyster's seventh great-grandfather Wilhelm Heyser.

The family's martial lineage, recounted in some of the brittle parchment rolls kept in the secure vault in the society's library, began in the hot, turbulent summer of 1776. On July 12, a week after the signing of the Declaration of Independence, Wilhelm Heyser was commissioned a captain by the Continental Congress. He prepared to set out from his farm in the hills of western Maryland to command a company of ninety soldiers in the German Battalion of the Continental Army. Heyser, a German-speaking immigrant, was born in Holland in 1748 and came to the colonies in his teens. A physician, Freemason, and master builder of the First Reformed Church of Hagerstown, he had already demonstrated his support for the cause of his adopted land, providing "rashons and drink" for the Maryland militia and feeding a company of Continental Army soldiers. He also served on the local Committee of Observation, convened in September 1775 to raise several companies of militia and serve as a clearinghouse for intelligence on British activities in the area. Patriotic fervor was strong in the area, where there were few known loyalists to the British Crown. The mostly German and Swiss immigrants responded in large numbers to the call to arms. Local communities provided uniforms, while gunsmiths struggled to keep up with the German Battalion's training and supply needs.

After taking command, Heyser's unit was dispatched to the outskirts of Philadelphia, where its first battle orders came on Christmas morning, hours after General Washington crossed the Delaware River to launch a surprise attack against the British forces near Trenton, New Jersey. Captain Heyser, who was now going by the Americanized William, gathered with his fellow company commanders on the Pennsylvania side of the river to hear their orders:

> You are to see that your men have three days' provisions ready cooked before noon, everyone fit for duty, except a sergeant and six men to be left with the baggage, will parade with arms, accouterments, and ammunition (40 cartridges) in best order and with provisions and blankets. No man is to quit his division on pain of instant punishment. Each officer is to provide himself with a piece of white paper stuck in his hat for a field mark. You will order your men to assemble and parade them at 4 pm in the valley immediately over the hill from McKonkey's Ferry, to remain there for further orders.

By late afternoon George's seventh great-grandfather and the main body of the attacking force, a little more than five thousand men, assembled near the ferry landing. Washington ordered they be read a new tract by Thomas Paine, the pamphleteer whose writings gave voice to the American cause. The troops, some wearing woolen cloaks, others clutching blankets to shield them from the wind, stood at attention as Paine's words were read:

> These are the times that try men's souls. . . . Tyranny, like hell, is not easily conquered; yet we have this consolation with

us, that the harder the conflict, the more glorious the triumph. What we obtain too cheap, we esteem too lightly.

As darkness fell, the formation was ordered to move. The 350-strong German Battalion forded the icy waters of the Delaware around midnight, just as it began to sleet. By 4:00 a.m., they were trekking southeast across open fields with their rifles and cannons toward the main road between Trenton and Princeton. The faint sound of musket fire pierced the stillness. Just after daybreak, the enemy opened up a full attack, their cannons raining down on the Americans and splitting open the hardened winter earth. Two enemy regiments tried to outflank them, and in the ensuing melee Washington, mounted on horseback, ordered the German Battalion to "throw themselves before them," which "they did with Spirit and Rapidity and immediately checked them," as the commander in chief reported two days later. The enemy troops, two regiments totaling about 600 men, fell by the dozens and finally surrendered to the smaller German Battalion.

Heyser spent the winter of 1777 encamped with Washington's Army at Valley Forge, where he received a letter from his eldest son, William Heyser II:

> *My Dear father, my greatest grief is, that I am incapable of the military Service, that I might enjoy the company of so loving a father, and serve my country in so glorious a cause, but tho' absent from you yet my constant prayer is for your safety, in the hour of danger, your complete victory, over the enemies, of the United States of America, and your safe restoration to the government of your family. I and my brother Jacob continue at school, and hope to give a full satisfaction, to our parents, and friends in our regular conduct, and progress in learning, my Mamma, my brother and sister do join me in their prayers and well wishes for you.*
>
> > *I am Dr. Father your most dutiful and obedt son,*
> > *William Heyser*
> > *Hagers Town*

Captain Heyser's military career came to an end less than a year later, on September 11, 1777, when he was severely wounded at the Battle of Brandywine. Upon hearing the news, Heyser's wife, the former Anna Trudy, rode on horseback to Philadelphia to nurse him back to health and bring him home to their Hagerstown farm. Heyser reported after the battle that his company was at less than half its full strength, with only thirty-eight men fit for duty. He also reported two of his soldiers "missing."

In nearly every succeeding generation, George's ancestors answered the call to defend the nation. Heyser's teenage grandson, upon hearing the news that the British had burned Washington in 1814, joined a unit of volunteers in Chambersburg, Pennsylvania, just across the Maryland border, where the family settled after the Revolution. To the sound of the drums and fife, William Heyser III, then only sixteen, marched off to the defense of Baltimore. Two of his sons later fought in the Union Army during the Civil War, while he watched Confederate troops burn some of his storehouses and, in the summer of 1863, tended to wounded soldiers from the battle at nearby Gettysburg.

It was Heyser III's son-in-law, J. Allison Eyster, from whom George got his surname, who was supplying equipment to Union forces when he was captured by the Confederates and imprisoned in the notorious Libby Prison near Richmond, Virginia. J. Allison Eyster's ancestors came to America from Germany and settled in Chambersburg in the early eighteenth century, also giving their share of sons to the defense of the country. One of his brothers was Captain George Eyster, who served as the provost marshal in charge of the military police for the Union Army in Pennsylvania during the Civil War. The first George Senseny Eyster was born in Chambersburg in 1795, his middle name derived from his mother's maiden name. It was a name that would stick.

By the twentieth century, the tradition was embodied in George's great-grandfather, who graduated from West Point in 1917. In World War II he served as chief of the operations branch on the staff of General Dwight Eisenhower, the top Allied commander in Europe. After the war he oversaw the withdrawal of American forces from Europe, and his last assignment before retiring in 1950 was as a brigadier general serving as the chief spokesman for the Army.

The ancestors of George's mother, the former Ann Pate, also had deep roots planted in the New World, arriving in Virginia from England in 1650, along with their own military tradition. Three Pate brothers were among several Pates who served in the Revolutionary War.

As he came of age, George was learning he had a pedigree that was about as all-American as it gets.

———

In the summer of 1985, twelve-year-old George Eyster knelt down next to his father on the rocky ridgeline known as Little Round Top. He listened intently as Big George described the ferocious fighting that had taken place there on July 2, 1863. His father gestured to where the federal troops had repelled the Confederate attack during the Battle of Gettysburg in the Civil War, pinpointing some of the locations on the granite spur where the decisive engagements took place.

The Gettysburg battlefield was one of Big George's favorite places to visit on long drives between Army posts or on family getaways. He knew intimately the history of the bloody battle, including all the skirmishes and the units and officers that played prominent roles in them. He was especially thrilled when his wife, Ann, was hired to type the manuscript for *The Killer Angels*, the Pulitzer Prize–winning novel about the Gettysburg battle that was later made into a popular film.

On this particular visit to the farmland of southern Pennsylvania, the Eysters spent several days at the historic site. They toured the military cemetery where President Lincoln gave his famous address and traced each battlefield marker. The patience of a young kid could grow thin after a few hours. One day as they took the battlefield driving tour, a restless George sat in the backseat with a picture book his father purchased at the gift shop. It showed image after image of the carnage that had taken place over those dreadful three days at the beginning of July in 1863. He looked intently at the grainy photographs of Union and Confederate soldiers lying dead and wounded on the sloping fields of corn and in culverts along the wooded dirt roads. It was difficult to tell the Union soldiers from the Confederates. They were stacked up like so many cords of wood. It was hard to see the glory in it all.

His was an early distaste for the cost of war that George learned later was shared by others in his bloodline. His ancestor William Heyser III expressed a similar disdain in his diary in late 1862 as the Civil War engulfed the nation and grew ever closer to his native Pennsylvania.

"Every day we hear the sad strains of martial music as the hearses pass carrying the dead from some distant battlefield to be buried at their home," wrote the veteran of the War of 1812, reflecting that "all lose in the end, the poor victims killed giving the most."

As he approached his teens, George began searching for glory elsewhere.

———

George's eyes were opened to a new reality when he entered middle school. Big George was assigned to the small Army base of Aberdeen Proving Ground in Maryland, and George was enrolled for the first time in a public school made up largely of kids with no military ties. He was now learning what lay outside the gate of an Army post, beyond the strictures and expectations of military life. They were living in Abingdon, Maryland, a middle-class suburb about twenty-five miles northeast of Baltimore. George was that in-between age when childhood begins to fade and a newly discovered independence fuels a desire to test one's limits.

He was blessed with a natural athletic ability, inherited from his father, who had been a football star and accomplished high school baseball pitcher. But George was drawn to the traditionally less popular sport of lacrosse, which not only was physically demanding but also required keen hand-eye coordination. As he entered seventh grade in suburban Baltimore, it was also clear that he had a knack for it. Before long, he was recruited to play with the high school kids and even found himself invited to practice games under the lights with college players from nearby Towson State University, who were impressed by the tenacious twelve-year-old's skills as a midfielder, a position that allowed George to roam freely, playing both offense and defense.

Nearly overnight, George was thrust from the sheltered world of an Army brat into a world of greater autonomy and self-reliance— and the pitfalls that came with it. Both on and off the field he found new acceptance among his lacrosse buddies, all of them several years older than he. Soon they were dragging him to high school parties. The adulation from his teammates and the attention he was getting from girls pumped him with a new confidence. Though somewhat shy and tentative in social situations, he started to gain a greater sense of himself than simply as the son of an Army officer dutifully playing his part supporting his father's calling and striving to meet his parents' high expectations.

His parents were wary of his newfound independence but could clearly see his love for lacrosse and didn't want to hold him back. But his wider berth soon proved too much for George to handle. He was drinking alcohol after lacrosse games, he grew more boastful and even bullying to his middle-school friends, and his grades sank. He acted out in other ways, growing his hair long like some of the other lacrosse players. In eighth grade he pierced his left ear with a safety pin.

George tried to hide the piercing from his parents, knowing that his buttoned-down father would be furious. He kept his head turned ever so slightly to shield the still-bleeding piercing when Ann picked him up from school that day. She took him to the mall, where they were to meet Big George for a treat of Boardwalk Fries in the food court. As soon as Big George arrived from work in his Army uniform, however, the game was up.

"What's happened to your ear?" Big George demanded as he sat down at the table.

Over the next year George's behavior only grew more troubling to his parents. He was punished, his after-school activities curtailed, and his participation in lacrosse limited to practices and games. Nothing seemed to work. It came to a head one day in the ninth grade when George was confronted in school by another kid whose girlfriend George had been flirting with. George head-butted the kid in the hallway and broke his nose. He was summarily expelled.

———

If the Eysters considered any place home, it was, as for many Army families, Fort Bragg in Fayetteville, North Carolina. They had been stationed there several times, and it was only a morning's drive to Grandma Harriet in Beaufort, South Carolina.

After George was expelled from school in Maryland, his father enrolled him on the sprawling Army base, and the two of them moved back to Fayetteville, in advance of Big George's next assignment. Ann stayed behind in Maryland until Scott and Teri finished the school year. George was now fifteen, and his parents hoped that Fort Bragg's more familiar environment would keep him out of trouble.

Before long, George's grades began to improve, and his parents were eager to continue encouraging his love for lacrosse. Because the sport was less prevalent in Fayetteville, it meant driving several hours to play in a league in Raleigh. After school Ann picked him up, plopped a TV dinner on his lap, and drove George the two hours each way for practice. After completing his homework in the car, he would climb into bed exhausted late in the evening.

George's interests were also beginning to broaden. He mostly viewed himself—as did most of his friends—as a jock: blond, brawny, and better suited for the ball field than the library. But as he prepared to enter the eleventh grade, he discovered that he had a more intellectual side, an impulse to draw deeper meaning from his experiences and a better understanding of the wider world. His mother and Grandma Harriet encouraged it, recommending various books for him to read. He got hooked on the novels of Pat Conroy, who captured the quaint exterior and inner demons of southern life in his acclaimed novels such as *The Prince of Tides* and *The Lords of Discipline*, which chronicled the Citadel military academy in Charleston. George not only was captivated by the stories but identified with the writer himself. Conroy was the son of a Marine who decided to become a teacher instead of following in his father's footsteps. One of George's favorite Conroy novels was *The Great Santini*. George saw some of himself in the fictional Ben, the eighteen-year-old son of a fighter pilot who is a born athlete but finds it hard to contend with the expectations of his overbearing father—the story, as Conroy described it, "of a boy's determination to be himself, whatever that may be."

George had not completely tamed his rebellious streak. The run-ins with his own father continued, like when he was caught sneaking out of the house when everyone was asleep to drink beer with his friends in the back fields of Fayetteville. One night he awakened Big George when he broke a window screen while gingerly climbing from the porch roof back through his bedroom window. After a middle-of-the-night confrontation that woke up the whole house, George found himself assigned to yard work and other heavy chores under the watchful eye of a stern Colonel Eyster.

But any resentment he felt toward Big George melted away in a flash on August 2, 1990, when Saddam Hussein's Iraq invaded Kuwait.

———

Within days Operation Desert Storm began, and George's father, who was now commanding the First Battalion of the 159th Aviation Regiment, received orders that his unit would soon be leaving for the Persian Gulf. The outlook was troubling. To build support for liberating the oil-rich kingdom, President George H. W. Bush took to the airwaves and likened the Iraqi dictator, Saddam Hussein, to Adolf Hitler. Iraq, listeners were told, also had one of the largest armies in the world. Unlike the conflicts in Grenada in 1983 or Panama in 1989, which only lasted a few days, this one looked as if it might drag on for months and be far more dangerous for Big George and his soldiers. The Eysters soon learned that two of George's uncles were also being deployed. George's stepbrother, Scott, was summoned home to help look after Ann and George—and to bid a tearful good-bye on the front porch of their house in Fayetteville.

Within weeks Big George was in Saudi Arabia. No one could say when he might return. The fall months dragged on. The nonstop news about the massive American buildup, broadcast from the front lines by CNN, only ratcheted up the anxiety of soldiers and loved ones alike. Would the Iraqi strongman back down, or would the United States and its allies have to go to war with the elite Iraqi Republican Guard? Their worries only grew deeper with reports of Hussein's stockpiles of chemical weapons and the grisly images flashed on TV of the Kurdish civilians he had ordered gassed a few years earlier. It was the longest that Big George had been away from the family, and they did their best to stay connected. George's father mailed home upbeat video greetings on VHS tapes, relaying how morale was high and his troops were ready for what might lie ahead. For Halloween 1990 he donned a bedsheet and dressed up as a cot, one of the goofy antics he and his men performed before the camera to keep up spirits on the home front.

Not to be outdone, Ann and the kids videotaped a series of skits they put together in the basement, staying up until dawn one night to complete the first of what they coined "Purple Heart Productions." In one sequence, George, displaying the awkward earnestness that would come to define him later, was dressed in a blue blazer and ascot, feigning an aristocratic accent. In another, he played a comical character named Commander Seagull. He took the roles seriously, almost too seriously. He insisted on shooting multiple takes before he felt the skits were just right, revealing a perfectionist streak like his father's.

The holidays were especially difficult without Dad. Saddam was refusing to back down, and as war seemed more likely, the tenor of Big George's video greetings changed. The one he taped on December 12, 1990, troubled the family greatly. His usually sunny and upbeat outlook had turned decidedly dark. They had never seen him so taciturn, almost melancholy. Looking somber in his flight suit and sitting behind a metal desk in an aircraft hangar, Big George shifted uncomfortably in his chair as he spoke in a low voice into the camera.

"Things are going fairly well here," he began, "but we are beginning to have a great deal of loneliness and some despair over how long this affair is going to take place. It seems that now staring us in the face is the reality that we are in fact going to war. . . . It may be a long time until you hear from me, but each and every one of you will be within my thoughts and in my heart."

He spoke movingly to his beloved Ann. "You have been the one thing in my life that has pushed me along to achieve bigger and better things," he told his wife of nineteen years. "I feel extremely lost and lonely when I don't have you there."

He then addressed each of his children individually, thanking his stepson, Scott, for coming home to help look after George and expressing his pride in his stepdaughter, Teri, who now had two young children. He then singled out George for praise but, as was his nature, also gave him a bit of advice.

"I am really proud of your academic work in school. . . . I got your report card, and you are doing, in fact, pretty doggone good," he told his namesake. "I still think you can do better."

Big George wanted to do something his own father never had a chance to do: tell them all how much they meant to him, in case he never saw them again.

"While I hope that nothing will happen, I am not above believing that there is always that possibility," he intoned. "If it does, I want you all to know . . . that I have loved each of you very much."

Watching the video message back at Fort Bragg, George couldn't help but think that he had not been the best son to his father and desperately wanted him back so that he could make it up to him.

When the Persian Gulf War finally commenced in the New Year, the United States scored a stunning victory over Iraq, and Big George returned home safely. His actions flying troops into heated battle further burnished the Eyster reputation for bravery in the face of danger, earning him a Bronze Star.

———

As George neared his high school graduation, the question was rarely uttered but hung over the Eyster household: What would Little George decide to do? Would he, too, go into the Eyster family business? A generation earlier Big George felt he had little choice in the matter and now seemed determined to let his own son decide for himself the path he would choose. He knew from his own experience the enormous pressure that came with the name George Senseny Eyster. In some ways, Little George's burden was even heavier than his own. Big George had a brother. George was the only Eyster heir.

For George, there were constant reminders of what so many expected of him—his family, his friends, his peers, and of course Grandma Harriet. As a favored guest at his grandmother's house, he sometimes felt as if he were being watched by all those photographs of George Eysters in their Army uniforms. Sometimes it even felt as though they were mocking him. The hallmarks of the family business—the Silver Star Grandpa George had earned in Vietnam, the endless citations and awards of his own father—were on display virtually everywhere. Even his step-grandfather, Frank Linnell, Harriet's second husband, who had become an influential presence in his life, was a retired Army general who had received the Distinguished Service Medal in Vietnam and had been one of the pioneers of Army aviation in the 1960s. Nearly everyone in his family was in the Army or had married into it, including most of his cousins.

One photograph in particular haunted him. Even as George was drawn to its almost Hollywood mystique, it conjured up painful memories of those violent images he had seen on television as an impressionable fifth grader. It was a picture of a grinning Grandpa George, one of the last ever taken of him. Standing in the tall grass of a Vietnamese rubber plantation, he was primed for combat, his weapon slung over his shoulder, a canister for launching smoke grenades tucked under one arm. Jutting from his lips was his ever-present cigar. The framed copy was inscribed by one of his beloved soldiers:

> When we were needed; we were there;
> When the call came out for freedom; we were there.
> Well it wasn't always easy, it wasn't always fair;
> But when freedom called we answered; we were there.

Part of George had always aspired to be the man in that black-and-white photograph. But he had privately decided after Dad returned from the Gulf War that whatever his future held, it was not to be a soldier. For starters, he didn't have the academic record to tackle the demands of the U.S. Military Academy at West Point, even if he could manage to get an appointment. He might not even qualify for an ROTC scholarship. In the end, it didn't really matter. There were too many things about the Army he found unappealing—the rootless existence, the need to constantly follow orders and bow to authority, and, yes, the prospect of real danger. It was an honorable calling, he knew, just not for him. And while Big George never said it in so many words, George had the distinct feeling that his father didn't think he should do it, either. It was too hard. And maybe he just wasn't cut out for it.

After the Gulf War, Big George was assigned to Army headquarters in the Pentagon, and the family moved again. This time they chose to live in the nearby Virginia suburb of Springfield so George could enroll for his senior year at Springfield High School, which had a top-notch lacrosse program. Fate would have it that the decision about his future was soon made for him when he was offered a scholarship to play lacrosse at Towson State University.

Towson State had one of the best collegiate lacrosse teams in the country, and George's scholarship to play for the Tigers was a true achievement that made his parents immensely proud. By the fall of 1992, Big George had retired from the Army after a career of more than twenty years. For the first time since Woodrow Wilson was president, there was no George Senseny Eyster wearing an Army uniform. By the looks of it, there probably never would be.

———

By the middle of his junior year at Towson State, George had already changed majors four times. First it was animal behavior, then mass communication, followed by zoology. He even toyed briefly with chemistry. As for lacrosse, for the first time he didn't enjoy it; being on the team felt too much like a chore. Many of his teammates were hooligans who seemed more interested in boozing than playing lacrosse. He decided he had had enough after a close game against the Naval Academy. Towson lost in the last minute when a goal was disallowed because of unsportsmanlike conduct; one of his teammates tried to attack a referee. In search of a new compass, George decided to drop out and go home to his parents to figure things out. Maybe, he thought, he could take a few classes at Florida State and then try to walk on at another lacrosse powerhouse like the University of North Carolina.

When he moved in with his parents in Tallahassee in early 1995, it seemed everyone else in the family was on a steady path but him. Big George, now out of the Army several years, was working as the chief of general services for the Florida Department of Agriculture. George's mom, Ann, had a job at the Florida Restaurant and Lodging Association, building on all her years as an Army wife and the director of community services during their posting to Maryland. Meanwhile, George's stepbrother, Scott, had been accepted into the Florida Highway Patrol, and his stepsister, Teri, was married and busy raising her two kids.

One weekend, as George was preparing to enroll in classes at Florida State, he and his father went to a baseball game on campus. As they were walking back to the car, Big George pointed out one of the campus buildings.

"That's where I did ROTC. Want to see it?"

It was Big George's not-so-sly way of giving his son a glimpse of what the Reserve Officers' Training Corps might offer—the same scholarship program he graduated from more than two decades earlier after he had opted out of West Point.

———

Inside the ROTC office, they were greeted by an Army major who hit it off famously with George's dad when he learned he was a retired colonel and a distinguished graduate of FSU's Seminole Battalion. The major warily eyed George, with his long hair. The officer's demeanor said it all. George was probably not what they were looking for. But outside, George noticed a rappelling tower that had been erected for the ROTC cadets. He was intrigued; it looked as if it might be fun. He turned to his father and asked him what type of commitment he would be making if he took one of the ROTC courses at the university.

"No commitment," Big George told him.

George went back to the ROTC office that fall. The colonel in charge was a gifted talker and charmed him. He highlighted the fun he would have—there were cadet challenges like "adventure training," he informed him—and skimmed over some of the other stuff, like ROTC boot camp in the summers. The athlete in George was drawn to the physical stamina ROTC would require. He was also attracted to the more regimented existence of the cadet, a far cry from his college experience to date. Besides, it was still an elective, and for the first two years he could participate "without incurring any obligation to serve in the military," as the promotional packet pointed out. George decided to give it a shot. He signed up for Military Science I: An Introduction to Military Arts. He also started attending weekly drill. Soon he was approved for an ROTC scholarship.

As he settled into FSU, George was pleasantly surprised that ROTC wasn't an all-encompassing experience. He had plenty of time to enjoy himself. He joined the fraternity Sigma Chi. He also met Vivian, a curvaceous dark-skinned Colombian girl from Miami. He was enthralled by her from the moment she walked into his Brazilian history class. He finally got up the courage to talk to her at a frat party. After that George and Viv were inseparable.

★

CHAPTER TWO

A TRUE CHARLESTONIAN

April 24, 1942, was a fragrant spring evening, with the bold scent of the tidal marshes carried on the breeze and the azaleas in full bloom. Wearing his freshly pressed dress blue uniform, Ryan parked Ma's car and walked down Meeting Street. He was exhilarated to be home on leave in his beloved Charleston. Its narrow streets, lined with centuries-old oaks, swaying palmettos, and colonial-era steeples, held a thousand cherished memories. Just a few yards away his mother, Grace, bought fresh flowers—two bundles for twenty-five cents—from the black ladies balancing baskets on their heads. One block south on King Street the shrimp man used to push his cart, shouting in a barely discernible twang, "Shrimp-de-rah, shrimp-de-raw." Just around the corner from there, on Queen Street, he had thrilled as a boy to the singing Irishmen, the street performers who outdid virtually every act he had seen since.

Ryan had been away at flight school for the past six months. He missed strolling with Ma and the girls around the Battery, the promenade along the shores of the peninsula. He and his youngest sister, Claudia, had dreamed up countless stories about the brightly colored eighteenth-century mansions with their wide porches and carefully sculpted gardens, competing to see who could come up with the most outlandish yarn about the mysterious people who lived behind the high brick walls and iron gates. How many afternoons had he sat with his sister Uranie in the shade of old Castle Pinckney, the masonry fortification constructed in 1810 in Charleston Harbor, or shared a steak with Ma at the Huguenot Tavern, that "hot, close, dusty little place" in the French Quarter, with its legendary desserts? The four of them—Ryan, "Claudie," Uranie, and Ma—had enjoyed countless pictures at the Riviera, the majestic Art Deco movie house on King Street, knocked around the white sandy beaches on the nearby Isle of Palms, and cooled off from the summer heat in the hidden coves snaking through South Carolina's Low Country.

The familiar sights and sounds of Ryan's Charleston were still here, but almost everything was now drowned out by the drumbeat of war. He continued a few blocks farther down Meeting Street and was engulfed by a hive of activity surrounding the City Market, the series of open-air buildings spreading northeast for four blocks to the Old Custom House on East Bay Street. The lazy seaport he once knew now swarmed with sailors, soldiers, fliers, construction workers, cooks, and countless other new arrivals. The restaurants and taverns were bursting with customers and the rooming houses crammed to capacity. Perhaps the starkest sign of the changes the war wrought were the military police keeping a watchful eye over the Friday night revelry.

The city's population had doubled to 220,000 in just two years with the expansion of the Charleston Navy Yard. Located about ten miles west along the Cooper River, the facility employed more than twenty-five thousand workers and operated around the clock, six days a week, building and repairing warships for the Allied invasions of Europe and the Pacific. At night, according to one observer, the sparks of molten metal from the welder's arcs and the glow of their forges made the shipyard look like a giant amusement park.

The hum of activity was fueled by the nearby Charleston Army Airfield and other military installations that had sprung up around the city, including the Army's Stark General Hospital in North Charleston, where wounded soldiers returning from the battlefields of North Africa were being nursed back to health. The changes had been profound in the five months since the Japanese attack on the American fleet moored in Pearl Harbor in Hawaii. County Hall was now the offices of the U.S. Army, the Calhoun Mansion was boarding Army and Navy personnel, and the Fort Sumter Hotel was headquarters for the Sixth Naval District. Charleston was struggling to keep up with the influx. On Broad Street the newly established Committee for

Congested Production Areas was overseeing the construction of new restaurants, cafeterias, and living quarters while working feverishly to improve the disposal of garbage and expand medical, fire, and police services.

Those not serving in uniform, meanwhile, worked in munitions factories, sold war bonds to finance the effort, volunteered for the Red Cross, or planted "Victory Gardens" to supplement the depleted supplies of fresh vegetables. Countless others served as nurses' aides, salvage workers, or aircraft spotters. Indeed, the dangers of the war were not just something feared from far across the sea. Earlier in the war German submarines had been spotted just outside Charleston Harbor. Beach patrols were established to prevent enemy infiltration, while the bridges over the Cooper and Ashley Rivers on either side of the peninsula were patrolled to look for saboteurs.

As in the rest of the nation, rationing was part of the new way of life. Shortages of sugar, meat, coffee, shoes, gasoline, tires, and other staples were common, while luxuries like perfume, whiskey, and nylons were almost impossible to come by, found only on the black market. City leaders were trying to locate enough rice and grits to keep the natives happy. They met with only modest success. Most Charlestonians, turning up their noses, had to settle for yellow grits instead of white grits for the remainder of the war. The signs of the collective effort were everywhere. "Support the War Effort. Make Do, or Do Without," urged one entreaty tacked to Charleston's faded brick storefronts. "Gasoline Is Vital. Save!" appealed another.

The tumult was wholly unfamiliar to a city that a novelist not long before described as "a beguiling old place with the smell of the sea, a place that spells leisure in a manner quite un-American." The Charleston *Post and Courier* summed up the new landscape in a recent editorial. "The old Charleston is one of the casualties of the war," the editors wrote, "and there is no time for mourning over it now."

But after all, this was still the same Charleston where Scarlett O'Hara in *Gone With the Wind* shops for her elegant accessories in the boutiques lining King Street. Some things were still sacrosanct, including the treasured tradition of socializing. The grand balls, hops, receptions, and debutante teas continued virtually unabated despite the war. Tonight was no different.

A few blocks beyond the City Market, Ryan arrived at the wrought-iron gate and glowing gas lamps of Hibernian Hall, the benevolent society and private social club where his sister Uranie was waiting in her white gloves and gown for him to escort her to the Medical Ball.

————

Ryan and Uranie ascended the stairs and proceeded through the six pillars of the imposing Hibernian Hall, a fixture of antebellum Charleston built in 1840. They stepped through the two heavy wooden doors and beneath the benevolent society's seal of a harp with the words, inscribed in Latin, *"Non ignara mali, miseris succurrere disco"*—"Being familiar with misfortune, I learn to assist the unfortunate." They stood in the grand foyer, a triple-tiered rotunda with two facing staircases. Along the ornately wallpapered central hallway hung the portraits of past presidents of the society, and on each side were spacious sitting rooms with imposing marble fireplaces furnished with plush antique lounges and billiard tables covered in red velvet. At the rear of the hall was a small, elegantly appointed ballroom decorated with large hanging mirrors and, just beyond it, a cozy barroom with high-backed leather chairs.

They ascended one of the staircases to the ballroom on the second floor but found it nearly empty, barring a stag or two. The orchestra was just setting up onstage for the dance. Undaunted by the lack of music, Ryan took Uranie by the hand, twirled his sister around, and they danced a few steps beneath one of the five golden chandeliers hanging in the cavernous room. They glided along the dance floor before the tall open windows, the curtains drawn, looking out over Charleston and the imposing stone spire of the Unitarian Church two blocks south on Archdale Street. The orchestra, Skura and His Boys, quickly took Ryan's hint and started up.

Uranie, with her brown eyes and dark curls cut attractively short, had creamy white skin and radiated a wholesome beauty like their mother, Grace. She was a student at the medical college and had a buttoned-down air about her. To Ryan, it seemed that the only time he got to spend with her was while driving her to and from her classes in Ma's car. But if anyone could bring Uranie out of her shell, it was her brother, Ryan. In earlier times the two of them went horseback riding in Hampton Park, the former plantation adjacent to the Citadel, sharing a bock beer afterward at Harry's Tavern or the Huguenot—once in a while even ordering a scotch and soda or a Bloater's Punch. Like Ma and their younger sister, Claudia, Uranie adored her older brother, who had been the man of the house ever since their father left, and was helping to pay for her schooling. When he had been ill, Uranie doted on him, making sure he took a cold capsule or a dose of salts. Last Thanksgiving, she went to visit him in Jacksonville, where he was in flight training, so he wouldn't be alone for the holiday. Ryan never forgot Uranie's birthday or failed to mark a special occasion with a postcard, telegram, or orchid.

Though just five feet seven inches tall, Ryan, with his wiry athletic frame, cut a dashing figure in his dress uniform. He wore a form-fitting flannel coat and collar with gold buttons, a white belt with a solid brass buckle, and blue doeskin trousers with a red stripe running down the side of each leg. His white cap—which was never worn indoors, of course—had a black brim to match his spit-shined shoes, and his shoulders glimmered with the gold bars of a second lieutenant. The ornaments of an eagle, globe, and anchor were pinned to both his cap and his collar. Most of all he proudly displayed the shiny new wings of a Marine Corps aviator on his chest.

He had sparkling sky-blue eyes and a stubborn cowlick that made almost a complete swirl of reddish-blond hair across the middle of his forehead. His most recognizable trait, however, was the left-eye squint. Ever since he was a boy, his left brow hung a little lower than his right, almost as if he were about to wink but the muscles around his eye froze in place just before he could do so. The feature accentuated a friendly, open face that smiled easily.

As a lifelong Charlestonian, he spoke in that low-sounding drawl where "cooper" becomes "cuppah," "house" sounds like "hoose," and one-syllable words are especially drawn out, so that "state" comes out sounding more like "stey-it." He also had a habit of turning nouns into adjectives, especially when talking about the weather, which as a pilot was never too far from his thoughts. It could be "rainy and squally" or "sunshiny." His favorite colloquialisms appeared frequently in everyday conversation—say, if things were going well, they were "smooth as cream." In the rare instances when they weren't, he would mutter, "No soup," or might propose that things were "tense as hang." When something captured his imagination, like a motion picture or an especially entertaining floor show, it was the "darnedest thing."

Marion Ryan McCown Jr., at twenty-five, was a mirthful spirit with a whimsical, even mischievous streak that gave him the urge to dance without any music or—as he did when he was a student a few years earlier at Georgia Tech—purloin a ladder from one of the dormitories so he could sneak a peek at Clark Gable and Vivien Leigh when *Gone With the Wind* was premiering in Atlanta in 1939.

The Hibernian Hall ballroom soon filled with more people, many also wearing the crisp uniforms of the Army, Navy, or Marines. The orchestra struck up a waltz, and a few of the fellas broke in to dance with Uranie. Ryan soon found a group of friends from the old neighborhood on Trumbo Street, where he and the girls lived for a time with Ma's brother after Dad had left, in the large three-story white house with black shutters on a sleepy palm-lined side street next to Colonial Lake. Harriette King, herself now a Navy ensign, arrived at the ball along with Ed LaRoche and Sue Legare. Ryan reminisced with them about when they were still in knickers and the neighborhood kids would pair up and pretend to get married in ornate mock weddings. They got a good laugh at the innocence of it all.

"What a thrill," Ryan wrote later in his diary, "to see a hall crowded with people you've known all your life."

Then, just before the intermission, Helen Miller arrived, "making the dance a mighty bright spot."

Ryan picked Helen out of the crowd in her blue dress, fitting snuggly on her petite frame. Her auburn hair was crowned with yellow flowers, and her lips were painted a deep red. Ryan vowed to dance with her during a no-break—when rivals couldn't interrupt the dance—before one of the other fellas beat him to it.

Four years his junior, Helen had been an acquaintance of his sister Uranie's from the hospital. She was now working as an X-ray technician up at Stark General Hospital, and he had been courting her during his intermittent visits to Charleston. They had been introduced the previous May in the Fort Sumter Hotel, when she had become the first girl who ever asked him, "Do you like to cast for shrimp?" Ryan and Helen quickly found they had a lot in common.

He danced with Uranie for the first no-break. It was a version of Tommy Dorsey's "I'm Getting Sentimental over You," and it brought back a flood of memories of his high school days. He waited impatiently for the second no-break to ask Helen for a dance, and when it finally came, the two of them pressed closely together, making hushed small talk, as Skura and His Boys started up a waltz medley with "I Love You Truly."

> Life with its sorrow, life with its tear,
> Fades into dreams when I feel you are near . . .
> Ah! Love, 'tis something to feel your kind hand,
> Ah! Yes, 'tis something by your side to stand.

How many times had he danced in this hall, to the same music by the same orchestra? Ryan thought. But Helen was different. He concluded privately that she rated as "old folks" but "with new ideas"— maybe just his type of gal. He vowed to see much more of her before his leave ended. He would be departing for the Marine Corps base in Quantico, Virginia, in a few weeks—and then who knew where? There was little time to waste.

———

Every chance he got, Ryan took advantage of his leave and the spring weather to inhale his beloved South Carolina Low Country. One of his first stops after he arrived home was Middleton Place, with its breathtaking gardens, near the banks of the Ashley River. Planted two centuries earlier, the gardens were patterned after Versailles with its bowling greens, canals, sculptures, and twin lakes shaped like a butterfly's wings—all designed with a mathematical precision that was especially pleasing to Ryan's eye for geometry. On another day, he and an old friend paddled in a heavy downpour through a black-water swamp of cypress and tupelo trees out in Moncks Corner, in Berkeley County. "Add under memories," Ryan scrawled in his diary after drying out.

Ryan had cherished the outdoors ever since he was a boy and joined the Boy Scouts. He loved to build fires under the moonlit sky on Folly or South Edisto Beach—an activity, he was recently disappointed to learn, that had been suspended due to the war. His urge to be in nature was also why he had decided long ago that he was "not open to clerical work." He liked to get his boots dirty scrambling up the riverbanks or, as he did one recent summer, being pelted in a squall while setting tidal gauges and recording sounding data in Charleston Harbor, rough work that required pulling cable and anchors for the sounding party. Nor was he afraid to drink river water out of a clamshell.

The job he previously held as a surveyor and draftsman for the U.S. Engineering Department made him intimately familiar with the waterways that snaked through the coastal areas of South Carolina. He knew where the eagles circled over the rice fields and recognized the green salt water of the marshes that gave way to the red tinge of the Santee and Sampit Rivers, where the ducks hugged the swamps. He had plied the Pee Dee and Black Rivers up to Winyah Bay and the old seaport of Georgetown, where young girls still stood on the shore shucking rice with a mortar and pestle, remnants of a bygone era. But it was the banks of the Waccamaw he liked best, with its old and twisted cypress trees that seemed to have died once, only to begin growing again. When he wasn't on the water, he traced the back roads on a motorcycle. He relished even the simplest of pleasures of his native surroundings, like the honeysuckle twining outside his open bedroom window at Ma's or the song of the mockingbirds in the moonlight.

The Low Country was in his blood. As the eldest child of Grace Emilie Aimar and Marion Ryan McCown Sr., he had deep roots in South Carolina. The first McCown who came to America was a Scottish Highlander from the clan Colquhoun, pronounced "Coheen," who arrived in 1756. John McCown later served in the Pee Dee Regiment of General Francis Marion's brigade in the Revolutionary War and provided provisions and cattle to the Continental Army and Militia. Family history held that John's three younger brothers, Samuel, Moses, and Alexander, all died fighting for American independence. In 1825, one Annie McCown, along with her classmates from the Female Academy, was selected to chant an ode of welcome to the Marquis de Lafayette, the French major general and hero of the Revolution, as he walked through a petal-strewn path on the green in front of Cornwallis House in Camden, South Carolina. Ryan's grandfather Robert Maxcy McCown had served as South Carolina's secretary of state from 1906 to 1916. Grace's family, too, boasted a storied tradition that began in the early years of the Republic. Her forebear Sebastian Aimar had been a soldier in Napoleon's army in France and was said to have hid under a coffee sack on a ship bound from Havana to Charleston in 1810 and later owned a store at 199 East Bay Street near the City Market.

Ryan's parents had been married in the Unitarian Church of Charleston in February 1916, and he arrived eleven months later, on January 14, 1917. Two years after that came Blanche Uranie, followed by Claudia Merritt McCown in 1921. But their parents' marriage didn't last. Ryan senior, a lawyer with interests in several hotels along the East Coast, divorced Grace in 1922, when Ryan was just five, Uranie three, and Claudia barely a year old. Gracie, as Ryan's mother was affectionately known, once remarked about her marriage that she and Ryan senior had one thing in common: three children.

The Unitarian Church, however, where Grace was active and her children marked key milestones, remained a stable force after the divorce and played a central role in molding Ryan and his sisters. The oldest Unitarian church in the South, the Gothic-style cathedral was built in 1772, its lush churchyard and cemetery thick with flowers, shrubs, and trees and rooted in history and legend. The church had been occupied by both American and British troops during the Revolutionary War, and one romantic embellishment was that the ghost of Annabel Lee, the heroine in Edgar Allan Poe's poem of the same name, haunted the faded headstones and overgrown pathways searching for her lover.

But while the church was a fixture of the Old South, its members left most of the traditional conservative beliefs of fellow Charlestonians at the stone archway. The Unitarians were guided by a Universalist compass that declared that every person had inherent worth. The ownership of slaves by some church members became a highly contentious moral dilemma during the Civil War. The church espoused a liberal acceptance of other religious denominations and a deep compassion for others. When Grace and her children attended, there were sermons on Shakespeare, and once even Hindu worship sheets were handed out to the congregation. The transcendentalist philosopher Ralph Waldo Emerson, who spoke before the congregation in 1827, described the church's worldview as living "through the fire of thought" and engaging in religious worship that does "not fence the Spirit." Amid the orthodoxy of 1930s South Carolina, the Unitarian Church was a welcoming and comforting shelter for a divorced woman like Grace working as a social worker at the police station while raising three children on her own to stake their claim in the world.

The church's teachings had an enduring impact on Ryan's own thirst for knowledge and understanding—for a deeper connection to the world around him. He fancied himself something of a Renaissance man who liked to draw and paint, especially scenes of his beloved Low Country. He read Poe and the short stories of Guy de Maupassant, the nineteenth-century French writer. He was also captivated by motion pictures, the way they transported him to exotic places, seized his imagination, and stoked his sense of wanderlust. If he had a down day or "busted" a physics quiz at Georgia Tech, Bing Crosby and Bette Davis or Gary Cooper and Gloria Jean on the silver screen would make it all right again. Some of his personal favorites were adventure movies like *Suez*, in which Tyrone Power played a diplomat who envisions building a canal on the Isthmus of Suez. He was naturally drawn to stories of chivalry like the serials of the comic book hero Captain Marvel that debuted in 1941. The romantic in him was drawn to fairy tales.

"Swell!" was his one-word verdict for *The Wizard of Oz*. When *Snow White and the Seven Dwarfs* opened at the Riviera to much fanfare in 1939, twenty-two-year-old Ryan McCown saw it three times.

He also had a deep appreciation for the simpler things in life. Ryan embraced—even relished—experiences that most others considered mundane. To him, taking a stroll down a traffic-clogged street in a downpour could be a grand activity. He was struck sometimes by how little feeling or emotion people around him often displayed, going through life barely noticing life itself. He had a name for them: "automatons."

———

Grace was initially less than thrilled when she learned that Ryan was dating Helen. She had been wary of all his female companions, a reaction stemming not only from her desire that he find the right match but also perhaps from a selfish impulse. When Grace had visited Ryan at the air station in Jacksonville the previous fall and he told her about a girl he had recently met there, he was surprised by her reaction, blurted out with a tinge of fear in her eyes. "Are you engaged to the girl?"

Tonight, he was planning to call on Helen at her parents' house and take her for supper at a nice place downtown. To his surprise, Grace offered to make dinner for them. "I wouldn't have asked [Helen] to go home with me," he wrote in his diary later, "but I noticed that in spite of Mother's negative attitude, she had set a nice table for a buffet supper, so Helen and I rode out there."

Ma's house at 1023 Ashley Avenue was a simple, one-story red-brick cottage with a small front porch and white awnings, located in a middle-class neighborhood a few miles west of downtown. The entryway to the right opened to the parlor, about twenty feet long but only six feet wide, leading to a small kitchen and laundry room in back. The other half of the cottage contained two bedrooms with a bathroom between them. The rear bedroom was partitioned so that Ryan and the girls had some measure of privacy; when Ma had a full house, which was rare these days, it was a tight squeeze. Ryan would sleep in a little nook created by a small supporting wall in the corner of the back bedroom.

After supper, Ryan, Helen, and Grace spent the evening sitting in the parlor. Ma identified Helen, as she did every girl Ryan ever dated in the insular world of Charleston, by who her mother was. "It turns out that Helen and I should have grown up together," Ryan discovered after hearing the two of them chatter. Helen's father, a pharmacist, had trained in Aimar's drugstore, which was owned by one of Grace's relatives. It turned out to be a pleasant evening as the three of them stayed up late talking, playing party tricks and parlor games, and even dancing to some music on the radio.

Helen sensed from Grace's increasingly friendly and welcoming demeanor that she was deeply appreciative that Helen was sharing Ryan with her for the evening. Helen could see how attached they were, in so many ways. Grace had bequeathed her bright blue eyes to Ryan, and her thick, wavy hair, usually tied in the back with a silk scarf, was the same hue of reddish blond as his. But their physical similarities were only the most immediate sign of their connection. They had that special bond of a single mother and her only son, whose identity from a young age was molded by a sense of responsibility to play the role of protector. Ryan had been the man of the house ever since Ryan senior left, and he had taken that role seriously. Whatever

Grace needed, Ryan was usually there, whether it was taking her to work, fixing a broken screen door, or scraping and painting the roof. When it came to raising Uranie and Claudia, too, Grace often sought his advice. When Claudia's fiancé, Leonard Almeida, an Army officer, wrote Grace a letter, Grace dispatched it to Ryan to get his opinion.

In turn, she doted on him, buying him new clothes and cooking his favorite dishes like rice and fried chicken with strawberries and cream for dessert. And like many mothers, she also tried to get him to go to church more often. But she didn't smother him. Grace was a full partner in her son's dreams and encouraged him in all his endeavors. When he was learning how to fly, she went out to the Charleston Army Airfield to watch him. When he got his license, she even went up with him on a twenty-five-minute flight. The previous spring the two of them took in the local air show, thrilling at the sight of the famous pilot Beverly Howard and his barnstorming aerial acrobatics.

Her boy was never far from Grace's mind, even if, due to his military duties, he was no longer around very much. When he was in naval flight training, she had dropped him a postcard from a whistle-stop. It read: "I keep seeing across the table an inquisitive little blue-eyed boy who was with me on another trip some 16 years ago. Remember?" Grace visited Ryan several times while he was stationed in Jacksonville, and as his training grew more intense and the war clouds inched closer, her letters and telegrams to him grew more frequent. Sometimes she penned one every day. For his birthday in January, she sent him a portable typewriter so he could write to her more often.

"Hope she isn't worrying," Ryan remarked in his diary at the time.

But spending time with Ma rarely felt like a chore. In many ways they were kindred spirits. The two of them went for drives in the countryside and enjoyed listening to Hans von Kaltenborn, the radio commentator known for his knowledge of world affairs. They liked to ride the bus downtown to see a picture and then enjoy a strawberry sundae at Walgreens drugstore. They saw the famed opera singer Lawrence Tibbett perform in County Hall—a grand experience despite the train whistle interrupting the show. Grace was an anchor in Ryan's life, and he showed it. He named his small sailboat after her, calling it the *Lady Grace*, and would often take it out on Wadmalaw Sound in search of a bed of oysters to take back for Ma to cook up. On his travels through the South he mailed her small boxes of sweets—pralines and marmalades were among her favorites. He recently bought her a cast-iron doorstop that she had fancied when she noticed it in a shop window. On other occasions he sent her bouquets of roses, especially right before he was planning a rare visit to see his father in North Carolina.

As for a twenty-one-year-old X-ray technician like Helen living in wartime Charleston, there was no shortage of invitations for dates. But Ryan was special. He had a maturity about him that many of the other boys lacked, but he was easy to talk to and interested in so many things. Helen, who considered herself a bit of a prude, would drink ginger ale or Coca-Cola at social events, and she liked that Ryan only drank and smoked on special occasions. In his mild-mannered way he was, she believed, the epitome of the southern gentleman. Perhaps the best compliment of all, she considered him a true Charlestonian. He had taken her boating in the marshes, for strolls along the beach on the Isle of Palms, and for dinner by the pool at the Villa Marguerita, the nineteenth-century mansion on South Battery and East Bay Street facing the White Point Gardens. And, oh, boy, the electricity Ryan gave off when he talked about flying, the way his eyes lit up when he recounted being at the controls in the cockpit, was infectious. Still, Helen couldn't help but think that what he was doing was dangerous. He was almost certain to be going overseas, and she knew from her shift at the hospital that a lot of boys were getting badly hurt and many weren't coming back at all.

When Grace finally retired to her bedroom for the night, Ryan and Helen sat for a while on the small swing on the front porch. Ryan unscrewed the lightbulb so that the two of them would have more privacy from the prying eyes of neighbors.

"Helen's mighty nice," Ryan wrote later in his diary. "Think I could go for her with half a chance—if I were sure she isn't a flirt."

———

"RHIP," as Ryan liked to say. "Rank has its privileges."

He grabbed Helen by the hand and led her through the crowded ballroom of the Fort Sumter Hotel. There was a wedding reception going on—"some lowly Citadel cadet," he quipped—but it was the swiftest way out to the hotel balcony, with its sweeping view of

Charleston Harbor and the historic Fort Sumter, where the Civil War began.

Ryan was wearing his dress whites with a gardenia boutonniere and set of small gold wings pinned on his chest, and Helen was wearing a yellow dress with matching gardenias pinned in her hair. They had enjoyed a Saturday evening supper in the hotel's restaurant. Now, as Ryan and Helen gazed out over Charleston Harbor, the moon hung low in the east, giving the June haze a reddish hue. Strangely, the view made Ryan think of something he had heard during night flight training in Miami: "The only way you can see a sub at night is up moon."

He glanced over at his girl.

He reached into his pocket for another pair of wings and, holding the pin between his fingers, handed them to her.

"They're like yours, aren't they?" she said, looking up at him.

"Exactly."

"I'm glad they're like yours, because then I'll look like you," she whispered.

"Take care of them," Ryan told her. "They're kinda special."

In the small box to store them, Ryan included a little inside joke on the note, a reference to how she wasn't like the other girls.

"Helen," he wrote in clear print, "you were always such a swell guy. Love, Ryan."

Not wanting the evening to end, they later sat on Ma's front porch, "enjoying a quiet summer night," he recorded. "I could notice the creamy odor of her flowers. It is so nice being with Helen even if she embarrasses me. She is a little vixen."

By the time he drove her home, it was past midnight, and the military police were clearing the streets.

"Migawd," he recorded in his diary later. "She even wore gardenias!"

————

At the end of April, after a precious few weeks of leave, Ryan was all set to take the overnight train north from Charleston to Quantico, Virginia, to report for duty. In the afternoon he phoned Helen one last time to say good-bye and tell her he would be back as soon as he could get away for a few days.

"There were a lot of things I wanted to tell her," Ryan wrote later in his diary, "and probably a good thing that I didn't say any of them. I am going to miss Helen."

With evening approaching, Ryan dashed to pick up Uranie at the medical college, then back to the house to collect Ma, change into his uniform, and take them both for supper at the Fort Sumter Hotel's dining room, with its "termite-eaten paneling and rafters." Just as they were finishing their meal, a chorus from the Jenkins Orphanage, established before the turn of the century for Charleston's African-American children, filed into the lobby to sing for the passersby.

"It couldn't have been better," Ryan wrote.

After dinner they barely had enough time to drop by and see Grace's sister before Ryan had to pack and head to the train station. They walked into her house just as the president's speech was coming on the radio, and they all gathered around to listen.

President Franklin D. Roosevelt's twenty-first so-called fireside chat was, like most of the nationwide broadcasts these days, about the war. Roosevelt's strong and steady voice filled the room at 10:00 p.m. sharp.

"My fellow Americans," the president began:

> It is nearly five months since we were attacked at Pearl Harbor. For the two years prior to that attack this country had been gearing itself up to a high level of production of munitions. And yet our war efforts had done little to dislocate the normal lives of most of us. Since then we have dispatched strong forces of our Army and Navy, several hundred thousand of them, to bases and battlefronts thousands of miles from home. We have stepped up our war production on a scale that is testing our industrial power, and our engineering genius and our economic structure to the utmost. We have had no illusions about the fact that this would be a tough job—and a long one. American warships are now in combat in the North and South Atlantic, in the Arctic, in the Mediterranean, in the Indian Ocean, and in the North and South Pacific. American troops have taken stations in South America, Greenland, Iceland, the British Isles, the Near East, the Middle East and the Far East, the Continent of Australia, and many islands of the Pacific. American warplanes, manned by

Americans, are flying in actual combat over all the continents and all the oceans.

In a call for national unity, Roosevelt then recounted for his listeners some of the exploits of those serving in uniform. One of them was about the crew of an Army Air Corps B-17 Flying Fortress on a mission over the Philippines:

As it turned back on its homeward journey, a running fight between the bomber and the eighteen Japanese pursuit planes continued for seventy-five miles. Four pursuit planes . . . attacked simultaneously at each side. Four were shot down with the side guns. During this fight, the bomber's radio operator was killed, the engineer's right hand was shot off, and one gunner was crippled, leaving only one man available to operate both side guns. Although wounded in one hand, the gunner alternately manned both side guns, bringing down three more Japanese "Zero" planes. While this was going on, one engine on the American bomber was shot out, one gas tank was hit, the radio was shot off, and the oxygen system was entirely destroyed. Out of eleven control cables all but four were shot away. The rear landing wheel was blown off entirely, and the two front wheels were both shot flat. The fight continued until the remaining Japanese pursuit ships exhausted their ammunition and turned back. With two engines gone and the plane practically out of control, the American bomber returned to its base after dark and made an emergency landing. The mission had been accomplished.

Roosevelt then closed:

As we here at home contemplate our own duties, our own responsibilities, let us think and think hard of the example which is being set for us by our fighting men. Our soldiers and sailors are members of well disciplined units. But they are still and forever individuals—free individuals. They are farmers, and workers, businessmen, professional men, artists, clerks. They are the United States of America. That is why they fight.

We too are the United States of America. That is why we must work and sacrifice. It is for them. It is for us.

After the speech, Ryan went home and finished packing his things. He decided to call a taxi to take him to the station in North Charleston—much against the wishes of his mother, who wanted to personally see him off on the train. After he settled into his berth in a Pullman car filled with soldiers and sailors, he noted in his diary why he didn't want Ma to see him off.

"I didn't want her hanging around the station then going back to the house." Without him.

———

It was Saturday, May 30, 1942, the morning of the regimental parade, and Ryan was up before dawn in his quarters at Quantico, the sprawling Marine Corps base on the western bank of the Potomac about thirty-five miles south of Washington, D.C. He was "awfully proud" to learn that he had been selected to lead the men as the parade formed and the band passed in review.

Ryan had taken quickly to military life when he joined the Navy Reserve back in 1937, at the age of twenty. With his affinity for athletics—boxing, tennis, swimming, and running—he liked the physical and mental challenge of drill, the highly choreographed and complex formations and movements that were military tradition. When he later enrolled in Georgia Tech and transferred to the Navy Reserve unit on campus, he found himself leading the student battalion's morning drill.

"How I like to be battalion commander," he remarked during his freshman year in 1939.

But even better than leading the men in that day's parade was Helen's upcoming visit. Ryan had been waiting excitedly all week to see her, especially after what happened three weeks earlier. He had hopped the Friday night train to Charleston after getting an unexpected weekend pass. After pulling in, he drove up to Stark General Hospital in Ma's car to see her and was crestfallen to find out she had a date—a previously issued invitation for the weekend at Porcher's Bluff—and planned to keep it.

"By all means, let's observe all the proper proprieties," he said then, rather caustically. "What do we care if the world is crashing around us, and it is later than we think. Let's be Charlestonian about this thing."

So when Helen proposed to visit him in Quantico, he didn't get his hopes up. "I seriously doubt it," he wrote that lonely weekend. He just wasn't sure if Helen was serious about him. She had a steady stream of invitations to balls and dances, he knew, and she probably had many other dates these past months while he was away. How he stacked up against all the other suitors in uniform competing for her affections, Ryan didn't know. Besides, Quantico was a long way from Charleston, at least twelve hours on the overnight train. So he was particularly delighted to receive her letter a week ago alerting him that she and her mother would be getting into Washington early Saturday.

After the Quantico parade, Ryan called for a taxi and headed north on U.S. Route 1 to Washington. His destination was the Willard Hotel, on the corner of Fourteenth and F Streets, across from the National Press Club and next to Garfinckel's department store. Ryan waited for Helen and her mother in the hotel's French-château-style lobby, with its pillars, ornately carved ceilings, and tiered chandeliers.

Helen and her mother soon arrived from Union Station, and Mrs. Miller retired to her room to take a rest after the long train trip, leaving Ryan and Helen alone together on a glorious afternoon in the nation's capital.

After getting a bite to eat, they stepped out of the hotel and joined the throngs of tourists, Red Cross nurses, and government workers enjoying the late May sunshine. They strolled a few blocks south down Fifteenth Street and crossed over Constitution Avenue in the direction of the Washington Monument, the obelisk gleaming white high over the nation's capital from its grassy knoll on the center of the National Mall.

But a landscape that had long been attractive parkland was now blighted by dozens of temporary war emergency buildings, or "tempos," the cheap and shabby-looking structures of concrete and asbestos board that were hastily constructed to house thousands of secretaries and bureaucrats supporting the war effort. They lined both sides of the reflecting pool between the Lincoln Memorial and the Washington Monument and were connected by two covered bridges. The dwellings could be seen nearly the entire length of Constitution

Avenue on the northern side of the Mall. They virtually surrounded the Washington Monument, and more were under construction. As Ryan and Helen ascended the knoll toward the monument, what open space was still left was now muddy pasture churned over by tractors. Trees had been transplanted and replaced by large stacks of lumber, neat piles of cast-iron pipes, kegs of nails, and concrete mixers. Mostly African-American street vendors sold soup, beans, coffee, corn bread, and succotash to the busy construction crews.

The entrance to the Washington Monument itself was surrounded by metal benches and posted with a sign informing visitors that no photography was permitted, a security precaution taken out of concern that saboteurs might single out the national landmark. Cameras would be checked at the door, they were informed, and the sign read "Violators Will Be Arrested—Film Confiscated."

To their southwest, across the nearby Potomac River, Ryan and Helen could see more commotion on a patch of ground that until the previous August had been mostly swamps. There, on the opposite shore, more crews were now hard at work on what would become the largest office building in the world, larger than the Chicago Merchandise Mart and the Empire State Building: the five-sided headquarters of the War Department that would soon be known as the Pentagon.

Walking that afternoon in Washington with Helen, Ryan later wrote in his diary, ranked up there as one of the most memorable experiences of his young life—a "thrilling moment" he would not soon forget.

As the sun descended lower in the sky on the Virginia horizon, Ryan and Helen hailed a taxi for the trip to Quantico, making a short stop along the way to look around Mount Vernon, George Washington's Virginia estate along the Potomac.

They arrived in Quantico just in time for a quick tour of the base in a friend's car before they had to get ready for supper and an evening in the Anchor Room at the Officers' Club, where Ryan was looking forward to showing off his girl to his fellow officers, especially the married ones.

Helen was fascinated by the sights and sounds of the Quantico base. To the Algonquin Indians who once called the area home, Quantico had been known as the "place of dancing." And now, in the middle of 1942, the hundred-square-mile Marine Corps base remained a high-stepping place. Known as the Crossroads of the Marine Corps, it was the nerve center of its training operations, where more than twenty thousand officers would be trained by war's end. The base was now an intricate network of barracks, classrooms, shops, warehouses, airfields, and training areas for both officers and enlisted troops. The complex was served by three major railroads, and U.S. Highway 1 ran directly through the base. Just before Ryan had arrived, fifty-one thousand additional acres were acquired west of the highway and named the Guadalcanal area—due to the dense vegetation, numerous streams, and deep, muddy ravines that were similar to the terrain Marines were encountering on the South Pacific island of the same name.

Ryan was attached to the headquarters squadron at the Marine Corps Air Station located on the base, where he was undergoing instruction at the air station's communications school and gaining more flight experience. He now spent most of his time in class, which he found covered a lot of material he was already familiar with from his engineering studies at Georgia Tech. He was also taking his turn, like all Marines, qualifying on the rifle range. In between he gained more flight hours in special aircraft designed to fly at night. He also was assigned some flights to deliver new aircraft to Marine Corps units on the East Coast and in the Midwest. There were ferry flights from Quantico to Floyd Bennett Field in New York City and on to the Squantum Naval Air Station in Quincy, Massachusetts, outside Boston. On other occasions the aircraft deliveries took him south and allowed him to drop in to see Ma, Uranie, and Helen for a quick visit—sometimes overnight but mostly for just a few hours, enough time for a meal.

These trips were not always routine. One in December took him to Detroit, Cleveland, and Pittsburgh in a blizzard, flying only with the aid of instruments because there was virtually no visibility from the cockpit. On several occasions the weather forced him to land on an alternate airfield and wait for the skies to clear. Even landing at Quantico could cause a little too much excitement at times. One day Ryan looked out to see a Navy pilot overshoot the runway and come around for another try. He then watched in horror as the pilot missed the runway again, landed in the marsh, and nosed over. The pilot was killed instantly. It wouldn't be the last time Ryan would see a perfectly qualified pilot die not at the hand of the enemy but in a crash. Aviation was still inching toward adulthood at the start of World War II, and equipment breakdowns, foul weather, and limited training all posed serious dangers.

Ryan gave Helen a tour of Turner Field, the main airfield where Navy SBD Dauntless dive-bombers, F4F Hellcats, and the Marine Corps's newest combat plane, the F4U Corsair, were being put through their paces. He showed her the tennis courts down in the Hollow, the boat dock where he went sailing in the Potomac on his days off, and some of his hangouts. One of his favorite haunts was Hostess House, the former bachelor officers' quarters in the Cinder City section of the base where a shabby old man did balancing tricks on a bicycle and a blind boy made change in the adjacent post exchange, or PX, where there was a theater and beer garden in the back. Hostess House was run by Mrs. Katherine De Boo, a wonderful, spectacled lady in her mid-sixties who had been a fixture at Quantico since 1925, when she arrived with her sergeant major husband and quickly became known and loved as simply "Mother." In her role as official hostess, she welcomed visiting parents, chaperoned girls on dates with Marines, arranged dinners and celebrations, and was a sympathetic ear to many. On Mother's Day she would receive flowers and gifts from Marines stationed all over the world. Marines fighting on Guadalcanal heard a radio message she recorded for them.

Ryan and Helen drove through the heart of Quantico Town, with its small, compact streets of residential houses and commercial buildings, whose motto was "Trouble-free and heart strung to the Marine Corps." The main thoroughfare, Potomac Avenue, led east from the train depot toward the river and was lined with barbershops, restaurants, and jewelry stores. To the sound of the frequent train whistles, shoe-shine boys hawked their services along the curb in the reflection of the shiny fenders of the black and white and gray sedans parked diagonally on both sides of the street. On the corner of Potomac and C Street was the Star Café, across from the Nationwide Grocery and the New Way Grill, the Greek diner with its stucco walls, wood-paneled bar with circular mirrors, and cozy booths with Formica tables, almost always crowded with Marines.

Ryan and Helen returned to his quarters to get dressed for supper. On their walk to the Officers' Club they stood at attention together for the evening colors. Ryan realized that in all the excitement he had forgotten to pin his lieutenant's bars on his shoulders. He dashed back to his room, but they were too late for supper with the officers. "So we ate at the New Way of all the places in the world," he recorded.

An evening of dancing in the Officers' Club followed before Ryan and Helen left at midnight for the ride back to her hotel in Washington so he could see her and her mother off on the 3:15 a.m. train for Charleston. Ryan then waited around the station for the "reveille special," arriving back in his barracks room just before dawn on Sunday, where he wrote a special "note" with the typewriter Ma had given him for his birthday and tacked it into his diary:

> Well, here I go again. I am in love—and this Miller girl is terrific. To say she is the most different girl I've ever known is being rather conservative. Her spontaneity, possible naiveté, straight-from-the-shoulder forwardness, absolutely un-subtle way she lets me know who's boss, is absolutely something new and different to me. I just don't know what kind of girl she is. She is, tho, absolutely charming—somebody that you definitely take pride in introducing to somebody else. She's just too much for me at times—such as when I handed her that corsage of red roses and then leaving the club in Nick's car. But she sure is some girl!

———

The biting wind blew in off the Potomac and whipped across Turner Field. From the confines of the control tower at Quantico, where he was pulling the code watch, Ryan peered at the mercury as it dipped to near zero, and looked out at the thick gray clouds that seemed to permanently block out the sun and the moon. The year 1942 was drawing to a close, and Ryan was "becoming bored actually to death."

Back in June, when he was preparing for the final exam in the communications course, Ryan received orders for his next assignment. He felt a tinge of disappointment to learn he wouldn't be going anywhere. Instead of being transferred to a Marine Corps unit heading overseas, as most of his fellow officers were, he would be staying at Quantico. He proved to be so adept in radio communications that the Marine Corps wanted him to teach the training course to new officers.

His daily routine usually began before dawn in Quarters 314B, followed by a workout in the gym—sometimes he was lucky enough to find a sparring partner—and then it was breakfast and off to teach the finer points of radio communications in one of the crowded classroom buildings next to the air station. In the afternoon he was back teaching another section.

Having been a highly rated math instructor for his fellow Navy reservists while he was at Georgia Tech in Atlanta, as well as a drill leader, Ryan was uniquely qualified for the instructor post. His military superiors had pegged him early as someone who should be given heightened responsibility, and he had striven to live up to those expectations.

"This is a student of outstanding ability who has been one of our company commanders for two weeks," one officer concluded in the fall of 1939, when Ryan was in reserve training at Georgia Tech. "Can give complete instruction in drill and manual. Was head of our mathematics department. And checked out with 16 words per minute in radio. Recommend that you give this student heavy responsibility."

When he was accepted two years later for flight training and reported to Jacksonville Naval Air Station in Florida, he was selected as the wing commander, responsible for the sixty flight cadets in his class. Soon he was showing other cadets how to wear their uniforms correctly and giving the men pep talks about willpower and heart.

His desire to lead also made him be hard on himself. He had a keen awareness of where he fell short, whether it was in his relationships, his studies, or his flying. "My flying smells from one end of the field to the other," he noted after one particularly disappointing checkout in the air. It was a drive that eventually propelled him to graduate second in his cadet training class.

Ryan had been preparing for an important role in the unfolding events since he saw the blaring headlines in the evening editions of the newspapers back in 1939. Germany had invaded Poland.

"Little man, what now," he wrote in his diary that day, spending the ensuing hours close to a radio to keep up with the hum of news about France and Britain declaring war on Germany.

Ryan had followed the advance of events with a growing anticipation that the American armed forces would have to act and that
ultimately he, too, would be called upon to play a part. Imprinted in
his memory, for instance, was May 27, 1941, while he was doing Navy
Reserve training near Atlanta, when Roosevelt declared a national
emergency. That October, when he arrived for flight training in Jacksonville, he learned that a U.S. Navy destroyer, the USS *Reuben
James*, had been torpedoed and sunk off the coast of Iceland by a German U-boat, the first American warship to be sunk in the war—two
months before Pearl Harbor.

Even in those early days he had detected a shift in people's atti-
tudes. It was subtle at first, but there was a collective anticipation that
America would not be able to stay out of the war and that the country
would have to come together to be ready. On a bus ride from Atlanta
to Charleston in April 1941, Ryan noticed the change in the passengers around him.

"People traveling are more friendly and talkative than they were a
year ago," he recorded in his diary.

Sunday, December 7, 1941, had been Ryan's traditional day off.
He awoke in room 239 in his barracks at the Naval Air Station in
Jacksonville, went to breakfast, and walked over to the 11:00 a.m.
base church services. He then took the bus into town and got off at
Riverside Avenue next to Memorial Park, where he strolled along the
banks of the St. Johns River in the Florida sunshine, enjoying the
warm, wet breeze and the hyacinths floating by the seawall.

In the late afternoon, as he walked into a mad rush of cadets at
the Hotel Roosevelt on their way back to the air station, he was told
of the news of the Japanese attack and jumped in a taxi with four
of them. He wired his sister Claudia the next day to tell her that he
would have to miss her and Leonard's wedding the following weekend
at Fort Benning, Georgia.

But as 1943 now approached, he was only reading and hearing
about the unfolding events from the newsreels in the base auditorium
or, in rare cases, fellow officers who arrived in Quantico from the
combat zone.

He was still flying but less frequently. There were more ferry hops
to deliver new planes to far-flung air stations and fields, others to trans-

port VIPs up to the Navy Yard in Washington and back. Much of it—like the flyover he did for a July 4 celebration near Richmond—was intended to keep him proficient and increase his total flying hours.

He was determined to be a tough but conscientious instructor, yet the days seemed to drag on as he watched his fellow Marine officers get their combat orders and depart Quantico. After one typical day of teaching a communications class, he wondered in his diary whether he was doing little more than "reading them to sleep twice a day." The only real action, and there wasn't much of it, came on the nights he was on the code watch, pulling a shift on the air station as the presiding communications officer for Quantico's flight operations.

"How bored can a man get?" he wondered.

He felt he should be doing more. His sense of purpose was only fueled by being a Marine. The Corps has always considered itself a breed apart from the rest of the military branches—a tradition that traced to its founding in the early years of the Republic. That was especially true in World War II, when the Marines were handed a singular mission. While the Navy, the Army, and the companion Army Air Corps were engaged against several enemies in Africa, Europe, and Asia, the smaller and more elite Marines trained to fight only one: Japan. Unlike the other branches, which to fill their ranks relied on the draft initiated by Congress in 1940, the Marines insisted on taking no conscripts and accepted only volunteers like Ryan. Those who flocked to the Marine Corps since Pearl Harbor—and so many did that the Marine Corps had to turn people away—were consciously signing up to fight Japan.

But to his increasing frustration, Ryan was not yet one of them. He grew more eager for a new assignment when one afternoon he walked down to the Marine Corps schools at Quantico to hear three officers—a colonel, a major, and a captain—give a talk about their experiences in the Solomon Islands. For the first time he was also shown confidential photographs of the brutal fighting against the Japanese on Guadalcanal in the South Pacific.

"My morale hits another low," he wrote in his diary. "I am just bored to tears with the lack of action. I can't stand being just another guy."

———

One high point came in early November when Ryan senior made a surprise visit to Quantico. Father and son weren't particularly close and seldom saw each other in the years since Ryan senior left Grace and the children behind. But each May, Ryan dutifully called Dad on his birthday, and the two exchanged letters and visits from time to time. Their relationship was rooted in the age-old desire of accomplished men to see their sons compete with their peers and strive to make their mark—and in sons' primordial yearning to make their fathers proud. Their early bond survived the breakup of the marriage, and while he had been fiercely protective of his mother, Ryan had fond memories of his father. Like when he had driven him to Charlotte, North Carolina, to participate in an amateur boxing competition. Ryan senior had watched proudly as his namesake, then a wispy teenager with outsized dreams of being a boxer, aggressively sparred with the bigger and more practiced boys.

Ryan's father was certainly proud of him now. He had come to visit several times during 1941, when Ryan was in flight training in Jacksonville. One afternoon Ryan got a surprise call at the training squadron telling him that his father and eight-year-old half brother, Vance, were waiting outside the gate. The two Ryans got a haircut and then rejoined Vance and Ryan's stepmother, Sarah, for dinner at the steak house in the lobby of the George Washington, the fifteen-story luxury hotel in downtown Jacksonville. The next morning, while Sarah went shopping, Ryan took Dad and Vance for a tour of the Jacksonville Naval Air Station. Little Vance was already well on his way to being an aircraft aficionado and gazed wide-eyed at all the airplanes taking off and landing. But he was even more mesmerized by his older brother, the real-life military flier.

The last time Ryan had visited his father and his new family in North Carolina was in the spring of 1941, when he was working on a crew surveying the runways for the U.S. Engineering Department in Florence, South Carolina. Ryan wired his father on a Friday night and after knocking off from work at noon the next day took a Greyhound bus north—though not before phoning Ma and sending her a corsage of yellow roses. Ryan senior and Sarah met him at the bus station in Spartanburg and accompanied him the rest of the way to Tryon, a small country town just across the border in North Carolina. Sarah fixed her stepson some beans and eggs before he "slept like a log through a deliciously cool night," as Ryan recorded after that rare visit. Early the next morning Dad took him upstairs to see Vance, who was in bed with the mumps but "was doing some pretty nice work in airplanes and stuff in modeling clay." On that last visit to Tryon, Ryan had also had a chance to see his grandfather and Maybelle, Ryan senior's parents, and to meet some of Sarah's family. But as always, he had little time just with Dad. He noted wryly after that visit that his stepmother "refuses with a bulldog tenacity to leave me alone with Dad."

But now, with Dad's surprise visit to Quantico—he was checking on some business interests in Washington—it was just the two of them. Ryan showed him the base, and then they drove to Washington for an oyster roast at the home of Ryan's uncle Moultrie McCown, where to Ryan's surprise Dad gave him two hundred dollars—in case, he was told, he was thinking of buying a ring for that girl he was dating.

A few days later, as Ryan waited impatiently at Quantico for word of his next assignment, he received a telegram from Georgia that lifted his spirits even further. His sister Claudia had given birth to a daughter, and they named her after Ma—Grace Emilie Almeida. The whole gang, he was told, was planning to spend Christmas in Charleston, and he vowed he would make it, too.

Ryan had hardly seen his dear Claudie, as he affectionately called his youngest sister. The last time she had burst into tears at the sight of him walking through Ma's front door. It still bothered him that he had missed her wedding when his leave was abruptly canceled after Pearl Harbor.

Ryan and Claudie enjoyed a sibling kinship that Ryan and Uranie, who was only two years younger than he, didn't quite share. Partly it was because Ryan was the big brother and Claudia was the baby. But they were also the most outgoing personalities in the family. Both had a gift for humorous banter and were equally quick-witted and adept at making a sarcastic crack at just the right moment in a conversation. They were compatriots in other ways. When they were younger, Claudia liked to wrestle her brother in the yard, proving to be a tenacious and determined foe, despite her physical disadvantage. When Ryan earned his pilot's license, Claudia was one of his first passengers as he carried her above their house and out over the marshes of Lagare

Island. Claudia had also been a smash hit with Ryan's friends at Georgia Tech when she came for the big football weekend against Auburn in the fall of 1940—especially the evening she went out on campus wearing tight-fitting riding trousers cuffed snugly at the ankle, "looking adorable in her jodhpurs," as Ryan recorded at the time. They also had similar tastes. Both craved the tangy and sour limeade at Walgreens and on a whim were known to go in search of a midnight steak. They naturally confided in each other about their romances, their dreams, and often stayed up late talking after Ma and Uranie went to sleep. Claudia had introduced Ryan to some of her friends, including Helen, but he was the protective older brother when it came to Claudia's boyfriends. Before Claudia met her husband, Leonard, an Army officer, Ryan had been wary of most of them; once, upon hearing that one of her relationships was on the rocks, he remarked that it was the "best news I ever heard." Ryan wrote his youngest sister long letters and relished her replies, including the lengthy one he recently received at Quantico that he deemed "a masterpiece of good literature."

In late December 1942 he arrived at the squadron to learn that his name was on the promotion list for first lieutenant. He was also informed by the commander of the air station that he was "being detached." He was being transferred, finally. After New Year's he would be leaving Quantico for Cherry Point, North Carolina, to be the communications officer of the Third Marine Aircraft Wing, a combat unit.

In preparation, the base commander, Colonel I. W. Miller, reviewed his performance during the eight months he had been at Quantico. Ryan was rated in a series of categories, including physical fitness, military bearing, attention to duty, initiative, intelligence, judgment, resolve, leadership, and loyalty. On all counts he was found to be "excellent." As for whether he would want Ryan under his command in battle, Colonel Miller wrote that he would "particularly desire to have him"—the highest rating. Ryan, Colonel Miller concluded, was an "excellent officer who is very much interested in his work."

———

Just before Christmas, Ryan finally got word from headquarters that he could leave for Charleston. Because Christmas was a Friday, he was told he had to be back on base for duty first thing Sunday morning. He was also granted permission to take one of the SNJ-2s, the two-seater training planes. But throughout the day the weather looked nastier and nastier. Winter storms stretched nearly all the way down the Eastern Seaboard to Atlanta. While waiting for the all clear, he bided his time sitting around the squadron watching the gloomy sky or back in his quarters, where he lay on his bed with a copy of *A Shropshire Lad*, the collection of rhythmic poems by A. E. Housman, the nineteenth-century British poet. It was a recent gift from one of the Quantico nurses who had been a steady competitor on the tennis courts down in the Hollow.

The poems were almost all obsessed with death:

Say, lad, have you things to do?
Quick then, while your day's at prime.
Quick, and if 'tis work for two,
Here am I, man: now's your time.

Send me now, and I shall go;
Call me, I shall hear you call;
Use me ere they lay me low
Where a man's no use at all;

Ere the wholesome flesh decay,
And the willing nerve be numb,
And the lips lack breath to say,
"No, my lad, I cannot come."

Finally, at 3:30 p.m. on Christmas Eve, Ryan shoved off for Charleston. He set down a few hours later at the Charleston Army Airfield and scrambled into town.

Everyone was eagerly awaiting his arrival at Ma's, where he got to meet his niece, Grace Emilie, and sat for hours on the front porch catching up with her parents, Claudia and Leonard. When they left for midnight Mass, Ryan stayed behind and visited with Ma and Uranie. It was a splendid evening all around, and by the time Ryan crawled into his bed in the back bedroom, it was just a few hours before sunup.

"Having mother close by" felt especially meaningful, he thought, as she was recuperating from what the doctors called her "cerebral accident" during the summer, a mini stroke that had prevented her from working. Ryan didn't know when he might be able to get back to Charleston.

Christmas Day dawned like spring. After only a few hours of sleep Ryan was up early. There were a lot of people he wanted to see, and he only had one full day before he was due to head back to Quantico. First he was off to call on Helen, who was spending the holiday at home with her family. Ryan promised to keep in touch with her and let her know where he was. Helen couldn't help but feel as if he were just saying that to make her feel better. They had talked on one of his last visits about getting married, but she said she wanted to wait until he got back. The future was just too uncertain. A lot of boys flying over Japan weren't coming back, Helen knew. Besides, she also thought, it wouldn't be fair to Grace, who should get his military allowance while he was gone. She would still be here when he returned, she assured him.

PART TWO

The fates lead him who will; him who won't they drag.

Lucius Annaeus Seneca

CHAPTER THREE

HEEDING THE CALL

At 2:00 on the afternoon of April 26, 1997, under the shade of sturdy southern magnolias and red maple trees, George straightened the creases in his uniform, squared his shoulders, and faced forward, chin up. He was now a "distinguished military graduate" of the Seminole Battalion of the U.S. Army Reserve Officers' Training Corps. Like his father a generation before, he stood at attention on the Natural Bridge Battlefield near Woodville, Florida, where he was about to be commissioned an officer in the U.S. Army.

George was lined up in formation with his fellow cadets before a monument topped with a bald eagle taking flight. On the granite were engraved just three words, "Lest We Forget." He glowed with a sense of achievement and had a look of determination in his slate-blue eyes as he raised his right hand and repeated the age-old oath uttered by so many of his ancestors. In a steady voice, with a hint of a southern twang that could only be called career Army, he recited the words slowly and clearly, his words carrying over the stillness of the park, where a bloody battle had been fought in the waning days of the Civil War.

"I, George Senseny Eyster V, do solemnly swear that I will support and defend the Constitution of the United States against all enemies, foreign and domestic; that I will bear true faith and allegiance to the same; that I take this obligation freely, without any mental reservation or purpose of evasion; and that I will well and faithfully discharge the duties of the office on which I am about to enter: So help me God."

Standing by his side were his proud parents, his father dressed in one of his old Army uniforms and a maroon beret, his mother in red. Along with his girlfriend, Vivian, also there to help pin on his epaulets was a beaming Grandma Harriet, looking as regal as ever in a black patterned skirt and matching coat.

His father had decided many years earlier that he would not pressure his only son to become an Army officer and would let him choose his own path. He understood that the pressure to become a soldier was strong enough without an overbearing father insisting on it. But when George belatedly decided to apply for an ROTC scholarship after transferring from Towson to Florida State, Big George could barely hide his excitement. In a Christmas message to his old Army brethren in 1995, he burst with pride recounting George's accomplishments since joining the ROTC.

"George was recognized as the outstanding cadet in his platoon," he bragged. "No sooner did he get home than he was offered the chance to go to Airborne School. It was a great experience for him and brought back fond memories for me as I was able to watch his final jump and present him with his 'blood' wings."

He took pleasure in relating George's apparent determination to stand out. "I thought I had him convinced that flying was better than walking," Big George wrote, "but he seems determined to become a grunt and eventually wants to go into the Special Forces."

Upon his commission as a second lieutenant, George soon found himself braving the stifling Georgia summer at the Infantry Basic Officer Leadership Course at Fort Benning, where he was learning the nuts and bolts of leading a platoon of soldiers. After a week of exercises defending against a larger opposing force of soldiers and armored vehicles, he took a few minutes to write an e-mail to his father.

"It was the toughest field problem we've had so far," he wrote. "It was about 100 degrees the first couple of days. . . . We dug fighting positions for two days. We also patrolled all night" looking for enemy troops in tanks and other heavy combat vehicles. "We set anti-armor ambushes along the roads and patrolled the forested areas of our sector. I really learned a lot about communications and the info flow between the platoon and the company. I also got a lot of practice calling for fire.

His unit's two Bradley Fighting Vehicles weren't much competition for the opposing force, which had sixteen armored vehicles and tanks. "In the end," he continued, "we got plowed. . . . They rolled our flank and pushed through us like butter."

George was learning some of the downsides of being an infantry officer humping it in the field, he told his father. "I came out of the field problem with a bad case of poison ivy," he related. "I've got it on my ears and my left eye . . . it swelled my eye shut on Wednesday morning, but there ain't much you can do for it except scratch so I wouldn't let them take me to the rear."

He was also getting a crash course in how dangerous his chosen line of work could be. One of the other new officers in the course was trying to clear an antitank weapon when the explosive charge went off while he was holding it over his groin. "It fried his testicles and other parts off," George wrote, sparing no details. "He has third degree burns from his balls to his knees. . . . He's probably done.

"I'm just starting to see how dangerous everyday ops can be," he told Big George. "You can get killed just as fast in training as you can in battle."

He closed by saying he was looking forward to visiting in a few weeks and attending the Florida State–Maryland football game with his father.

"Three things keep me going in the field. You and Mom, Vivi, and the upcoming football season!"

He signed the e-mail "George #5."

———

Big George received a letter from George's commander at Fort Benning in late September that made him even prouder. He was informed that George's performance in infantry officer training made him eligible for the commandant's list, recognizing the top 20 percent of each graduating class.

"Your son has been both physically and mentally challenged during the past 16 weeks and has met every challenge with a high degree of professionalism and confidence," the letter stated. "He has proven that he is a true leader among his contemporaries, and that he is ready to accept the highest trust that this country can bestow upon him, that of leading American soldiers."

But even with their new bond, George still found it difficult to connect with his father. Dad had always been reluctant to talk about what it was like to be the son of a dead war hero, and he rarely spoke of his emotions. He had a tough exterior difficult to pierce. The only time George could remember seeing his father cry was when he returned from the Persian Gulf War to learn that their dog Schotzy had died. Conversations between father and son were a bit too professional, especially now since they often reverted to soldier talk and how George's experiences were similar to Dad's when he was coming up the ranks.

Still, little gestures from Big George let him know how pleased he was, like making the long drive to watch him complete Airborne School at Fort Bragg. George desperately wanted to find a way to reach him, to thank him for the example he provided and for helping steer him off the wrong path he had been heading down in high school and college.

For his father's birthday, George penned a poem. He titled it "The Once and Future Soldier."

> Old soldiers never die,
> They just fade away up into the sky;
> An old soldier will remember the day
> When his old soldier passed away
> And too he'll recall the day
> When his future soldier began to play.
> There in his mind's eye he vividly replays,
> The first of all his past days.
> The times, the places,
> The names, the faces.
> Rucker, Carson, Aberdeen and Bragg,
> Grenada, Panama, Iraq and D.C.,
> Always duty, to defend the free.
> And in his time,
> He was the best of the best,
> Never afraid to take on the test.
> But perhaps his trial greatest in life,
> Ladened with endless more strife,
> Wasn't fought to the tune of the fife.
> He raised a son, and called him the same,

He gave him his love,
His guidance and name.
And as the next chapter is penned and weighed,
He has wrought a man,
Who is proud to say,
"In the old soldier, I have seen what is best,
Give me the guidon,
I will stand the test."
And in all the days that come to me,
I will remember the soldier, in all I see.
In the country I protect,
And the place I defend,
The once and future has come again.

The next stop in the Army would prove to be George's biggest test yet. He returned to Fort Benning, Georgia, in the fall of 1997, where he had been selected to attend the Army's elite Ranger School. Like his father and grandfather before him, he was committed to earning the coveted "Black and Gold" tab of an Army Ranger. Big George dropped him off at the Ranger Training Brigade like everyone else selected for the program—with his military and medical records in hand and no rank or insignia on his uniform.

Politely called a "handshake with reality," Ranger School is designed to mold the Army's best soldiers into resolute and highly skilled combat leaders by exposing them to unrelenting physical and psychological pressures like those experienced in close combat. The Rangers traced their roots to before the American Revolution and the New Hampshire Regimental Rangers, a militia unit whose men, armed with their own muskets, wore deerskin frocks that came down around their knees to help them blend into the forest. Now, to join the exclusive fraternity, those good enough to be selected had to brave nine weeks of intensive field training in the backwoods of Georgia and the swamps of the Florida Panhandle.

There are three phases. The first, known as the Benning Phase, builds physical and mental endurance and forces soldiers to operate in the field under extremely difficult conditions. It includes a host of increasingly demanding physical tests like a twelve-mile march in full combat gear. To pass the water confidence test, soldiers must walk across a log thirty feet above the water and then crawl out on a suspended rope and drop thirty-five feet into Victory Pond. Then they must climb a sixty-foot-high tower and hold on to a pulley as it carries them down a two-hundred-foot cable known as the "slide for life" into the water. Moving in pairs, they must also crawl through, jump over, or slide past nearly two dozen obstacles on a densely wooded hillside to complete the dreaded Darby Queen obstacle course. It is also during the first phase that Ranger candidates are drilled in their ability to navigate during the day and at night. The second part of the course is known as the Mountain Phase, in which students must lead small units on ambushes and raids in the treacherous mountainous terrain of northern Georgia. George had one advantage in this phase over his fellow students: he had spent a couple of summers on a forestry crew cutting down trees in some of the same forests. The last part of the Ranger course is the Florida Phase, which introduces the most extreme mental and physical stress, when trainees have to plan and mount operations against a sophisticated foe on land, from the air, and using small boats.

Many never make it through Ranger School. Indeed, nearly half of the officers and enlisted soldiers who start it fail to graduate, while only 25 percent who do complete the course do so with the same class they began with. The rest have to repeat one or more phases of the course before they pass.

After one particularly tough day in the field in October, George had a few precious moments to rest. Sitting on the ground in the middle of the Chattahoochie Reservation, in rural Georgia, he scrawled a letter to his parents on the back of a map.

"Things are going well enough," he scribbled. "The only way I know what the days are is when I check my watch. The first week was the hardest of my life. But it's not so bad now. We just don't get any sleep."

He had no envelope, so he folded the letter, secured it inside the cardboard packaging for a field ration, and addressed it to his parents back in Tallahassee.

Several weeks later, on Monday, November 24, with just twelve hours to go in Ranger School, George was tapped on the shoulder during a maneuver in the Florida swamps and told he was to report immediately to training headquarters. He hadn't had a good meal in weeks and virtually no sleep. His mind began to race out of control. What had he done wrong? Where had he made a mistake? He couldn't think of a single reason why he was being removed from the course. He was so close to the end, just hours away from completing the nine-week version of hell. He was stunned.

As he sat alone in the small trailer that served as the command post, waiting to be informed of his fate, he was nearly delirious. His heart pounded, and he felt faint. Then, after what seemed an eternity, he saw something out of the corner of his eye that focused his mind like a laser. Approaching the trailer was a Florida Highway patrolman. With him was a chaplain. As the pair walked purposefully toward him, George studied the expressions on their faces. He felt a sharp pang and immediately thought of his mother. Something terrible must have happened to her, he was sure of it. But in a hushed whisper from the chaplain, he finally learned why he had been taken out of the field and brought here. His father had suffered a heart attack. Big George, only forty-nine years old, was dead.

There were no tears at first. The state of shock that quickly set in was compounded by the physical and mental trauma he had already undergone in Ranger training. George simply couldn't believe it. Big George had always seemed invincible to him. It all combined to put him into what could only be called a trance. George's stepbrother, Scott, had seen to it that the state trooper was there to drive him home to Tallahassee, and George remembered very little of the nearly two-hour drive on Interstate 10 through the dead of night in the state police cruiser—only that he had no wallet with him and the patrolman was thoughtful enough to stop at a rest stop along the way and get him something to eat.

It was the week of Thanksgiving. The holiday passed like a blur amid the family's grief and preparations for the funeral, which was to be held the day after Thanksgiving. No college football was watched at the Eyster household, a first. It was just too painful without Big George. That evening, George met privately with the family's pastor, who wanted his help in crafting the service. His father, he told him simply, as he fought back tears, had equipped him for life—from how to survive and prosper in the military to how to love and succeed in marriage.

"He encouraged my faith," George said of his father.

He later sat alone in meditation with his father's casket and read from Psalm 91:

A thousand shall fall at thy side,
And ten thousand at thy right hand;
But it shall not come nigh thee.

The funeral service was held at the Temple Baptist Church in Tallahassee. The pews were filled with longtime family friends, old Army buddies and neighbors, and the friends and colleagues Big George and Ann had met in his new career working for the Florida state government and hers at the restaurant association. The eulogy was delivered by Ann Wainwright, the deputy commissioner of the Florida Department of Agriculture, who had first met George and Ann when they were dating more than twenty-five years before.

"He loved to serve. He thrived on it," she recalled of a public servant who even after leaving the Army insisted on being referred to by his radio call sign, Pegasus 1. "In Greek mythology Pegasus was a legendary and mighty flying horse," Wainwright intoned. "So was George. Sure-footed, strong, swift, and dependable."

She recalled something else about her friend and former colleague that she thought captured his essence. "You see, George came to the department after a brilliant career in the military. I remember on his official application in the space where you describe your past experience, George simply wrote: 'Defending Our Country.'"

The pastor recounted Big George's dedication to his family, especially to Ann but also to his two stepchildren, whom he raised and loved as his own. His description of his relationship with his namesake was particularly poignant, extolling his "patience and willingness to encourage the young George, even when he was finding his way."

The life of the late lieutenant colonel George S. Eyster IV offered lessons for everyone who had come to bid him good-bye. For George those lessons now meant far more than he ever realized, one in particular. His father, the pastor said, "raised people's expectations of themselves."

As if on cue, hours later George was presented with a new dilemma that tested his ability to live up to those words. He was informed that even though he had been a few hours from completing Ranger School when his father died, the Army wasn't going to pass him. To earn his Ranger tab, he would have to complete the last thirty days of the training course again. He felt as if he had been hit while he was down, and disbelief quickly turned to anger.

"Who needs this? I just won't do it," he told one of his Army buddies.

——

As the only George S. Eyster left, George now found himself the recipient of a growing collection of family heirlooms. When it wasn't Ann, it was Grandma Harriet who made sure of that. Each time he visited her, he left with another artifact to remind him who he was— of the name he was now steward of. He also hit upon a convenient way to explain to those who were inevitably curious about what it felt like to come from such an illustrious military family. It was a line from a popular movie that nearly everyone understood and usually put to rest a subject he had never felt comfortable with, let alone talking about.

"I have a Lieutenant Dan complex," he quipped when asked by his fellow officers or acquaintances who discovered his pedigree. He was referring to the character in the popular novel and motion picture *Forrest Gump* who hailed from a long line of battlefield heroes and was singularly focused on living up to the glory of his name.

What George didn't say, however, was that unlike the fictional character, who was obsessed with dying in battle as his forefathers did, he had been decidedly wary of the family business from the start.

Now he was surrounded by that history. He had the desk plate that his great-grandfather used during World War II, along with the textbooks that General Eyster used as a cadet at West Point and his metal rod pointing stick. Other relics of the Eyster line he inherited from Grandma Harriet or were bequeathed to him by his late father included a more-than-hundred-year-old solid-gold pocket watch with twenty-seven ruby jewels, a German Nazi sword, and a nearly priceless cherrywood grandfather clock. One of the most mysterious items was an ornate saber and scabbard of a 32nd degree Freemason, which had been passed down through the generations after the Civil War.

Before long, there were sheaves of old letters and faded postcards penned by his forebears and military records he had never seen before. One of the first he inherited was a copy of a letter that Grandpa George had written to a fellow officer a little more than two weeks before he was killed in Vietnam. The three-page typewritten message included detailed advice for other units that were heading into the war zone—down to how much salt, sugar, baking soda, and extra nails to bring. George learned it was later put on display in the West Point Museum as a classic example of one officer taking the time on the battlefield to counsel another back home who would soon be following him into combat. The copy George was given was still in the envelope from when Grandma Harriet had given it to his father.

There were also letters from Grandpa George to George's father that offered new insights into a relationship that Big George was so reluctant to speak about. One written from Vietnam a few months before his death provided a peek into the pressure that George's father must have felt to carry on the family tradition.

"Things go pretty well here—we've killed a lot of Vietcong at the expense of 12 of our own plus 87 wounded," Grandpa George reported.

Yet the bulk of the two-page handwritten letter dated November 30, 1965, was about his expectations for his son's future.

"I wish you all the success in the world in getting to" West Point, Grandpa George wrote, before adding, "if that is what you want to do. . . . You will also hear from the Army on the four year ROTC scholarships but they are only good if you have been accepted by a college that offers four year ROTC. So be sure you apply to one or more that meet this requirement," he instructed.

The letter, which would be the last that George's dad would receive from his father, was almost completely lacking in feeling, save for the final sentence.

"Much love son," Grandpa George wrote. "Take care and have fun. Devotedly, Pop."

These were some of the raw materials that had built and sustained the George S. Eyster legend. But George wasn't ready to digest it all. He was trying his best to catch up with the parts of the story that he already knew. Indeed, most of the letters, news clippings, and other items he was now the custodian of filled up a box that he stashed away in a closet.

———

For the next two years George sought, with mixed success, to write his own chapter in the saga. But his rightful place in it remained elusive. In some ways he found being in the Army even more difficult than agonizing over whether to don the uniform in the first place. He struggled to achieve a level of professional satisfaction—a search that would soon exact a high price in his personal life.

Despite his resentment at how the Army treated him, after some soul-searching George reluctantly agreed to repeat the most grueling phase of the Ranger course. He simply couldn't stand the thought of not wearing the Ranger tab after coming so close. Then, when he went off to Fort Bragg to command his first platoon, Viv came with him. She had studied to be a schoolteacher, planning on a career that she thought would befit a future Army wife likely to have to move every few years.

But before long, it became increasingly clear the rootless existence, the foreign culture, and the long stretches that George was away for training just weren't for her. They fought a lot and steadily grew apart. It came to a head when George was selected to participate in an elite training exercise in Belgium. He didn't have to go, and she didn't want him to. He insisted that it was important for advancement in the fiercely competitive officer corps. The day of his departure they had a heated argument. In a flash of anger and frustration, George told Viv it might be a good idea if she wasn't there when he returned.

As soon as he boarded the flight to Europe, George regretted it and the way he had treated her. But despite his repeated entreaties over the phone when he arrived, it was too late. When he got back, Viv was gone. The truth was hard to swallow, but George knew he had chosen the Army over the woman he loved and believed he would marry.

After Viv left, George grew even closer to his mother. Following her husband's sudden death, Ann had been in deep mourning, her loneliness brightened by very few things. George's familiar greeting of "hey, pretty lady" was one of them. On Fridays he often made the nearly six-hundred-mile trip down Interstate 95 to spend Saturday with her in Tallahassee before heading back on Sunday in time for duty on Monday.

Then, in the spring of 1999, a series of events forced George to take stock of what he was doing with his life. The first occurred one morning in March when his platoon was out on maneuvers at Range 77 at Fort Bragg. Asleep in his tent, George was startled awake by the loud report of a weapon followed by the shuffling of feet. One of his soldiers, Wayne Gajadhar, a twenty-year-old specialist from Columbia, South Carolina, had been on duty the night before guarding the ammunition. After daybreak, he walked behind a shed, just steps away from the forty or so of his fellow soldiers asleep in their tents, inserted a bullet into the magazine of his M4 carbine, placed the barrel of the gun in his mouth, and pulled the trigger. He apparently pilfered a single round.

The incident, as well as the effect it had on his men for months afterward, was a defining moment for George as an officer. He had cared for Gajadhar a great deal. In fact, he was one of his favorite paratroopers and singled out by the company commander twice for Trooper of the Month. George had big plans for the young soldier and was going to recommend him for Ranger School. George thought he had known the kid but realized he didn't know a thing about him, really. The suicide was a painful blow, both personally and professionally.

Then, later that summer, George's platoon was conducting a parachute jump at Camp McCall, a nearby practice range. They jumped out of a C-130 cargo plane into low and heavy clouds. As he descended quickly toward the ground, he saw a Humvee directly in his path. Trying to maneuver out of the way, he lost control and landed on his backside. He was knocked unconscious. When he came to, he was in agonizing pain. He had broken his tailbone and suffered a ruptured disk in his lower back. Meanwhile, his first sergeant broke both his ankles, while a fellow lieutenant broke his pelvis. Other troops were badly hurt.

George was informed by the Army docs that his parachute-jumping days were probably over and his back was likely to be a long-term problem. A few months later, still grappling with the pain from his injuries, he was out on a field maneuver one morning when he awoke wet and cold in his tent. He rolled over stiffly and muttered to the soldier next to him, "This sucks."

Just then, as he poked his head out at the gray dawn, he saw a pair of Kiowa Warrior scout helicopters zip by overhead.

"I could do that," he thought.

————

George hadn't informed his superiors at Fort Bragg when he decided to send his paperwork to an old friend of his father's in the Pentagon who offered to help him get into flight school. His request was finally approved in the late summer of 2000 as George was completing the Eighty-Second Airborne Division's annual training rotation in California's Mojave Desert, where the Army prepared its combat units for full-scale war. A blazing sun beat down on the arid terrain, and George dripped with sweat in his full battle gear in the back of a cramped and dusty Bradley Fighting Vehicle. His platoon was in the middle of a maneuver, with dozens of Bradleys spread out across the vast desert plain, when he was pulled away from the action. One of his commanders glared at him from beneath his helmet. He brusquely informed George that his request for a branch transfer had been approved. He was no longer an infantryman. He was now officially an aviator.

As he stood there sheepishly, George was curtly reminded that he still had a platoon to lead and was expected to complete the exercise. George did as ordered, but he couldn't help but smile at the thought that he must be the only "aviator" in the Army leading an infantry platoon. Also, for the first time since Dad died, he was excited, filled with anticipation, if a little bit nervous about what he had gotten into.

He didn't fully appreciate it until much later, but he was now following in his father's footsteps in a different way. George's father had also originally been an infantry officer and had once told him that he had decided to transfer to aviation later in his career after he looked at the talent field around him and knew he couldn't compete with many of his fellow infantry officers. George, too, now felt that he couldn't keep up with the gazelles of the infantry branch, whose physical demands were never-ending. He also remembered his father telling him that flying was more cerebral, a thinking man's pursuit. The problems an infantry officer had to solve mostly got bigger but didn't change much. It had stung when Big George once told him that his strengths might be better suited for the infantry. It was time to prove him wrong.

George was older and more experienced than the other cadets when he arrived at the Army Aviation School at Fort Rucker in Alabama. He had been an infantry platoon leader for more than two years. His classmates were fresh out of West Point, ROTC, or officer candidate school, while a few others were specially selected enlisted soldiers known as warrant officers. At first his instructors didn't quite know what to do with him, but his maturity was apparent. They decided to appoint him class leader.

Located in the southeastern corner of Alabama, near the border with Georgia and Florida, Fort Rucker was only a ninety-minute drive from Tallahassee, which meant that George could hop into his Audi sports car on Fridays and spend the weekend with Ann or drive a bit farther down I-10 to have lunch with Grandma Harriet in Atlantic Beach. Sometimes he would even drive to Ann's for dinner during the week. The two of them grew closer than ever. George made her laugh with some of his favorite cartoon voices, well honed over the years. He liked to shower her with little gifts, scouring bookstores and art galleries across the South for scenes of South Carolina's Low Country, her favorite. He also bought a small fishing boat to keep in Florida and took to calling it the Low Country Lady, a nickname of hers; some of their fondest memories were of weekends boating in the Chesapeake Bay when they lived near Baltimore and his father kept a motorboat. They now watched countless movies together—action flicks for George, romantic comedies for Ann—and took day trips to some of Big George's favorite places. As 2000 turned into 2001, they were becoming best friends.

————

In the summer of 2001, as a newly minted member of the air cavalry, George entered an exclusive fraternity of fliers. Kiowa Warrior pilots pride themselves on being the last generation of military aviators to manually fly their own aircraft. The armed scout helicopter is a remnant of the Vietnam War, where it was first introduced in 1969. It still has few automatic functions, and the two pilots, sitting side by side in the all-glass cockpit, manually control most of the flight operations with a maze of dials, switches, and green monitors that are a throwback to another era. Kiowa pilots liked to brag that all those other pilots were just pushing buttons.

Built by Bell Helicopter, the Kiowa was named for the Native American tribe that originally hailed from the northern Great Plains and shaved the hair around their ears to prevent arrows from getting tangled when let loose from a bow. The aircraft, with its telltale dome-like structure above the main rotor, resembles a large mosquito bobbing up and down and darting quickly in and out of canyons. Sometimes flying a few dozen feet off the ground, the pilots' mission is to enter enemy territory quietly and undetected—during the day or at night—to identify distant targets for artillery or other attacking forces. They are, in effect, the modern version of the horse-mounted cavalry. Under a secret program in the 1980s the helicopters were outfitted with weapons, which now include more than a dozen 70-millimeter rockets, a .50-caliber machine gun, and a pair of Hellfire missiles targeted by the spherical laser targeting system perched on top.

Compared with other combat aircraft, the Kiowas are exceedingly small, about the size of a large SUV. First-time pilots describe feeling as if they are strapping on the Kiowa, as opposed to boarding it. The cockpit glass comes over the top and wraps under the pilots' feet, giving them greater visibility but also creating a sense of being suspended high over the earth. Strapped in nearly shoulder to shoulder, the pilots have virtually no extra space and are exposed to ground fire from both sides of the aircraft, protected only by a small swinging armor plate to cover their haunches and another underneath their buttocks. With no air-conditioning or heating, the Kiowa crew must contend with freezing temperatures or blistering desert heat, for up to eight long and stiff hours at a time. Both pilots can fly the helicopter and fire its weapons using the control sticks between their legs, but the one in the left seat, usually more senior in rank, is commonly hunched over the small display in front of him, which includes a recordable TV and a thermal imaging system, providing instructions to the pilot next to him.

George found training to be a Kiowa pilot a thrilling experience and one that challenged him physically and mentally. Dad had been right. This was a thinking man's pursuit. Getting through his course work and flight training took every bit of brains he had and all the study skills he could muster. Yet he still felt a strong connection to his infantry brethren. It was because of them, when the time came to choose the type of helicopter to fly, that he requested the Kiowa Warrior. He would be providing direct support to troops in battle.

He was also beginning to feel a greater connection to his lineage and had a growing urge to delve further into his family's past. He began to read the letters he had hidden away and was eager for Grandma Harriet to pass down more Eyster history. Now that he had decided he would make the Army a career, he wanted to know more about his forebears' experiences, to learn from them. Early in 2001, George published a notice in the newsletter of Grandpa George's old unit from Vietnam, the Black Lions, seeking to contact some of the men who served with him. He included his phone number and address in Alabama where they could contact him.

Within a few months he received letters from several of them, all eager to tell him about their dealings with his grandfather. Some thought he was their former commander's son rather than his grandson. They spoke glowingly—even lovingly—of a man whom they clearly revered. Despite his image of his grandfather as a stern disciplinarian, George learned that Grandpa George was also considered a sensitive man. One of his young lieutenants told of the patience and concern he had personally shown him after his unit was ambushed. The chaplain who had led a memorial service in Lai Khe, Vietnam, for Grandpa George and three of his soldiers also killed in action mailed George a worn copy of the program.

"He was a kind and understanding leader," the retired lieutenant Jay Whitcomb, who had served under his grandfather, told George in April 2001. "He believed in being with his troops."

———

After a long stretch of night flying, George was asleep in his two-bedroom town house in Enterprise, Alabama, on the morning of September 11, 2001. The telephone rousted him from bed with the news of the terrorist attacks in New York, Washington, and Pennsylvania.

He quickly got dressed and in a few minutes drove through the gate at Fort Rucker, where he learned that all flights were grounded. George and his fellow pilots spent most of the day watching in disbelief the wall-to-wall news coverage of the attacks. As the day wore on, there was a deepening sense that this meant war.

Two weeks later George was on his final nighttime checkout in the Kiowa. Under the cover of darkness, he was flying with an instructor out near Lake Tholocco in the middle of the sprawling base. Wearing his night-vision goggles, he was instructed to put the helicopter through its paces.

"Fly the shit out of it," the instructor told him.

George took the controls and demonstrated a series of attack maneuvers he had learned in flight training. He performed "hover fire," in which the weapons are released as the helicopter is hovering in a fixed position. He then moved on to "running fire," when the weapons are released while flying at high speed, followed by "diving fire," descending at a steep angle toward the target. When the instructor was satisfied, he told George he wanted to show him something new, something he hadn't learned in the course. He wanted to demonstrate what he called "bumping fire."

The instructor took the controls and climbed high over the Alabama wilderness. When he reached about five thousand feet, he put the helicopter into a dive. He swooped down at high speed, and as he neared the ground, he pulled up and banked the helicopter behind some trees. Emerging into the open, he fired the Kiowa's weapons. George watched in fascination. The maneuver, the instructor told him, was designed to use the terrain as a natural shield, as the Kiowa was notoriously vulnerable to enemy fire. Bumping fire could be used with virtually any terrain feature, including buildings.

"Pay attention," he instructed George. "This is going to keep you alive."

George repeated the maneuver several times before thick storm clouds started rolling in above them. Within minutes, visibility was so limited that they had to fly five feet off the ground to see where they were going. Finally, they had no choice but to bring the Kiowa down in a dry lake bed.

Days later America was at war in Afghanistan, but George's turn would have to wait. He didn't have enough flying experience. He had never commanded an aviation unit. The best way to gain experience, he was told, was to do a tour in South Korea. There he would get his first command of a Kiowa troop and have the opportunity to fly, both patrolling the demilitarized zone and in countless war games with the South Korean military preparing for a possible renewal of hostilities with the Communist North. George could have stayed at Fort Rucker but he was recently promoted to first lieutenant and felt he needed to catch up with his contemporaries in the field.

"I'm stuck here," he thought. "I could do this for another twenty-four months and not see combat." So he volunteered for a tour in Korea.

————

By the end of 2003, George was back at Fort Rucker, where he was frustrated to find himself serving as the operations officer of a training battalion instead of in a combat unit pulling duty in either Iraq or Afghanistan. He completed two consecutive tours in Korea, where he earned an Army Commendation Medal, won the "top gun" award for Kiowa pilots, and received high marks for commanding Dagger Troop in the Seventh Cavalry Regiment. By now a captain, he had been in the Army nearly six years and felt he had not yet done his part. Moreover, he knew, without a combat tour his career prospects would be significantly dimmer. The pull to get into the war was growing stronger and stronger.

"I need to do that," he decided.

He soon found a way when he saw a bulletin from the Army's aviation branch saying it was looking for helicopter pilots to volunteer for a tour in Iraq. The catch was that it was with the Forty-Second Aviation Brigade, part of the New York National Guard. The part-time soldiers needed SMEs—subject matter experts—to help prepare them and then deploy for a year in the war zone. They would be leaving in the fall of 2004 along with the rest of the Forty-Second Infantry Division.

George immediately contacted a representative in the Army's Human Resources Command to put his name in.

"Well, I guess if this is what you want to do, man," was the tepid response on the other end of the phone.

Not every officer would jump at the chance to go to Iraq, let alone with the "weekend warriors" of the National Guard, who often had more limited experience than those on active duty.

The decision to deploy the Forty-Second had sparked criticism in some of the local communities that its members hailed from, mainly in New York and New Jersey. The Forty-Second was the first National Guard division being sent into combat since the Korean War—just as anti–Iraq War sentiment in the country was moving beyond the fringe and becoming a key divide between the political parties in the unfolding 2004 presidential campaign.

George had watched with interest from his perch in Korea as antiwar protests were organized at home and around the world in the lead-up to the war in the spring of 2003. Now, as he prepared to report for duty, the mood in the country was nearing a crossroads. It had been more than a year and a half since the U.S. invasion to topple Saddam Hussein, and no hidden arsenal of nuclear or biological weapons—President George W. Bush's key rationale for the war—had been found. Meanwhile, U.S. casualties were steadily rising, and the price tag for the war was climbing into the hundreds of billions of dollars. In the spring of 2004, public anxiety about the war reached its high point when the investigative reporter Seymour Hersh revealed evidence of torture at the hands of U.S. soldiers at Abu Ghraib prison. The scandal set off an uproar at home and around the world and marked a turning point in many Iraqis' view of the Americans, whom they increasingly saw as occupiers, not liberators, and brutal ones at that. George was also closely following the U.S. presidential election, in which the Democratic Party's nominee for president, Senator John Kerry of Massachusetts, was running to unseat Bush on a platform to end the war.

"Public opinion in New York won't stand for these guys to be extended much past a year," he wrote to Ann. "It was very controversial to deploy them in the first place, so I'm not sure Big Army can afford the negative press."

Some of George's fellow officers, meanwhile, were incredulous when he told them about his next assignment. "What the hell were you thinking?" was one common refrain. But he was committed to playing his part and saw this as his best opportunity in the near future to lead men into combat.

Another question soon popped up: What would he do after Iraq?

His energies were focused on getting things squared away at Fort Rucker before reporting to the Forty-Second, so it hadn't yet occurred to him. But the U.S. Army is nothing if not good at planning, and his branch representative soon contacted him to talk about his future after his combat tour.

George was told that his decision to volunteer with the Forty-Second would earn him a chit on the back end, and for his next assignment he had more choices than was traditionally the case. The Army's Human Resources Command at Fort Knox in Kentucky sent him a list of possible assignments to read over the weekend. Several appealed to him. He could be an ROTC instructor, teaching military science on a college campus for a few years. Another was a position overseeing some of the training ranges at Eglin Air Force Base near Pensacola, Florida, not far from Ann. Or he could return to Fort Rucker, where he now owned a town house, to be a flight instructor. After a few days going over the list, George was still undecided about which he should choose.

In a follow-up call to inquire further about the possibilities, George was asked if he might be interested in another job, something a bit more unique. What did he think about being a recovery team leader in charge of searching for prisoners of war and soldiers missing in action? George asked the branch representative to read the job description. He would be responsible for traveling worldwide to recover the remains of MIAs and POWs. George assumed this meant another tour in Iraq or Afghanistan. It didn't sound very attractive immediately after returning from a year in Iraq, he responded.

"No, this is for guys lost in previous wars," he was told. Vietnam, Korea, World War II.

"How am I qualified for that?" George wanted to know.

The Army's aviation branch, the officer on the phone explained, had never recommended one of its officers for the position and was eager to do so.

"You have the right background," George was told, especially with a stint in the infantry.

Moreover, George was informed that the branch representative in charge of placing infantry captains in new assignments was going to the same command.

"If one of the guys in charge of placing officers in new assignments was going, it might be a pretty good gig," he thought.

Another detail intrigued him even more. The command he would be working for was based in Hawaii.

Still, George wanted to think about it. He knew exceedingly little about what he would actually be doing. In all his years as an Army brat and after nearly seven years as an officer, he hadn't been aware that military personnel—let alone a dedicated unit—were still actively searching for missing personnel from previous wars. To find out more, he logged on to the Web site for the command. He read some of the latest press releases about the search for MIAs and learned about the high-tech laboratory that was using DNA and other cutting-edge science to identify the remains, bringing long-awaited closure to families that, unlike his, never knew what happened to their loved ones. He was particularly interested in what the outfit was doing in Vietnam. The war in Southeast Asia was such a prominent theme in his life. It was a subject he wanted to learn more about.

George had recently been reading about the tunnels of Cu Chi, where Grandpa George lost his life, and caught a documentary about the Vietnam War hosted by Peter Arnett, the war correspondent who had been with his unit that fateful day in 1966 and so movingly eulogized him in an Associated Press obituary at the time. George had also just finished reading *We Were Soldiers Once . . . and Young*, the Vietnam War memoir of the retired three-star general Harold Moore and the war correspondent Joseph Galloway recounting the Battle of Ia Drang, the first major U.S. engagement of the war. It took place just weeks before Grandpa George was killed and set the stage for a conflict that would drag on for ten more long and bloody years. George was fascinated reading about Moore and Galloway's experiences returning to the scene of the battle twenty-five years later to meet some of the very men Moore had fought.

"Wow," George thought, "I could have the opportunity to wander around in Vietnam on the battlefields where my grandfather had fought. Who gets that opportunity?"

He had every reason to say yes to the assignment. He called his branch representative back to tell him.

"I'll take it."

Soon it was official. At the end of 2005, George was to report to Honolulu and the Joint POW/MIA Accounting Command. But that was more than a year away. First he had to report to Fort Dix, New Jersey, where the Forty-Second Aviation Brigade was preparing for its yearlong tour in Iraq.

CHAPTER FOUR

★

PREPARING FOR WAR

On July 8, 1943, Ryan stepped out of the hangar and into the sweltering heat. He was wearing his summer flight gear—lightweight flight suit, boots, flight jacket, and unlined helmet. A face mask and goggles clung to his forehead, along with a headband to hold his radio assembly in place. He strolled over to his assigned plane, tail number 17419, climbed the ladder on the right side, and stepped into the open cockpit. He settled into the pilot seat and fastened his seat belt, and adjusted the seat height. He was instructed not to slide the canopy shut with the bright yellow handle until he was airborne, in case he had to get out quickly.

In front of him, on the outside of the aircraft, a member of the crew inserted a cartridge, about the size of a shotgun shell, into a small breech. He pressed the starter. With the sound of a muffled pop, the large propeller started to turn, and the aircraft's 1,850-horsepower engine coughed and sputtered to life.

Ryan proceeded through his checklist. He tested the wing flaps by pulling the small lever to his left and opened the cowl flaps slightly to let cool air into the engine. He checked the fuel indicator to ensure it read "reserve" and tapped the magneto on the instrument panel in front of him to make sure there was sufficient combustion and power. With the engine idling in the background, he turned a dial to release the brakes and taxied toward the runway.

The plane's wide nose and large three-bladed propeller in front of him blocked his field of view. To make sure he didn't run into anything, he made a series of S-turns, turning left and then right as he moved forward along the apron. After a few minutes, he came to a stop at the end of the runway and waited for instructions. When he got the signal, he pushed the throttle carefully forward. The plane quickly picked up speed and roared down the runway. Within moments the aircraft lifted off the ground, and Ryan was climbing high and fast over the North Carolina woodlands. It was his maiden voyage in the Marine Corps's newest fighter plane, the F4U-1 Corsair.

Along with its telltale blue-gray paint, one of the most recognizable features of the Vought aircraft was its bent-wing shape, creating a gull-wing silhouette, which was an aerodynamic feature resulting from the most powerful piston-engine in a fighter plane and one of the biggest propellers in the world, at more than thirteen feet long. The Corsair was among the first fighter planes to exceed four hundred miles per hour and in many ways was a pilot's dream. Its landing gear was capable of being enclosed completely within the wings, and it could climb exceptionally fast, up to over thirty thousand feet, and travel over a thousand miles on its nearly four hundred gallons of fuel. Designed to nose-dive ten thousand feet, it could also outmaneuver any American fighter plane that came before it. The fighter would come to earn its share of nicknames like Old Bent Wings and Hose Nose. To the Marines who fought there, it would endearingly be called the Sweetheart of Okinawa. It also had another distinguishing feature: a high-pitched whine that was caused by the air entering the engine inlets underneath the wings. A Navy evaluation of the plane described it as a "banshee scream." The Japanese, it was said, were calling the Corsair by another nickname: Whistling Death.

But in early 1943 they had only been used in combat a few months and, to meet the ever-rising demands, were being rushed off the production line at Vought's plant in Connecticut. As a result, the early models suffered from more than their share of mechanical problems and design flaws. Indeed, the Corsair's very name, conjuring up images of a privateer, or pirate, was a fitting description of the traits required of the men who first flew it—gutsy, independent-minded, even fearless.

For starters, the pilot had limited visibility from the cockpit, which was situated low behind the nose and propeller. One Corsair pilot described the shape of the fuselage as similar to a baseball bat, with the cockpit barely visible poking out from where the bat is nearing its thickest point—not necessarily the most aerodynamic shape. A crew chief would often lie on the wing beside the pilot and use hand signals to help guide him along the runway. The canopy covering the cockpit above the pilot had so many crisscrossing bars that it came to be known derisively as the birdcage, and a mirror housed in a small bubble in the cockpit was the only means the pilot had to see the rear of his plane.

Pilots did enjoy one unusually clear view, though: through a hole in the floor. Next to the two small heel panels for the pilot's feet there was a three-foot-deep gap, sometimes covered with Plexiglas, sometimes not. Much later the hole was covered over with steel to better protect the pilot, not to mention his flight chart, which was said to have been dropped through the slot by some very unhappy fliers. Shorter pilots were at a particular disadvantage because the cockpit was quite roomy and they had trouble reaching the pedals to control the plane. Some stashed a pillow or two behind them.

When it came to actually flying the plane, meanwhile, the operating instructions were riddled with special warnings. Some were carefully worded so as not to sound too alarming, such as when referring to the procedures for landing the plane. "This airplane is sometimes subject to noticeable momentary directional disturbance just after it makes contact with the ground," pilots were informed. In other words, the aircraft often pulled to the left during landing, requiring pilots to engage the right rudder to keep the plane from flipping over. It became such a concern that United Aircraft, which owned Vought, asked one of its premier consultants to make an assessment. Before Ryan flew it for the first time, he and his fellow pilots received a personal tutorial from the consultant, Charles Lindbergh.

The world's most famous aviator conferred with pilots, mechanics, and the Marine Corps brass before imparting some blunt advice about landing the Corsair.

"Forget everything you were taught about flying," the first man to cross the Atlantic told them. "Just fly it in."

He told them they should come in level and bring the main landing gear down first, rather than with the nose up and rear wheel down first, as was the traditional practice. But that also meant coming in at a higher speed than was normally considered safe. One pilot overseas warned only half jokingly at the time, "You might lose control of it when you're landing. If you do get in real trouble, I would aim the damn thing between some of those neat, orderly rows of coconut trees, to shear off the wings and slow you down."

Lindbergh's guidance gave them confidence that they would eventually get the hang of their new planes. The famous flier even insisted on sleeping in the barracks with the pilots instead of the more comfortable accommodations his stature afforded him. His only request was that he be allowed to sleep on a top bunk.

The new Corsair pilots' mettle was constantly tested that summer. The early-model Corsair, they learned, was prone to stalling at various speeds while flying level and making turns, and it usually occurred abruptly, with few of the traditional warning signs like buffeting or wing heaviness. The pilot manual also noted that the early batches like the one Ryan was flying did not have a stall warning light. The Corsair's right wing so habitually stalled out that a temporary workaround was identified until Vought instituted changes in later models: a carved block of wood was taped to the end of it to improve stability.

There were other problems. When the Navy first ordered the plane in 1938, it wanted the pilot to be able to recover from eight spins. That requirement was eventually scaled back to two, and pilots were ordered never to try it at all. It was simply too dangerous. "NO INTENTIONAL SPINNING OF THE F4U-1 AIRPLANE IS PERMITTED," Ryan's manual stipulated in capital letters. If a pilot unintentionally went into a spin, it informed him, a recovery had to be made quickly—within one second or so—or the human forces required to do so will "become very high and the pilot cannot apply fully reversed controls which are necessary."

The problems didn't stop there. They were only compounded. The fuel tank made of reclaimed rubber and housed right in front of the cockpit leaked. A small spark could set the whole thing on fire. The leaks were especially problematic when the plane flew upside down and the highly flammable gas started seeping into the cockpit. The preferred remedy overseas was to place long strips of white tape around the edges of the gas tank where it met the windshield of the cockpit to prevent the pilot from being blinded. It also minimized the vapors that could ignite and blow the plane to pieces.

The early-model Corsairs had so many development problems, in fact, that at one time the plane was officially considered a "failure" by the Navy Department. Though it was designed to operate off the decks of aircraft carriers, it was not deemed safe enough to land on them until the end of 1944, after adjustments had been made. In the meantime, it was decided, the Marines could operate Corsairs from land bases.

After serving as communications officer for the Third Marine Aircraft Wing and then assistant operations officer, Ryan was assigned to Marine Fighter Squadron 321. Established in February 1943, the unit was stationed at Cherry Point Marine Corps Air Station in North Carolina, where in 1941 a new air base was constructed in the densely wooded marshland between the New and the Neuse Rivers in the southeastern part of the state.

The new squadron, officially designated VMF-321, was part of the Marine Corps Reserve. But with the war expanding each day, the reserve distinction made little difference. The Allies were desperate to get reinforcements to the fight, particularly in the Pacific theater, and the squadron was to undergo "vigorous training" before going overseas in a few months.

Ryan had been assigned to help set up and train the new unit. Most of the squadron's pilots were younger second lieutenants fresh from flight training and with little flight experience compared with Ryan's 650 total flight hours. A number of them had been trained to fly the OS2U Kingfisher, a slow and lumbering seaplane that operated mostly in the Caribbean hunting German submarines. It could fly at a maximum speed of ninety miles per hour and bore little resemblance to the high-performance combat fighters they would be operating against the feared Japanese Zeros and battle-hardened anti-aircraft gunners. Other pilots assigned to the squadron, meanwhile, had flown the PBY Catalina, another flying boat designed for search-and-rescue operations at sea. When some of the fresh cadets reported for duty, they inquired where the seaplanes were. A colonel in charge responded: "There are no Kingfishers here. You are going to fly fighters." When they protested that they had not been trained in fighters, his response was similarly simple and direct: "We're gonna train you."

Very few of them, including Ryan, had experience in fighter tactics. Indeed, even the squadron's commander, Major Gordon H. Knott, was a U.S. Naval Academy graduate who had previously flown

Kingfishers. His knowledge of the Corsair and overall fighter operations was exceedingly slim.

It was not an uncommon set of circumstances for units headed
to the Pacific theater in World War II. After Pearl Harbor, Allied
leaders decided to give priority to the war against the Germans in
Europe and North Africa. MacArthur and his Navy counterparts in
the South and Southwest Pacific were in desperate need of reinforcements from the very start and chafed at the knowledge that better-
prepared fighting units were heading to the European theater. Indeed,
the first American fighter unit dispatched to defend Australia in February 1942, the Forty-Ninth Fighter Group, arrived with 102 pilots,
89 of whom had no experience at all in fighters. Their aircraft, a mix
of Bell P-39 Airacobras and Curtiss P-40 Warhawks, were not considered modern fighter aircraft. In fact, the only truly modern American
fighter plane in existence at the time, the P-38 Lightning, had been
strictly reserved for operations in Europe until later in the war.

Despite their divergent experience and backgrounds, however,
Ryan and the other pilots of VMF-321 quickly bonded over their
shared experience of being at the birth of a new combat unit, flying
a new, relatively untested aircraft, and their chance to put their collective imprint on the squadron's character and future exploits. Ryan
was particularly close with some of the other more experienced pilots,
like Harold Jacobs of St. Cloud, Minnesota, the squadron's operations
officer, and Newton "Zombie" Blount of Hattiesburg, Mississippi.

Ryan and Zombie, a feisty boxing champ from the University of
Mississippi, became fast friends, sharing their experiences growing
up in the South and their time in the ring. Blount was always challenging officers and enlisted men alike to arm-wrestling contests,
which he usually won. The squadron's card shark proved to be Roger
Brindos, a fearless pilot with dark, wavy hair and chiseled features
from Duluth, Minnesota, whose outsized bravado made him seem
indestructible. Brindos found in Ryan a willing, if novice, poker companion. Another one of the founding members of the squadron whom
Ryan quickly bonded with was Robert Woodson Marshall, a young,
baby-faced lieutenant from the small town of Amite, Louisiana, who
in his quiet southern manner and gentle speech swapped stories with
Ryan about their engineering studies back home—Ryan at Georgia
Tech and Bob Marshall at Louisiana State University.

Before long, Ryan's squadron mates took to calling him Mac, while some of the younger pilots gave him the nickname Pop, a reference to, at least in that setting, his advanced age. At twenty-six, Ryan was at least a few years older than most of the others. To some of the fresh lieutenants, at twenty-one or twenty-two, he was downright old—and more than a bit wiser.

But the thrill of flying still tickled him, just as it had when he was a teenager and Grace first took him out to the Charleston Army Airfield to watch the barnstormers do their stunt flying before crowds of gasping onlookers. He was hooked then and had jumped at every opportunity to fly since. He had almost lost count of how many times he had scrounged together the money to fly to school at Georgia Tech in Atlanta, often as the only passenger on the Delta Airlines flight that stopped in Columbia, South Carolina. Those trips had only fueled his dream to be a pilot. His diary entry for July 17, 1940, the summer he took his first flying lessons, said it all: "SOLOED!" When he was accepted as a Navy flight cadet, he almost couldn't believe his luck. Nearly every day he got to climb into one of the two open cockpits of a Stearman Model 75 biplane, wait excitedly as the whir of the propeller stuttered to life, and experience the thrill as the spunky little seven-cylinder engine carried him up into the clouds. Sometimes, when he was flying solo without an instructor, he would unfasten his safety belt for a few brief moments, exhilarated by the feeling of being untethered thousands of feet above the earth as the wind gusts bracketed the sturdy little aircraft. If he thought he could get away with it, he sometimes took the training plane up to 11,800 feet, the highest altitude at which it could fly safely. In Jacksonville and later in Quantico he spent hours practicing splits, loops, cartwheels, snap rolls, touch-and-go landings, and what to do in a whole range of emergencies—from engine failure to the loss of oxygen. He also gained some modest experience in gunnery practice, firing dummy rounds at a target towed by another plane. One of his favorite maneuvers was peeling off en masse as part of a formation. "Sure do have fun stunting," he recalled after one long afternoon of flying out over the Atlantic.

When he wasn't in the cockpit, Ryan was often studying the finer points of navigation, sitting in his room in the bachelor officers' quarters plotting a course by the stars; in his barracks in Jacksonville, he spent many nights looking out his window at the constellation of Scorpius in the southern sky. Like all pilots, he also did his share of "hangar flying," sitting around the squadron or in the Officers' Club swapping stories about being at the controls—like the one about how he got his first full taste of the dangers of flight when a fellow trainee out at the Charleston Army Airfield tried to land his plane on top of his, cracking up both aircraft. Or when, during that same summer he learned to fly, he had to ditch in a plowed field on Johns Island after his engine cut out.

Now Ryan familiarized himself with the Corsair. To his left was the engine control box, with several levers situated next to a small wheel to maneuver the ailerons—the control surfaces on the trailing edge of the outer wings—and to trim the rudder. Nearby was the lever to bring the landing gear up or down and the dive brake to increase drag. To his right, at about knee level, was the radio control box, just above a leather pouch to store flight charts or other personal belongings. In front of him were red warning lights and a series of gauges and indicators for fuel, air, hydraulic pressure, altitude, and airspeed, as well as the all-important artificial horizon. On the floor to his left were two charged CO_2 bottles, one for extending the landing gear if the plane's hydraulic power failed and the other to stabilize the air in the fuel tank to protect from an explosion when engaged in combat with an enemy plane.

He could see immediately that this plane was wholly different from others he had flown. It was made purely for destruction. This particular model, the F4U-1, carried six .50-caliber machine guns—three in each wing—and could fire 2,350 rounds more than three hundred yards. Directly in front of him, between his legs, was the control stick, with the weapons-release button for his thumb. Below the main instrument panel and to his left was a pair of switches for the guns, covered by round gray safety caps. Up above, directly in Ryan's field of vision, was the gun sight, housed underneath armored glass.

Ryan had precious little time to become proficient in the Corsair. While the squadron had its full complement of forty pilots by May, it only had a handful of Corsairs to train with as it waited in frustration for new planes to come off the production line. Much of the experience the squadron did get was not very promising. By midsummer, three pilots in the squadron were already dead from accidents. In May, Second Lieutenant Minard Baker flipped over while coming in for a landing, and just days after Ryan's maiden flight, two accomplished fliers, Captain John Sanders and Major Joseph Leising, were killed in a midair collision of their Corsairs. The squadron's pilots were also receiving gloomy reports about Marine aviators flying the Corsair in combat. Some were well on their way to becoming Japanese aces—a tongue-in-cheek reference to how they were personally responsible for destroying five Corsairs. Those were the lucky ones. Many others were killed in crashes, while the Japanese were claiming even more. Ryan's squadron was in turmoil. Its members were wholly unprepared for combat, and they knew it. Their few months of training consisted mainly of formation flying and acrobatics in single-seat training aircraft.

As their departure date approached, Ryan and other officers worried that low morale was becoming a grave problem. They felt leaderless. Major Knott, the squadron's skipper, may have had movie-star looks and been a magnet for girls, but he had also grown more and more unpopular. He had a reputation of not listening to advice. For instance, he insisted early on that pilots fly in formations of three rather than two, a basic tactic of fighter operations meant to ensure each flier had a fellow pilot keeping an eye on him for mutual protection. Those who raised the issue were brushed off. Soon enough, words like "arrogant" and "conceited" became some of the kinder descriptions whispered about him. Knott also privately held deep concerns about the spirit of the men, recounting how haphazardly they were thrown together and rushed toward combat. "It was one hell of a way to get ready to fight a war," he wrote years later.

Ryan would get only a few dozen flight hours in the Corsair—and just two hours of dogfighting practice—before going to war. Many of the other pilots got even less—if any at all.

They had also missed out on the highly valued counseling provided by the plane's main test pilot, who didn't visit Cherry Point until more than a month after they had shipped out. They would have to learn fighter tactics in the war zone.

It was not until the afternoon of September 1, 1943, the day before they were scheduled to leave Cherry Point for the West Coast, that the squadron finally received its full complement of Corsairs.

———

The cross-country journey of VMF-321 began on Thursday, September 2, 1943, from Oak Grove Field in nearby Polkville, North Carolina, one of the outlying airfields. The squadron had received orders to report to Naval Air Station, San Diego, where it would spend a few weeks getting equipped for combat before boarding an aircraft carrier bound for the Pacific. With forty fliers, the squadron had twice as many pilots as Corsairs, so only half of them were needed to fly the newly delivered fighter planes to California for the sea voyage to the combat zone. The others would travel by rail, along with enlisted Marines to serve as mechanics and other ground crew. Meanwhile, four of the pilots were married, and their wives set out for the West Coast in a red Ford convertible so they could see their husbands off to war. Before leaving Cherry Point, the pilots drew playing cards to see who would be lucky enough to fly and who would have to put up with the weeklong train trip. Ryan was among the luckier lot and drew a high card.

With Ryan serving as navigation officer, the flight echelon set out on a preselected route with stops to rest and refuel. Their first stop was Atlanta—and they barely made it in one piece. Lieutenant Bob Norman—who's shiny new Ford was carrying his wife and the three others to the West Coast—flipped his plane over trying to land. Luckily, he was skinny enough to crawl out of an opening in the canopy before being burned alive. Still stunned from his near-death experience, he continued the journey as a passenger in a training plane that was assigned to follow the group. From Atlanta they moved on to Shreveport, Louisiana, where they spent the night. The next day, they set out for Denison, Texas, to refuel, before heading on to an Army airfield in Dallas.

The skies were clear over the Texas prairie the following morning, the third day of the cross-country journey. They planned to stop in Midland, Texas, for lunch before continuing on to Arizona. The Texas sunshine was nearly blinding as they lifted off from Dallas. But about thirty minutes after takeoff, black storm clouds appeared on the horizon. The wind picked up and the Corsairs were knocked violently in the swirling gusts. The pilots tried to get around the storm. Some peeled off to the south, others went north, but soon the thick rain clouds were all around them. The storm severely damaged Lieutenant Bluford P. Mauldin's plane, and he had to ditch in the prairie. He considered himself lucky to be alive. He actually landed a few miles from where he grew up and hitched home. Lieutenant Eugene "Vic" Smith was tucked closely underneath his flight leader, Captain Ray Lemons, when his fellow pilot flew into a dark thunderhead and disappeared. Suddenly, Smith couldn't see a thing and quickly lost his bearings. He feared he would crash into Lemons. Then, with only seconds to spare before he spiraled uncontrollably toward the ground, the Ohio farm boy glimpsed an opening in the sky. He was able to use the point of reference to emerge from the storm. But there was no sign of Lemons.

By the time it was all over, the squadron was spread across West Texas. Most of the pilots rendezvoused at an Army field in Abilene after locating a radio beacon before continuing on as planned. When they arrived that night at Davis-Monthan Air Base in the Arizona desert, their skipper soberly informed them that Lemons was dead. When his Corsair hit the ground it had gouged a hole the size of a basement, Major Knott reported. That brought to four the number of pilots killed since the squadron was born. And they hadn't even left the States.

The group finally pulled in to Naval Air Station, San Diego on September 6. It was clear to Ryan and many of the others that most of their pilots needed additional training on how to fly using only their instruments to guide them. In what was still the infancy of aviation, they relied too heavily on visual flying. They needed to be able to confidently "uncage" their instruments and switch on the gyro compass, the artificial horizon, the needle ball, and the airspeed dials and use the information to fly through the kind of weather they had encountered over the Texas prairie. But few of them got the necessary training in the Corsair. Their planes spent nearly all three weeks the squadron was on the West Coast undergoing repairs.

So with combat on the horizon, the men of VMF-321 spent their few weeks in San Diego doing what millions of young men do before shipping overseas. They enjoyed the surf, dined out, and took in some of the city's nightlife. The married men stayed at San Diego's US Grant Hotel, while some of the others took a quick trip to Tijuana,

Mexico, to get tailor-made leather shoulder holsters for their Marine Corps–issued .45 caliber pistols.

During the day they attended lectures on how to prepare for the months ahead, down to small but enormously useful tips like why they should bring a lot of prophylactics. Not for the girls. There most likely wouldn't be any of them in the combat zone. But rubbers had proved to be the best way to keep small personal items dry in the tropics. They were also unofficially instructed to bring as much whiskey as they could, to trade with the natives. So they went down to the Officers' Club to stock up on bottles of Teacher's Highland Cream scotch whiskey, which they wrapped in towels and stored in their footlockers.

They were also encouraged to get their affairs in order. On September 17, Ryan filled out paperwork to leave 100 percent of his accrued pay—$351 a month—to Grace should he fail to return from his tour of duty. To support her and Uranie while he was gone—he would no longer be able to send them money himself—he designated that they receive $100 per month, effective immediately, directly from the Marine Corps. He had also recently directed that $37.50 be deducted from his pay each month to buy U.S. Savings Bonds. In the event of his death, that, too, would go to Grace, he instructed.

Finally, at noon on September 25, 1943, with calm seas and a light wind blowing at eight knots under cloudy skies, the USS *Nassau*, a newly constructed escort carrier, steamed out of San Diego and set a northwesterly course. Ryan and his fellow pilots were headed to war.

——

A few days before Ryan's squadron was scheduled to ship out, its number-two officer, the profanity-prone Major David Drucker, convened a secret meeting of the men. They took a vote. It was unanimous. They had no confidence in Knott, their commander, and desperately wanted a new leader to take them into combat. But there was little they could do about it.

The atmosphere those first few days on the *Nassau* bordered on mutiny. They were only reminded how ill prepared they were as they watched the *Nassau*'s crew conduct daily drills, including how to defend against a torpedo attack and to abandon ship. What lay ahead was also clear by the complete blackout enforced on the ship for the ten-day journey so as not to attract attention from Japanese vessels.

About the only thing that kept up their spirits was playing cards by the dim light of the ship's heads, or bathrooms; in fact, their journey was quickly turning into a marathon gambling session, under the stewardship of the outsized personality of Lieutenant Roger Brindos, who in addition to poker and blackjack was steadily teaching Ryan the finer points of gin rummy, casino, and hearts.

"I never went for cards before—but now—while I took this up to pass time, I do have a lot of fun from them," Ryan wrote to Grace. "I haven't tackled contract bridge yet, but I think with a little more time I will."

About halfway through the voyage, on September 29, all the pilots were hastily ordered into the *Nassau's* wardroom. Major Knott, looking stunned, told them he had news. He was being transferred. They would be getting a new commanding officer, effective immediately. Before they had a chance to digest the welcome news, they were introduced to their new skipper.

Major Edmund F. Overend, or "End Over End," as the men soon got to calling him in private, was a tall, muscular officer with a furrowed brow and unmistakable air of command. He was a deeply spiritual man who grew up in Coronado, California, where he was an avid Boy Scout and worked his way through college before earning a commission in the Marine Corps before the war. He was already something of a hero. Earlier in the war Overend had flown in Burma with the Flying Tigers of the American Volunteer Group, fending off Japanese air attacks over China in P-40 Warhawks with shark teeth painted under the nose.

The Fighting Tigers were legendary. In the spring of 1941, before the attack on Pearl Harbor, President Roosevelt approved loans to the Chinese to finance the purchase of warplanes to beat back the Japanese onslaught in the Pacific. The deal also permitted the Chinese to recruit American pilots as long as they resigned their commissions in the U.S. military. The volunteers were effectively well-paid mercenaries, but in the view of most Americans the good kind.

Overend was already a highly decorated ace, the pilots aboard the *Nassau* learned, with Japanese planes to his credit. On Christmas Day two years earlier, he had been reported missing in the skies over Burma after being shot down in a dogfight with a Japanese fighter. To the surprise of his fellow Fighting Tigers, however, "Eddie" showed up back at their base the next day. Overend's arrival to take the helm of the new squadron lifted morale immeasurably.

On the night of Friday, October 1, as the *Nassau* steamed west, he regaled the pilots of VMF-321 with tales of the fearless men he served with in Burma. Men like Gregory "Pappy" Boyington, who was perhaps the most famous Marine Corps fighter ace, for his proficiency in the air and his whiskey drinking on the ground—both of which had been exhaustively covered by the papers back home. Boyington, who had two dozen Japanese planes to his credit, and his Black Sheep Squadron of Corsairs were now on their third combat tour in the South Pacific.

Overend was eager to impart all his knowledge to his new squadron about how the air war against Japan was being fought. If they believed in each other, he told them, and in what they were doing, they could surmount virtually any obstacle.

"I took a green, eager Marine fighter squadron into the South Pacific," he recounted soon after the war. "I strove to teach it all I knew about the Japs and aerial tactics—also all that I had learned about human relationships."

A U.S. intelligence assessment at the time described in no uncertain terms what they could expect to face in the coming months: "The first-line Jap pilot is well trained and resourceful, and he handles his plane in a skillful manner; he will initiate attack, is aggressive in combat, and is a fighting airman not to be underestimated. . . . They will change their methods with alacrity whenever they find their aerial operations successfully countered. . . . They are alert and quick to take advantage of any evident weakness."

Japanese pilots, the men of VMF-321 were also briefed, were known to concentrate their fire on stragglers or a disabled plane. They could be ruthless in their determination: several cases had been reported by late 1943 of American pilots being machine-gunned as they parachuted to earth. Japanese Navy pilots, meanwhile, were especially feared.

The Corsair's main competition would be the Mitsubishi A6M Zero, also known in American lexicon as the Zeke. It had a less powerful engine than the Corsair but was lighter and therefore more maneuverable, especially at higher altitudes. Japan's confidence at Pearl Harbor was in no small measure due to its faith that the Zero would rule the skies against any other fighter. The Japanese had also recently introduced a souped-up version of the Zero known as the Tojo, which was faster and had a greater rate of climb. Yet the planes' relatively scant armor protection made them vulnerable to American firepower; the Corsair's weapons load alone was equal to the total weight of a Zero.

Ryan and his fellow pilots were enraptured as Overend spoke of the excitement mixed with fear that came with looking out from the cockpit for the first time to see the dreaded "meatball"—the big red dot painted on the side of Japanese fighters. He also impressed upon them the importance of constantly harassing the Japanese with strafing runs on their ground positions and bases whenever possible.

That night on the *Nassau*, as they steamed toward the rising sun, the squadron also finally got a name. Its members settled on the moniker of one of the three squadrons in the famed Fighting Tigers: Hell's Angels. They also chose an emblem to paint on the sides of their planes, one befitting their boyish zeal: a scantily clad woman with wings and a halo set against a blood-red background.

———

Ryan descended the gangplank and drew fresh sea air into his lungs. As he stepped onto the pier, the warm equatorial breeze, moist from the frequent tropical rains, licked at his cheeks, and the faint smell of freshly caught tuna wafted over the waterfront. It was the afternoon of Wednesday, October 6, 1943, and the USS *Nassau* had tied up earlier in the day in the narrow harbor at Pago Pago on Tutuila, the largest of the three islands known as American Samoa.

At first glance, Ryan's first overseas post, code-named Strawstack, looked like anything but a war zone. As the sliver of land came into view in the predawn darkness, the men aboard the *Nassau* were surprised to see the lights of the harbor in the distance. No precautionary blackout here. Now Ryan could see tall palm trees swaying in the breeze as aquamarine waters splashed white across the coral reefs. The vegetation radiated brilliant greens in a majestic landscape all framed by the Rainmaker, the volcano that stood sentry over the harbor and was so named because it seemed to catch the passing rain clouds. Most striking of all were the young, barefoot Samoan girls, wearing only short grass skirts called lavalavas with flowers in their long black hair. Their bare, sun-kissed breasts beckoned the men ashore.

As Ryan and his fellow pilots waited for their seabags to be dropped from cargo nets onto the dock, their reverie was broken by the drone of Navy Dauntless dive-bombers being catapulted off the deck of the *Nassau* and landing on the coral airstrip at nearby Tafuna Airdrome that jutted into the blue waters of the Pacific about four miles south of the harbor.

Here, on the thickly forested mass of volcanic rock that had inspired Robert Louis Stevenson's *Treasure Island*, Ryan and the rest of the squadron would spend the next five weeks preparing for combat. The port, which was pronounced in the Samoan tongue as "Pango Pango," had been the site of a small American naval base since 1900, when a U.S. warship first anchored in the harbor. The natives, for the most part, were still living in their simplicity, gathering coconuts and fishing from their canoes, or *pow-pows*, beneath the cliffs in the islands' small bays. They lived peacefully in thatched sugarcane huts, known as *fales*, with deep oval roofs and coconut leaves tied under the eaves to shut out the elements. The natives themselves were festooned with garlands of ferns, tropical flowers, and brightly colored tortoise shells. They loved to sing, especially, in their broken English, "You Are My Sunshine." Christianity was imported by missionaries beginning in the nineteenth century, so on Sundays nearly everyone went to church, the women in white dresses and parasols, the men in planter hats, white suits, and white shirts.

The harbor, largely hidden by the surrounding mountains, had been shelled once by a Japanese submarine early in the war, causing minimal damage to the naval quarters on Centipede Row and a stone wall outside the customhouse. Otherwise, the most pressing threat to the American military came from mosquitoes, which carried a number of tropical diseases and the dreaded elephantiasis, which later in the war would require the withdrawal of most Marines from American Samoa.

The chain of islands now offered considerable elbow room for training, and situated along the main trade route between the United States and Australia, Tutuila had become a major staging area for Marines fighting across the Pacific.

Ryan and the other pilots climbed into waiting trucks. The vehicles snaked down the narrow sand-covered streets of the town, brushing the thick bushes on both sides of the road. The new arrivals could quickly see the island was a small armed camp. Schools had been commandeered into machine shops. Concrete pillboxes were erected on every beach that might be vulnerable to an amphibious landing and manned around the clock with the help of a native guard known as the Fiti Fiti, the well-built Samoan men who towered over many of the Americans.

To help ward off possible air attacks, large anti-aircraft guns were nestled on Blunts and Breakers Points in the hills around Pago Pago, and a communications and radar station had been erected high up in the island's central mountain spine. Naval Construction Battalions, the legendary Seabees, had turned the single-lane track connecting the island's main villages into a two-lane road surfaced with coral rock, where a constant stream of military vehicles kicked up clouds of choking dust. Marines now outnumbered the islands' ten thousand Polynesian inhabitants, who referred to their guests as *malini*.

By nightfall, Ryan had settled into one of the *fales*—four men assigned to each—at the squadron's new beachfront camp out near the airfield, where some of the exotic tropical plants gave off a fluorescent glow at night that helped lead the way to the bathroom.

The next morning, after breakfast, Ryan and the others were trucked back to the harbor to begin unloading their Corsairs and the rest of the gear from the *Nassau*. Rather than drag the planes through the town, a drawn-out process that could delay the ship's departure and make it more vulnerable to Japanese submarines, Major Overend decided to catapult them off the deck like the Dauntless bombers a day earlier, even though none of the pilots had ever done a carrier takeoff.

The pilots were a bit jittery about their prospects. For starters, the ship had been so weighted down with men and equipment—four squadrons and ninety-five planes—that upon its arrival a day earlier some aircraft had to be hoisted off before the Dauntless bombers could safely take off while the ship was anchored. The Corsair, meanwhile, was heavier than the bombers, and the prevailing winds were blowing directly across the deck of the *Nassau*.

So Overend, as any good leader would do, went first. His plane coughed and sputtered to life and with the catapult's combination of compressed air and oil eased off the end of the flight deck and over to the airstrip at Tafuna. The rest of the pilots soon followed, and at the end of the day Ryan penciled his first carrier catapult into his pocket-sized flight log with the brown canvas cover.

The new skipper had interviewed all the pilots in the squadron aboard the *Nassau* to learn more about their individual flying experience in order to organize their on-the-job training in Samoa. By the end of the first week, the pilots completed a series of familiarization hops to acquaint themselves with their new planes and the surrounding geography. Takeoff, they quickly learned, was a bit too thrilling with the strong air currents funneled between the mountains overlooking Tutuila. Pan American Airways had once experimented with using Pago Pago as a way station but decided against it due to the strong wind currents. Meanwhile, the surrounding mountains required aircraft to climb very quickly to avoid crashing.

The shortage of spare parts was proving to be a huge problem for the maintenance crews. Overend set a goal of keeping at least twelve of the squadron's seventeen planes in flying shape, and even that was a struggle. Some planes were just used for spare parts and never flown.

On October 12, after less than a week on the island, the squadron lost its first plane. Coming into Tafuna for a landing, a pilot nosed his plane over on the runway. Luckily, he only suffered a minor laceration on his scalp. But the plane was a total loss.

Overend, determined to get the Hell's Angels in dogfighting shape, pushed ahead with the training. The morning after the crash, several planes flew in a Lufbery Circle, a defensive formation dating back to World War I in which aircraft fly in a horizontal circular formation so that an enemy plane that tries to attack any one of them will theoretically come under fire from the plane flying directly behind. The Hell's Angels practiced attacking the circle from above and drawing the planes out of position to make them more vulnerable. Overend's verdict on their performance was positive. But when a few days later the squadron rendezvoused with some bombers to practice an escort mission, weaving above the formation at various altitudes, the daily report recorded that "a great deal of such work needs still to be done." Yet with each passing day, the men grew more and more confident in the cockpit and tighter as a unit. To show their appreciation for the enlisted mechanics who kept their planes flying against long odds, the officers threw a beer party for them after their first week on Samoa.

Along with Overend, a great influence on the men was Doc Wolfe, the flight surgeon who was quickly becoming the squadron's surrogate mother. Lieutenant Russell Wolfe was a surgeon from Iowa who had been assigned as the squadron's doctor. He played an instrumental role in helping Overend establish a new squadron spirit. He also spent a lot of his time counseling both the officers and the enlisted men, listening to their problems, trying to calm their nerves. Many of the men found comfort sitting on a cot in Doc Wolfe's hut, where he was often seen doing cat's cradles with a piece of string to keep his fingers nimble for his delicate medical work back home in the Midwest.

But they were all focused on a singular goal: preparing for their turn to get into the fight. Overend sent them on strafing runs, showed them how to attack a Zero and how to get away from one, and had them fire their guns at an oil slick a few miles off the island. With rounds dipped in paint, they practiced firing their guns at a white banner towed behind another plane as a target.

The pilots, flying in pairs, or sections, would practice a series of defensive maneuvers to confront attacking enemy planes. One primary tactic was to fly in a scissoring pattern, in which they weaved back and forth, taking turns covering the other's tail. In another maneuver, two sections flew about half a mile apart. The planes on the outside, with their guns outward, maintained a 180-degree view of the sky. If they saw something, they would turn in, and the others would follow, keeping the Zeros from penetrating the formation.

The section leader and his wingman needed to know each other so well that they could predict the other's actions. When flying at night or in a tight formation or through a storm, "the wingman must trust his leader more than he trusts himself," one Marine Corsair pilot explained. "If he wavers in his decision to follow his leader into what seems to be a hopeless situation and goes off on his own, he will be lost sooner or later."

The squadron was beginning to get its rhythm, but the incessant downpours on Samoa curtailed operations on many days. On other days the weather kept them completely grounded. They wiled away in their *fales* or sat through a "fighter direction lecture" by more experienced pilots. By the end of October, their flying had nearly stopped altogether. More than half of the planes were grounded due to tail wheel problems, and a cargo ship bringing repair parts was not scheduled to arrive for another ten days. It was on November 1, as they waited to get back in the air, that Overend told them they would be leaving Samoa in two weeks—first to the New Hebrides, an island chain to their south and west, and then "up the line" to the Solomon Islands. There, they all knew, the epic struggle against the Japanese was reaching its crescendo.

Ryan also received some welcome news from home that gave him more reason to want to get this over with. His stepmother, Sarah, had given birth to his half sister. Her name was Jane.

★

CHAPTER FIVE

A LOSS OF FAITH

By Thanksgiving 2004, George found himself in a sprawling tent city in northwestern Kuwait near the Iraqi border. Camp Buehring, named for a New York soldier who had been killed in the opening salvos of the Iraq War, was one of four major staging areas where American units could get used to the desert climate, complete last-minute training, and make equipment repairs before "crossing the berm" into Iraq.

In just the two weeks since George arrived, he watched the base quickly expand, the frenetic pace of construction a testament to the size and seemingly enduring nature of the conflict he had volunteered to fight. Before long, the place would be a self-sufficient slice of America, he thought. There was a small post exchange, or PX, to shop for personal items and another preparing to open in a few weeks. A nearby coffee shop would be at home in any American city, along with an Internet café and a gym. To his pleasant surprise, he found the food at the chow hall, a large warehouse-looking structure, quite acceptable. There was even a Burger King and a twenty-four-hour pizzeria. Much of the base was still a maze of big-top tents, but permanent structures were going up everywhere. George had just moved into a new barracks with eight rooms, four officers in each.

"Not too bad!" he wrote to Ann after he arrived.

There was little downtime, though. George's days and much of his nights were filled doing three jobs. Each morning he reported to the Forty-Second Division's tactical operations center, where he advised the assistant commander on how to employ helicopters in the division's battle plans. After lunch, he headed over to the aviation brigade to fulfill a similar function for that unit's helicopters. He was doing a lot of "coaching, teaching, and mentoring," as he put it. Although most of the officers were quick learners, as part-time National Guard troops they were a bit rusty or had limited experience. "Unfortunately none of them have been in the active Army for over ten years," George recorded, "and we have changed the way we do business drastically."

But the Forty-Second Infantry Division had battle streamers that would be the envy of any active-duty unit. The Army's storied "Rainbow" division had been gassed in the trenches of Europe in World War I and had liberated the Dachau concentration camp in Germany in the waning days of World War II. It was now made up of National Guard troops from twenty-eight states and territories, many of them police officers, construction workers, paramedics, schoolteachers, and firefighters, including some who had been on duty in New York City on September 11, 2001.

George was uniquely suited for the role of mentor with his assignment in Korea and experience helping to train fresh pilots in Alabama. He felt as if he were making a critical contribution, preparing the Guard troops for the battles that lie ahead. But it was his third task, beginning each day in the late afternoon, that he looked forward to the most. That was when he went out to the airfield and reported to the "Cav."

The First Squadron of the Seventeenth Cavalry Regiment was an active-duty unit from Fort Bragg, North Carolina, usually attached to the Eighty-Second Airborne Division. The squadron was the most deployed Kiowa unit in the Army and over the previous two years had served tours in Iraq and Afghanistan. On this deployment, it would be operating alongside New York's Forty-Second. The 1-17 was a storied Army scout unit, tracing its lineage to the early twentieth century and the hunt for the Mexican revolutionary Pancho Villa. The unit's patch still displayed a soldier on horseback set against a Native American headdress. Many members treasured their cavalry Stetsons emblazoned with crossed swords. Only now they rode into battle with night-vision goggles in the cockpits of Kiowa Warriors. Although George had technically deployed to Kuwait with the Forty-Second's Aviation

Brigade, the Kiowa squadron soon plucked him up and installed him as their assistant operations officer.

"It's the only time all day that I get to stand back and observe and learn," he wrote home to his mother. He was immediately impressed with what he saw. "They are uncommonly strong. . . . They may be one of the strongest command teams I have ever observed."

Before long he got another assignment—not the kind he bargained for. When the air cavalry unit moved north, it would need an experienced pilot, someone who spoke fluent "aviator," to serve as a liaison with the ground troops—to be in the "hip pocket" of the ground commander when he needed to call in air support from helicopters operating overhead. The commander seized on George's unique background as a pilot and an Army Ranger to fulfill the special duty. It meant he wouldn't be flying. He would be "outside the wire," patrolling with the infantry, face-to-face with the enemy.

The "upside," he wrote to Ann to give her the news, is that "I will be doing valuable work that will challenge me and will certainly keep the boredom at bay." It would be a "really great experience," he added, "the opportunity to participate in a way I hadn't expected—and to potentially really impact the outcome of the battles for Samarra, Taji and Baghdad."

He was also proud to report that the assignment meant he would get to wear the combat patch of the Eighty-Second Airborne Division, just as his father had in Grenada, instead of the Forty-Second, which was sure to help his career. Going into combat with a National Guard unit simply didn't look as good on a résumé as such a premier unit in the professional Army.

But he made no bones about the drawbacks of his new job. A guerrilla war was intensifying, and U.S. forces had recently invaded the restive city of Fallujah to dislodge insurgents who had taken control of several major population centers in the so-called Sunni Triangle, north and west of Baghdad. George would likely be right in the middle of it.

"Downside is that I will be outside the security of the forward operating bases," he told his mother, "in the streets . . . not the safest of environments."

As he waited apprehensively for the go order to move north, George received a touching letter from his stepbrother, Scott, who tucked inside a photograph of Little George and Big George taken around Christmastime when he was in high school. Father and son were sitting contentedly on the couch eating dinner, Dad wearing what he jokingly called his "birth control Army glasses," the ugly wide-rimmed black ones provided by the government.

"It was bittersweet," he told his mother about it.

George thought a lot about his late father, now dead seven years. He imagined what it was like back in 1991, when it was a fretful Lieutenant Colonel George S. Eyster IV who as commander of a helicopter battalion was camped in the same desert awaiting orders to invade Iraq. Still fresh in George's memory was that somber image of Dad in the video greeting he mailed home to Fort Bragg at the time. So was the story of how difficult that time had really been for Big George.

After his father died, George's mother received a letter from Gordon Terpstra, who had been his father's battalion chaplain during the first Iraq War. Terpstra wrote to Ann that he was deeply saddened by the news of the untimely death of his former commander. The two families had first met when they lived on the same street at Fort Bragg in 1989, where a teenage George played ball behind the house with Terpstra's two sons. In his letter, written on the letterhead of the church in Washington State where he had become the pastor, Terpstra recalled how emotionally fragile Big George had been in those weeks leading up to the 1991 invasion. The two of them, who were exceptionally close for a lieutenant colonel and a junior captain, had been living in adjacent tents at their camp in the Saudi Arabian desert near the Iraqi border, where they often huddled on cold evenings over a wooden crate playing chess by the light of a kerosene lamp. As the 1991 invasion approached, Terpstra could see that his commander was on edge; on one occasion Colonel Eyster slammed his fist down on the chessboard before quickly apologizing for letting his frayed nerves get the best of him. Then, on the morning of January 14, 1991, Big George came into Terpstra's tent and asked him to sit with him in the privacy of a nearby vehicle. He wanted to tell him something and didn't want anyone else to hear. Almost immediately after they closed the doors, Big George, whose military bearing had inspired so much confidence in his men, hung his head and his shoulders slumped.

"Today is the day my dad died in Vietnam, and today is the day we are launching an operation north," he confided. "I'm scared. I don't have a good feeling about this."

Terpstra clasped his commander's hand and asked him if he wanted to pray. The chaplain then recited some verse from scripture, asking the Lord to protect him and his men on their mission. It was all over in a few minutes, and Colonel Eyster regained his composure and went about his duties. Later that day, when Big George and his men returned safely from their mission, he took Terpstra aside and thanked him for giving him the courage he needed.

Now, almost fourteen years later, it was Little George's turn to face the uncertainty of combat—on the front lines.

————

George finally got his turn at one of the computer kiosks set up in tents around the base for soldiers to hop on the Internet.

"Mom," he typed into the small Yahoo! chat screen and hit the send button. He waited a minute or two to see if she was near the computer back in Tallahassee.

It was about half past six in the morning on the East Coast, and Ann was still sleeping when her computer came alive with a *ding.*

George tried again. "Are you there? Momma . . . are you there?" He felt a little guilty he might wake her up, but he was getting ready for another night patrol and didn't know when he'd have another chance to reach her.

After stirring for a few more moments, Ann realized in her half slumber the source of the sound and scrambled out of bed and across the bedroom over to her desk.

"Yes," she typed quickly and hit return. "I'm here."

"Hey there. I am so happy I finally caught you."

"Me, too. My hands are shaking. I thought I was dreaming," she replied. "I have been worried about you because it has been a week since I heard from you."

"Sorry about that," George typed. "I have been really busy. I've been trying to get off an email to you and every time I come in here we get attacked."

It was a week before Christmas. George was now at Camp Anaconda, the sprawling former Iraqi air base north of Baghdad that was now the largest American installation in Iraq, with some twenty thousand personnel and its own weekly newspaper. This was the first time mother and son communicated by Internet chat. Telephone calls, George had discovered, would be rare, but computers were set up all over the base for soldiers to communicate with family and friends back home. So he had given Ann instructions on how to set up the chat program so they could talk in real time—and how she could leave it on and update when she would return if she was out on an errand. It would be much more intimate than letters or e-mails, and as long as no one was waiting for a turn, or he didn't have to be somewhere, they could "talk" as long as they wished.

Ann was delighted to hear from her boy and wanted to know if he'd received the two packages she had sent. He got the books and magazines but no sign yet of the Christmas decorations Ann had collected to spruce up his bunk with some holiday spirit: a hand-carved Nativity scene; a small, American-flag-themed Christmas tree; and, for good measure, a DVD of a burning Yule log. Ann told him to also be on the lookout for his Christmas presents, which were on their way separately.

How was his back? Did he need a hot-water bottle? Ann peppered George with all sorts of motherly questions. It was still sore, George reported, but it got better as the day wore on, as he started to move around. It hurt most when he woke up and at the end of the day, but he was managing. "I've weaned myself off the drugs and am relying on Motrin now," he told her.

George uploaded a photograph of himself, taken after a recent mission. Wearing dark sunglasses, he was outfitted in full body armor, his night-vision goggles perched atop his helmet and his gloved hands clutching his M4 carbine. He was standing next to a Humvee with a walled compound in the background.

"Got it! It's great! Thank you!" Ann responded after opening the attachment.

"That one was taken just after sunrise on Friday morning," George explained. "We had done a raid of the house behind to pick up a couple of suspected insurgents."

"I don't like to think of you doing that kind of job," she replied. "Please be careful."

"Well . . . it's a job anyway," George wrote stoically. "There won't be any flying for me anytime soon."

Then, just as abruptly as he woke her, George's time was up. "Ohh . . . gotta go . . . I am getting kicked off. . . . I love you very much. . . . I'll write soon."

"Love you too very much."

———

George rolled through most of Christmas at a hundred miles an hour, literally. He spent much of the holiday on patrol near an American outpost called Camp Paliwoda, an abandoned Iraqi military training center beside a canal that was believed to be surrounded by insurgent safe houses and hidden weapons supplies. The road between Anaconda, where he was based, and Paliwoda, about twelve miles away, was one of the most dangerous in Iraq. So unless they were engaging a target, the members of George's unit never took their feet off the gas for the full eight hours they were outside the wire in their Humvees. George jokingly called it a "highway man's paradise" because they drove "as fast as the chariots will take us" to avoid being ambushed. By traveling at such high speed, they also held out hope that if they hit one of the improvised explosive devices—the makeshift bombs insurgents were increasingly burying in the road—they would "blow right through" and come out the other side unscathed.

Ann knew George would be outside the wire for Christmas and didn't expect to hear from him for at least a few days. Over the holiday she watched the news out of Iraq with growing trepidation. There had been a large bombing in the city of Karbala to the south of Baghdad, and she felt even more anxious after a suicide bombing on December 21 inside a dining hall at an American base in the northern city of Mosul. Fourteen U.S. soldiers and eight others were killed and nearly eighty wounded in what commentators said marked a new, macabre twist to the escalating violence.

So Ann felt especially relieved when George surprised her and signed in for a quick chat on Christmas night.

"Hey mom. . . . Merry Christmas. I love you and miss [you] very much."

"Merry Christmas to you! I love you and miss you very much, too."

George had been on the go for much of the last twenty hours and was soon going on another raid in a nearby village. She asked him about the Mosul attack. He didn't try to sugarcoat things for her. The bombing—by an Iraqi soldier who had been working with the Americans—was a new technique and "a bit dismaying," he acknowledged. And there were new threats from what the brass were calling "vehicle-borne" IEDs, or car bombs. "We've also had an increase in activity," he reported.

Still, George assured her, he felt the American forces were making good progress. They were seizing weapons and explosives, along with suspected enemy fighters and bomb makers. What they were doing, he told her, was critical, as Iraqis were preparing to go to the polls at the end of January in the first elections since the fall of Saddam Hussein. Ensuring the election of a national assembly went off successfully was now the main effort of the U.S. military, and heavy emphasis was being given to helping prepare Iraq's nascent security forces to secure polling sites. U.S. military leaders saw the January 30 elections as a key step toward democracy that would provide a much-needed incentive for some of the warring groups to lay down their arms and join the political process.

The voting "will strike a blow [against] terrorism," George wrote, sounding confident. "It will go a long way towards marginalizing insurgent efforts I think."

The pace of operations was steadily picking up, he told her, though he spared her a lot of the details. Those weren't always pretty. Nor did they always make a lot of sense to him. Like the first time he had to fire his weapon.

It happened one recent morning after a nighttime raid. They were headed back to base just after dawn when they heard a distress call over the radio net. Another patrol traveling in a combination of tanks and Humvees near the banks of the Tigris River had been attacked with a roadside bomb. There were no major injuries, but reinforcements were needed to search the adjacent homes and fields for the perpetrators or witnesses who might know where to find them.

When he arrived at the scene a few minutes later, George tried to make sense of the shouted orders from several members of the jittery patrol, which had fanned out around their vehicles. They seemed confused and disagreed about what to do. He was struck by the incon-

gruence of it all. A massive armored tank was sitting in the middle of
the road, where the bomb had gone off underneath it. The explosion,
believed to have been set off by a cell phone signal, had done minimal
damage to the iron behemoth, but the patrol couldn't seem to figure
out what to do next. "This is nuts," he thought. The U.S. Army was
literally stopped in its tracks with no enemy in sight.

A senior officer on the scene finally took control of the situation.
George's unit was ordered to search in an adjacent citrus orchard that
spread out to a steep incline and the Tigris below. There, just out of
sight from the orchard and hidden along the steep riverbank, they
found a cache of weapons. The order was given to destroy it by setting off a controlled explosive charge. Just as the "fragging" ricocheted
across the Tigris and back, George spotted what looked like a teenage
boy in the distance darting down the bank. The platoon watched as
the kid jumped into the river and began swimming toward the opposite shore. George raised his weapon, took aim, and fired warning
shots into the water. The boy put his hands up and was taken into
custody for questioning. Whatever happened to him George had no
idea. But all he kept thinking that morning was, "He was just a kid." If
he set off the roadside bomb, he had almost single-handedly paralyzed
a combat unit of the mightiest military in the world.

Some of the other raids that George went on that first winter were
simply bizarre. Like the nighttime operation when they blew open the
door of a suspected insurgent's home with a shotgun only to run right
into the rear end of a massive milk cow in the middle of the living
room. There was no one else in sight. On another raid, they kicked in
the door of a home to find the husband and wife in the middle of having sex. Embarrassed, George's patrol turned around and left.

It sure beat having a desk job, though. And, he confided to Scott,
what really kept him going, often in the face of grave danger, was
something else: he was becoming an "adrenaline junky."

———

When he wasn't on patrol or spending long, caffeine-fueled hours
in the command center, George escaped to the confines of his bunk,
the so-called containerized housing unit that was alternately beastly
hot from the overpowering heating system or bone-chilling cold. Even
in the desert, the mercury dipped into the thirties at night, and he

was grateful for the "snuggly blanket" that Ann had shipped in one of her care packages to keep him warm. Not to mention some of the comfort food that arrived from Tallahassee every few weeks like Tostitos corn chips, which they had learned somehow didn't crumble on the long journey.

When he could keep his eyes open, he wrote letters to Grandma Harriet, who had recently fallen and broken her arm, and a few other pen pals or played video games with his "Joes," the enlisted soldiers in the squadron. Another escape was watching movies on his portable DVD player. Every Tuesday he went down to the PX on Anaconda to buy another movie to add to his collection, already up to twenty-five by the turn of the year. One of his favorites was *The Big Lebowski*, a comedy about an out-of-work ex-hippie, and some of his other standbys were action and war films like *Gladiator* and *Black Hawk Down*.

Then, one day in late January, while he was in between missions, George caught a television special playing in one of the R&R tents. It was about the MIA unit in Hawaii, where he would be going after his Iraq tour. What captured him most was the exotic location where it was filmed.

"They were in Palau. Some beautiful little island in the Pacific . . . recovering a plane that had crashed in World War II," he told Scott. "Looked like hell . . . not."

Scott was excited for him. "Everybody I talk to about the [Hawaii] thing thinks that sounds outstanding," he told his little brother.

————

The last thing George saw before he fell fitfully asleep each day was the collage of family photographs he had taped to the bunk above him. There was the one of George with Mom, Dad, and Schotzy, the little cockapoo they had owned years before at Fort Bragg, along with a few of his two step-siblings, Scott and Teri, and her two children. They all kept him company in those quiet moments. He also worried about them.

In recent years George had taken a particular interest in Teri's teenage kids, his niece, Tara, and nephew, Stevie, at times even filling the role of a stand-in father figure. He desperately wanted to see them avoid some of the struggles of their parents, who were now divorced and facing mounting financial troubles. What would become of Tara and Stevie wore on him even more now that he knew Teri had filed for bankruptcy and her home was threatened by foreclosure. George sought ways he could help and encourage the kids to strive for something better. He feared most that Stevie, who was now nearing high school graduation, would squander his opportunity to go to college and make something of himself. George saw a bit of himself in Stevie, a headstrong kid with all the right instincts and brains. But just as George had been at his age, Stevie was vulnerable to others around him who weren't the best of influences.

In an Internet chat from Camp Anaconda, George raised the prospect with his mother of doing something special for young Stevie, who he knew was working hard in school. He proposed giving him his pickup truck, which had just been paid off, as a reward for his achievements and an incentive to keep at it. "Seems to me that his schoolwork and attitude are more than enough," George told Ann, "when compared to what I got when I was 16 . . . meaning he is certainly more deserving than me."

Ann wondered if the truck might be too much responsibility for him, but George insisted. "Kids need cars. He needs to be able to do his own thing."

———

The early months of 2005 brought key milestones in the war, but like the wet weather, which caked everything in mud, they were mostly discouraging.

The Iraq Survey Group, a special American unit set up after the invasion, officially ended its search for weapons of mass destruction, reporting that none had been found. The conclusion further fueled antiwar sentiment back home, as the main rationale for the war—the threat of Saddam Hussein's secret arsenal of doomsday weapons—proved faulty. In the view of a growing number of Americans, the war had been launched under false pretenses.

Then, on Iraq's Election Day, the Sunni population, the minority that had held power under Saddam, largely stayed home from the polls, as many had predicted, while the country was engulfed in bloodshed. More than a hundred attacks shook Iraq, killing forty-five people; nine of the attacks were set off by suicide bombers, an ominous sign of what might lie ahead. This was despite the fact that U.S. forces imposed curfews, closed Iraq's borders, and banned the carrying of weapons in public, and more than 130,000 newly trained Iraqi security forces guarded polling stations.

To George, the security situation looked bleaker by the day. It was getting harder to have faith that their efforts were making a real difference. For every success they were having on the battlefield, the insurgents often simply moved to a new battleground and recruited new foot soldiers to replace those who had been killed or captured. While there were restrictions on what he could reveal to Ann about the situation, he cryptically alluded to the enemy's resilience.

"Bunch of new kids on the block," he relayed one day when she asked how he thought the war was going, his code for how many of the bad guys who had been driven from one area were showing up to sow chaos somewhere else.

"Why, what happened to the old kids?" Ann didn't quite understand the lingo.

"I'm not supposed to answer those questions from my mother. I am supposed to say that everyone waves and throws flowers," George answered wryly.

"Oh, okay. But it won't work for me."

Ann knew what the news reports were saying, including that insurgents were building more powerful roadside bombs to attack American troops.

"It's getting more gamey across the country," George allowed. "We've definitely had more incidences."

Camp Anaconda itself was now the target of almost daily mortar attacks from insurgents hiding in the warren of neighborhoods just outside the perimeter. On a number of occasions George had to cut short an Internet chat with his mother because the base was taking incoming fire. The whine of air raid sirens frequently sent him and hundreds of other soldiers scrambling into bunkers for safety. The attacks rarely caused significant damage, but they contributed to the growing sense that the enemy was everywhere and nowhere at the same time.

It soon became a running joke that those who were launching

mortars and rockets before melting back into the population might not even know whom they were attacking. They might not care. George had learned that the base had also been rocketed when Saddam's troops had been using it. He couldn't help but suspect that in the view of many Iraqis the American forces that had liberated the country weren't any different from those of the toppled tyrant who had enslaved it.

"They are just mad that anyone is here," George reluctantly concluded.

Such awareness only increased his desire for a greater understanding of Iraq's tortured history and politics, and he began scouring the Internet for articles on the country's different ethnic and religious groups. What he learned only fueled his doubts.

"One thing you can be assured of is that the Sunni margin will not be happy," he told his stepbrother Scott at the time. "They will be disenfranchised completely." The Sunnis, he knew, were most responsible for the insurgency, and their hardening position could only spell more violence.

It was with Scott, who had been in his share of scrapes as a Florida state trooper, that George felt comfortable discussing some of the more gruesome details of what he was experiencing when he was outside the wire. The two of them had a special bond. Scott was supplying George with those most important of care packages: cigars and Copenhagen long-cut chewing tobacco, which became part of his daily routine. George had a tradition of lighting up one of the cigars Scott had sent just before he went on night missions. He joked that they helped him look the part of the "dog-faced" soldier.

"Just like Dad!" Scott ribbed him.

As a police officer, Scott patrolled some of Tampa's most dangerous neighborhoods and could relate to what George was seeing in ways that their mom never could. George confided in him in terms he knew Scott would understand.

"This place is really the wild wild west," he said. There was no rule of law—at least not until the U.S. military showed up, and "only then if the locals aren't packing more heat." George found it hard to see how all the bloodshed would abate. It was probably not unlike what Scott was seeing in gangland Tampa, only worse, fueled by ancient animosities and religious differences.

"They'll knock each other over all day long," George ventured. "Everybody wants to be king of the block."

It was also getting harder and harder to know who the bad guys were. "I can't help but see a terrorist in each boy," George confided to Scott after the elections. Whether the locals were friendly often depended largely on whether he was pointing a gun at them or giving them candy. The toughest challenge was figuring out when to use force to protect himself and his fellow soldiers. One thing that he thought might make it a hell of a lot easier would be if—like Scott—he carried a Taser.

"There are about 100 kids a day I'd like to ZZZZZZZZZap," he told him.

The worst thing U.S. troops were facing, though, was the IEDs. Insurgents were simply too creative, George reported to Scott, planting the makeshift bombs in old tires and under signs or underpasses. George had recently encountered a cannon shell hidden in the carcass of a dead dog. The ballistic and armored protection installed on their vehicles made a difference—"I'm living proof," he offered—but all too often it wasn't enough.

"Doesn't save everybody. . . . They've figured out how much it takes to wreck a [Humvee] and how much it takes to rip a Bradley" armored troop carrier. "We just can't fight them."

——

The explosion was almost half a mile away, but it shook George's vehicle. A huge plume of smoke began to billow in the sky ahead. His patrol rushed to the scene to learn that a large car bomb had gone off and a young trooper from a fellow unit had been killed. The blast had been so large that George was surprised more people hadn't died. It nearly destroyed all the adjacent shops.

George thought very highly of the dead soldier's platoon leader, a bright and engaging young lieutenant from Virginia who had learned to play the bagpipes at West Point. George had gone on a number of patrols with him in recent weeks and was slated to go out with him again the very next day. As a higher-ranking officer, George quickly found himself counseling the distraught lieutenant.

"Please remember to say a prayer for that fallen soldier, and for the confidence of my young friend," he wrote to Ann afterward. "He is shaken by the events of the last few weeks . . . where he has lost two soldiers and had his own vehicle destroyed twice. I sat with him for several hours after we returned home."

The circumstances couldn't be more different, but George drew on his experience as platoon leader when the young soldier under his command at Fort Bragg had committed suicide out on the range.

"I shared my experiences, where as a young platoon leader, I too had lost a man," he told Ann. "We talked about the leadership challenges that would follow this tragedy and how he had to find the means necessary to show strength in this most trying of times."

The next day George was on patrol in the same area of the city of Balad when his patrol got it.

"We had a kid in the turret doing all the right things . . . down under the turret shield," he recounted in an e-mail to Scott. "Should have been safe. But when the IED blew . . . the base of the shell punched right through the shield and took most of his head off."

Ann didn't like what she was hearing, either. "I like it better when you are off the streets," she told him after the incident.

George's mother also noticed that her boy had a shorter fuse. His demeanor could be brusque, even angry at times, not the George she knew. Simple queries prompted him to lash out—for instance, when she asked whether Iraqis changed their clocks for daylight savings. The U.S. military abided by daylight savings, but the Iraqis didn't observe it, he responded. Whatever time it was, it was killing time. "So now instead of shooting at him at 0900 we shoot at 1000."

Indeed, time meant little anymore. "I have no conception of time or day here," he told her. "It's either light or dark . . . that is it. Don't even know the month without thinking about it."

But the ground patrols outside the wire would continue. "The boss likes what I am doing too much," he said, warning her they were moving into even dicier territory.

By the spring, George had left the relative comforts of Camp Anaconda for a remote FOB, or forward operating base, farther to the north near Samarra.

Samarra, located deep in the Sunni Triangle, was where five thousand American troops had recently launched an offensive to wrest control of the violence-racked city from Sunni insurgents. The U.S.-led command was now trying to build up the local security and spending tens of millions of dollars on public works projects in the hopes of building a viable local government to hamstring the insurgents' recruiting efforts. George knew they were having only mixed success and he was in for a tough fight.

FOB McKenzie, formerly known as the Samarra East Air Base or al-Bakr Air Base, was eight square miles of sand, concrete blocks, and barbed wire. It had been bombed by the United States in the first Iraq War in 1991. By the time George arrived, it was still one of the more primitive American outposts in Iraq, with few amenities; there was one shower for every twenty soldiers. The only exception to the paucity of creature comforts was a movie theater and library with Internet access that had been cobbled together in one of the dozen aircraft bunkers on the base. The American forces stationed at the base were responsible for a vast desert area about the size of the state of Vermont. They had their hands full. Sunni insurgents were still moving freely through the area, bringing in weapons, explosives, and new recruits from elsewhere in Iraq. Sunni extremists allied with al-Qaeda were also slipping in from neighboring Syria, Saudi Arabia, and Kuwait to wage war against the Americans and Iraq's Shia Muslim majority. FOB McKenzie was now the target of nightly rocket and mortar attacks—twenty-one on a single night.

"There are different levels of paradise around here. And different levels of hell," George told Ann about his new post. "Next stop Hell."

The relative isolation also forced George to take greater stock of his life. As he reflected in the solitude of his bunk, his thoughts often turned to how, unlike most of his fellow officers, he was still single. There was no special girl waiting for him to come home. Yet the passage of time, a series of failed relationships, and his duty to the Army gave him unsettling doubts that he would find her.

He opened up to Ann in their lengthy Internet chats about how he worried that it was getting too late for him to find what she and his dad had. Why hadn't his relationships succeeded with Viv or his high school girlfriend? They kept him around, he proffered, to "pick them up when they were in trouble . . . or they cried on my shoulder when they needed one . . . but of course . . . blew me off when it was important." He was corresponding with a few girls he had met back in the States, he told her, but their interest seemed to have faded. Maybe he simply wasn't good enough for the kinds of girls he liked.

He sounded depressed about it, and Ann tried to reassure him, imploring him not to lose hope.

"You are an attractive, interesting, extremely well-read, funny, sensitive, well-traveled person, with integrity and values," she told him. "And there is someone for you." There was, to paraphrase the Bible, "a season for all things."

"Well, we're getting late into said season," George offered. "Leaves are starting to turn."

"Yeah. But you are not exactly over the hill—is that what you are talking about?"

"I am getting a bit too old to be screwing off and not thinking seriously about dismounts," he responded, using the Army term for soldiers getting out of a vehicle. "You know . . . kids. . . . I am getting impatient."

"Well, we will continue to pray," Ann assured her son, though privately she was more worried than ever about his state of mind and well-being.

"Thanks mom," George typed. "It really helps me to be able to talk to you . . . gives me a bit of peace."

He also felt a bit more at ease when he thought about what he might do if he left the Army. Sometimes it was a vision of a beach-front house on the Gulf Coast of Florida, where he could buy a fishing vessel and start a charter business. Sometimes George and Ann talked about going in on a beach house together.

His mother, conjuring up the image from the movie *Forrest Gump* that they both loved, sometimes ribbed him about the life he was planning when all this was over.

"When you get back are you going in the shrimp business?"

"No I am going to run across America ten times," he wrote, playing along.

"Oh, how disappointing . . ."

"Okay . . . maybe not . . . But I would like to find a nice girl and have a little boy named Forrest . . . or George."

On other occasions, George envisioned what it might be like to get away from America altogether, perhaps buy a place in Costa Rica or Mexico and find a local girl to settle down with.

He also still held out hope that his next post, even with all the expected travel, would allow him to develop "some sort of root system."

———

The expectation of living in Hawaii for his next assignment planted the seeds of a plan: to live on a boat. Some of George's fondest memories were of boating in the Chesapeake Bay when his father kept a small motorboat while he was stationed in Maryland, and he was determined to make the most of the opportunity.

"A lieutenant of mine turned me on to the idea," he told Ann of his plan. "I've done some research and it is not unreasonable. . . . Question is what to do with it on the backside . . . have it sailed to mainland or sell."

He was also adamant that he didn't want to live anywhere near a military base if he could help it. "I want to be as far away from everyday military as possible," he told Scott.

George surfed the Internet looking for vessels for sale in Hawaii and how to get a boat out there if he bought it on the mainland. Ann sent him copies of *Boat Trader* and other fishing and boating magazines. He had his sights set on a forty- to fifty-foot motorboat that he could finance as a second home.

To further stir his imagination and keep him thinking about the future, Ann also sent him a copy of James Michener's epic novel *Hawaii*, the saga of the first Hawaiians who arrived from Bora-Bora. For a little while each day, as his grimy fingers turned the dog-eared pages of the thick paperback, George was transported from the barbed wire and blast walls of the base to a chain of bucolic islands with sandy beaches lapped by the brilliant blue waters of the Pacific— about as far away as one could get from the dust, dirt, and danger that was his daily existence in Iraq.

George was mesmerized by the descriptions of thousands of years of volcanic fury that left a crater, in the shape of a punch bowl, in the middle of Oahu and another, at the very edge, in the shape of a diamond head. He was captivated to learn that the Hawaiian Islands were the youngest landmasses on earth, still forming after the Bible was written and Jesus and Muhammad walked the earth, where no man had arrived until the end of the first millennium. "Raw, youthful islands, sleeping in the sun and whipped by rain, they waited," Michener wrote. Nearly everything that grew on the islands grew nowhere else; in Michener's telling, it was "an authentic natural paradise where each growing thing had its opportunity to develop in its own unique way, according to the dictates and limitations of its own abilities."

The novel spoke to George, who longed to be born anew, to etch his own story on a new slate.

———

One day out on patrol George befriended a mentally handicapped boy, earning a winning smile when he gave him some candy.

"The thing is about a foot tall, with coke bottle glasses," he wrote to Ann. "Adorable."

George was increasingly troubled by the mounting number of innocent Iraqis who were victims of the conflict, caught in the cross fire of what looked more with each passing day like a full-blown civil war. Especially hit hard, he knew, were the new Iraqi security forces fighting alongside the Americans. "Bad to be in the Army or Police right now," he told Scott.

Now it was also common for multiple car bombs to go off in downtown Baghdad and other crowded Iraqi cities. Many of the victims were not soldiers or police but women and children. The spreading violence was affecting nearly everyone and only increasing the number of Iraqis living in abject poverty, with little hope of a better life.

He was most distressed by the plight of women, especially the young girls he encountered in Iraq's dusty, garbage-strewn streets. They were unbelievably beautiful, he thought, almost angelic. They were being treated so poorly by Iraqi society, forced to do manual labor and afforded so few rights.

"You could never imagine what it means to be a woman in this country or society," he reported home. "It breaks my heart."

He longed to do something for them, to brighten their bleak existence, even for a little while. Scott had been sending him a seemingly never-ending supply of travel shampoos, and George began handing them out to the young girls he encountered on his patrols. Before long, some of them recognized him and came running up to his vehicle, eager to get their hands on a simple luxury that most of them had never known.

George needed to feel that what he was doing here might ultimately help improve the plight of some of the most vulnerable. He snapped a picture of the mentally retarded boy who brightened an otherwise tough day out on patrol to help him remember whom he was fighting for.

"It's my favorite of all that I have taken," he told Ann.

He also learned that beginning in April, he would no longer be a liaison with ground troops and would finally get to fly. With the blazing-hot summer quickly approaching, the good news couldn't have come soon enough. What he didn't tell Ann when he relayed the news was that flying Kiowas was now one of the most dangerous assignments of the war.

———

One of George's all-time favorite movies was the 1979 Vietnam war film *Apocalypse Now*. He had seen it so many times he had lost count. One character he particularly got a kick out of was Colonel Kilgore, the fearless air cavalry officer played by Robert Duvall whose bravado in the face of combat is matched only by his obsession with surfing. A caricature of a fanatical military officer, Kilgore even embraces chemical warfare, exclaiming in one of the movie's most memorable lines, "I love the smell of napalm in the morning," as he paces before his men, shirtless in his cavalry Stetson.

"It's my favorite part," George told Ann in an Internet chat from FOB McKenzie after she wrote that she stayed up late watching the movie on television for the first time with her new husband, Mike, whom she had married the previous fall.

The famous line was also something of an inside joke in the Eyster household. When Big George oversaw the spraying of pesticides in Florida citrus groves after he retired from the Army, a critical newspaper cartoon at the time pictured him as Kilgore bragging how he loved the smell of malathion in the morning, referring to the controversial chemical that was being used to fight the agricultural infestation.

"I went and got the scrapbook and showed Mike the cartoon of Daddy saying he loved the smell of malathion in the morning," Ann reported. "I re-read everything this morning—haven't done that in a while. A great guy," she said of his father.

George and his fellow pilots weren't playing Wagner's "Ride of the Valkyries" on full volume as they flew into combat, like the cav guys in *Apocalypse Now*, but what they were doing would certainly have impressed the thrill-seeking Kilgore and his men.

Kiowa pilots in Iraq were being deployed more than any other helicopter crews and were routinely flying within the range of insurgents' AK-47 machine guns and rocket-propelled grenades, or RPGs. Most of them felt that if they weren't getting shot at, they weren't doing their jobs. The need for Kiowas to support ground troops was exacting a heavy toll. By the summer of 2005, nearly a dozen Kiowa pilots had been killed in Iraq, more than any other military fliers. They had been shot down or crashed after clipping power lines or striking other obstacles, while excessive heat and sandstorms were causing a host of mechanical problems for their aging aircraft, many of which were older than the pilots flying them.

"We are the only pilots in country doing anything," George boasted a few weeks after getting back in the cockpit, telling Ann how other pilots flying in the war were mostly just going from point A to point B, dropping bombs from twenty thousand feet, or weren't seeing any action at all.

When he wasn't flying, George was filling the role he briefly held in Kuwait as the squadron's assistant operations officer, overseeing a staff of ten—four captains and six enlisted soldiers—managing what he called "nugging," the nuts and bolts of the squadron's daily activities. On good days he was on the clock sixteen hours.

He was flying missions at least two to three times a week, most of them lasting up to five hours. His job was mostly to circle near ground units and await a radio call to help locate suspected insurgents or, if needed, provide supporting fire. George, usually sitting in the left seat, flew many of his early missions with Matt Lourey, a tall and lanky forty-one-year-old chief warrant officer with fair skin and a shaved head whose long legs could barely fit in the cockpit. Married to an Army officer, the enlisted Lourey had a reputation as one of the kindest and most intelligent pilots in the squadron. Many looked up to him as a mentor, including officers like George.

What made their missions even more dangerous was the enormous pressure to be restrained when using the Kiowa's firepower, even in the face of a hail of bullets or rocket-propelled grenades. They were flying mostly in densely populated areas where they could kill large numbers of innocent bystanders with their powerful weapons if they weren't judicious in their use of force. As a result, they often chose to simply aim their M4 carbines out of the sides of the cockpits to shoot at insurgents rather than open up with the Kiowa's cannons or missiles. It wasn't a tactic George had learned in flight training, but like his fellow pilots he had to quickly get the hang of it. The learning curve was not without its challenges; some pilots firing their weapons out of the cockpit of a banking Kiowa shot up some of their own rocket pods underneath.

"This isn't exactly the Fulda Gap and we ain't shootin' missiles at tanks," as Big George had trained on the plains of Europe, he told his mother in April. "Not too hard to lean out the door and shoot back. You can be much more accurate . . . precise."

Sometimes the Kiowas were called in to determine if a neighborhood was friendly or hostile simply by flying over it. If they elicited cheers and waves, it was probably friendly territory; if the people opened fire, it was probably an insurgent stronghold.

As the insurgency continued to expand, the cowboy grit and street-fighter instincts of the so-called flying infantry were earning Kiowa pilots a special place in the hearts of the ground pounders, who had grown to love the *thwump-thwump-thwump* sound of the twin rotors arriving as if out of nowhere on the scene of an ambush.

———

Late on the night of Thursday, May 26, 2005, as George was pulling a shift as assistant operations officer in the command post on FOB McKenzie, the terrible news flashed over the radio. Matt Lourey and another pilot, Josh Scott, who had been flying a mission near the insurgent stronghold of Baquba, went down. George scrambled with other pilots and flew to the scene, where air cover was needed to secure the area around the crash site while ground forces tried to reach the downed pilots.

Lourey and Scott had been flying cover for four Humvees patrolling down a narrow street in the village of Buhriz, a known insurgent stronghold framed by date palms and orange groves along the Diyala River. When the Humvees got about halfway through the main market street, an RPG fired from a rooftop sailed past the hood of one of the vehicles. Within moments the entire patrol was under attack from three sides by a flurry of RPGs and insurgents wielding AK-47s. The troops tried to escape, but the last vehicle got pinned down.

Just as the situation appeared desperate, Lourey and Scott swooped down with their .50-caliber guns blazing. The soldiers in the Humvee had enough time to hit the gas and speed out to the open road. As they exited the market, they looked up to see the Kiowa barrel into the thick palm groves. A round had entered the cockpit above the two pilots and struck the engine below the main rotor, causing a catastrophic power failure. Lourey and Scott had no time to recover before hitting the tops of the trees.

For most of the next three hours, George and a swarm of other Kiowas and Apache helicopter gunships struggled to keep the insurgents in the area at bay while fellow troops reached the crash site. Together, they expended thirty thousand rounds of .50-caliber ammunition and fired at least thirty rockets. Finally, the news came over the net that Lourey and Scott were dead.

——

That same day, as she was preparing to go to bed on the East Coast, Ann saw a news report on television that a Kiowa had been shot down over Baquba. The identities of the pilots were not yet being divulged, but she was pretty sure they were from George's squadron when the report cited the Forty-Second Division. The hours ticked slowly by as she lay awake wondering how long it might take for the military to pay a visit to the mother of a soldier killed in combat. She listened for a car pulling up the gravel drive in the middle of the night. But no one came. As Thursday became Friday, Ann pushed aside her gnawing worries and went to work. But she could barely think about anything else. She searched every news story every hour all day for more information. When nearly twenty-four hours had passed, she started to breathe a sigh of relief that she probably wasn't going to get a dreaded visit from a military chaplain. But there was still no word from George.

Finally, late that night, her computer buzzed with an incoming message. "Mom," George typed from FOB McKenzie.

"I am very relieved to hear from you," she replied after running to the keyboard.

"I am sorry. . . . Could not write or call until Mr. Lourey and Mr. Scott's wives and children were notified," George reported matter-of-factly, his way of telling her they had suffered losses.

"Oh, my goodness. I felt it was probably your unit," Ann wrote, letting him know she had heard the news. "It gave me a very rough time today."

George's responses to her questions were clipped, almost without feeling. No banter about home, boating, rug shopping in the local bazaars, or Ann's new life with Mike, his stepfather. He had been appointed to oversee the disposition of Josh Scott's remains and to comb through his personal effects to prepare them for delivery to his wife, he told her. Ann tried her best to comfort him, but George deflected her attempts. He was in a different place right now. "You've never had anyone killed in the Army," he wrote. "This is my second time."

Matt Lourey's death hit him hard. The two of them had spent hours together in the cockpit, shoulder to shoulder, talking about home and what they would do when they got back. They had flown together over those very same orange groves just days before, one of nearly two dozen missions they had flown in the past two months.

Matt, whose wife, Lisa, was an Army captain, had been groomed as the ultimate team player. He grew up one of twelve siblings in East Bethel, Minnesota, where his mother, Becky, was a state senator. She and his father, Gene, had four birth children, including Matt, and had adopted eight others, with each new adoption put to a family vote. But he was an unlikely warrior. Both his parents actively protested the Vietnam War. Matt's mother, meanwhile, had circulated a petition around the Minnesota statehouse urging President George W. Bush not to invade Iraq in 2003. "The Bush administration's stated goals of a potential war with Iraq, such as replacement of the Iraqi government, economic redevelopment of Iraq, disarmament of the Iraqi military, are as likely to be achieved without war as with war," it concluded. She had even gotten Matt's blessing beforehand. But all

Matt Lourey had ever wanted to do was be a military pilot. When he was a boy, he donned a World War II aviator's vest and white scarf to play the part. Gene tried unsuccessfully to talk his son out of a career in the military. When he volunteered for a second tour in Iraq, Matt said it was because his fellow soldiers needed him.

Everyone in the squadron had a favorite story about him. George remembered the time that one of the soldiers who wore his Christianity on his sleeve started ranting about how he was going to kill all the Iraqis he could. Matt, his face buried in a manual, remained silent at first. Then, at just the right moment in the tirade, he peered over the top of the manual. "That's very Christian of you," he admonished the soldier, putting an abrupt end to the tirade. Now George couldn't stop thinking of the picture Matt kept showing him of the two-seat convertible Pontiac Solstice that he was going to buy as soon as he got home. So much for that.

George had other comrades he previously served with who were killed in the war. There were nine, in fact. Men like Captain George Wood of Utica, New York, a quiet guy who played football at Cornell University whom George had met during summer ROTC training. Wood was killed by a roadside bomb, not far from where Matt Lourey died, earlier in the war. There was also the twenty-three-year-old warrant officer Michael Blaise of Macon, Missouri, who served under George in Korea. He was killed when his Kiowa crashed near Mosul just days before the end of his tour, leaving behind his wife and high school sweetheart, an Army captain. But as tough as it was to hear about the losses of those men, whom he had lived and sweated with, George hadn't been there when they were killed. Their deaths hadn't touched him like Lourey's—hadn't been so close. The only consolation was that Matt probably didn't suffer much. George learned later that the Kiowa had been flying in a downward direction at a pretty good clip when it was hit. Matt likely died almost instantly when the chopper hit the trees and burst into a fireball.

As for Matt Lourey's co-pilot on that fateful night, George had never flown with the twenty-eight-year-old warrant officer and father of three from Sun Prairie, Wisconsin. But he had been one of his fiercest Xbox competitors back at the base.

George was nearly overwhelmed with emotion at their loss, and he wasn't prepared for the reaction of others in the squadron. The commander of the aviation brigade openly sobbed at a memorial service they all held for their brethren on FOB McKenzie a few days later. It was then that George couldn't fight back the tears any longer. He had reached a crossroads with the deaths of his fellow pilots and now felt very differently about the war and his role in it. The official line on what they were trying to do here was constantly drummed into him—to bring stability to a war-torn nation and give it a chance to make democracy work—but he just didn't believe anymore that the U.S. military could really do that. It probably never had a chance.

"What did Matt Lourey and Josh Scott die for?" he thought as he lay awake in his bunk. What would he tell their families if they ever asked him? He didn't have a good answer.

———

"I am afraid."

The simple words, confided in an Internet chat to Ann one Sunday as she was getting dressed for church, summed up the mounting pressures weighing on George in the late summer as his tour entered the home stretch.

There was the fear of death, of course, which had always been there. But now it felt as if insurgents were lurking around every corner, hiding on every rooftop, or preparing to fire at him from the camouflage of each palm grove. About a week after Lourey and Scott were killed, George and his co-pilot were flying over FOB McKenzie to test fire their guns when the "Guard" emergency channel squawked with a report of a downed aircraft in the area. As he flew in the direction of the reported coordinates, George relived in his mind the night his fellow pilots went down. His heart was pounding, every inch of his body seemed to tighten, and his mind raced with fear. What was he flying into?

He breathed a sigh of relief when the report turned out to be a false alarm, and they returned to McKenzie. Yet he was troubled by how he reacted, how he had to fight off what was almost a mental and physical paralysis in the face of danger. The sense of foreboding also came from something else, he realized. George feared that he had given up his chance to live the life he really wanted—and for what?

As he later sat at a computer and typed to Ann, his dreams of marriage and children felt further away than ever. First, he had set aside his desire as a young man to chart his own path away from the one that he felt had been chosen for him. Then, when he had committed to military service, he chose it over Viv. He had since set aside his personal goals in striving to achieve status and rank in the Army—goals he now confided that he doubted he would achieve in the end anyway. Now he feared it might be too late to have a more fulfilling life. He was only thirty-two, but he harbored a dark view of his future.

George felt he was being chased by what he morbidly called the "GSE curse," the bad genetics that had made victims of more than one George Senseny Eyster before their time—his father at the age of forty-nine and his great-grandfather General Eyster at the age of fifty-three. At his most recent flight physical, George's cholesterol was over 220, and his blood pressure was also too high.

"Just goes to show you," he told his mother, "I better get the old family started soon. Or maybe not at all."

He had also put on a few pounds since the ground patrols had ended, and while he was trying to exercise regularly, he told her, there was little time with his frenetic schedule. Even when he could, he was frustrated at how difficult it was to go for routine runs. "This place is horrible . . . can't find an even pavement in the whole damn country," he complained.

The long hours hunched over in the cockpit didn't help his outlook on his health, either. Some missions flying up north lasted eight hours from the time he took off and returned to base, and he had re-aggravated his old parachute-jumping injury. His back pain was now worse than ever.

"Sitting in the same rigid position for five hours or more at a time is not the best for people with broken tails," he wrote. He was now taking several narcotics prescribed by one of the military docs for the pain.

"The tide is working against me," he told his mother. "There are only so many years in a GSE's life."

He had too much going for him to be so down, Ann wrote, trying to lift his spirits. His future was still so bright, and he would meet someone to share his life with.

But he only grew more morbid. Even if he did meet someone, he responded, how much time would he have to enjoy it?

"It'd be nice to get it all together . . . just in time to get dead."

Not even in Ranger School had George felt this depleted, both physically and mentally. He had an overpowering feeling of dread and a tightness in his chest, especially when he was about to go on a mission. For the first time he also regretted agreeing to the posting in Hawaii. He should have called it quits after this, like all those other officers who were heading for the exits in droves.

"I'm not sure that I will not regret going to Hawaii," he told Ann.

It was clear to Ann that her boy's commitment to the Army was at an all-time low and the Iraq experience was changing him.

"I absolutely agree," she responded.

In conversations with his stepbrother, Scott, George was even more direct.

"Hawaii better let me have a life or I am done."

———

A Gallup poll in the summer of 2005 showed that more than two-thirds of Americans disapproved of the way President Bush was handling the war and a strong majority agreed the country had "made a mistake" by invading Iraq. More than half, meanwhile, also believed the effort was not worth continuing. Even the parents of some dead U.S. soldiers were insisting that "Operation Iraqi Freedom" not be etched on the tombstones of their fallen sons and daughters.

By late summer, as a bloody civil war raged, members of Bush's own Republican Party were beginning to openly call for an American withdrawal. "We're locked into a bogged-down problem, not dissimilar to where we were in Vietnam," said Senator Chuck Hagel of Nebraska, a Vietnam vet. "We should start figuring out how we get out of there. . . . I think by any standard, when you analyze two and a half years in Iraq, where we have put in over a third of a trillion dollars, where we have lost almost 1,900 Americans, over 14,000 wounded, electricity production down, oil production down—any measurement, any standard you apply to this, we're not winning."

Later, the retired Army general William Odom, another Vietnam veteran, who ran the National Security Agency during the presidency of Ronald Reagan, made headlines when he called the Iraq War the "greatest strategic disaster in United States history, far worse than Vietnam." Also feeding the antiwar movement were reports that tens of thousands of Iraqi civilians had died since the invasion. By the fall, a British medical journal, the *Lancet*, was estimating that the civilian death toll since the war began was between thirty thousand and a hundred thousand. The headlines, when he paid attention to them, only fueled George's own doubts about the mission he had volunteered for. "Don't pay attention much to the news anymore," he confided to Ann, "can't get my hands around it mostly."

Despite all the good he and his fellow soldiers were trying to do, he could now understand why so many Iraqis viewed the Americans as occupiers whose motives were more sinister than simply removing the hated dictator Saddam Hussein. George, too, began to suspect that the United States was here for less valiant reasons. He couldn't say with certainty what they were, but he felt it wasn't simply to fight terrorism and build a more stable and free society.

"They don't think we are here solely to liberate Iraq and keep the world safe," he told Ann. "I don't either. It's just part of it."

In July he got word he would be moving again, this time up north, where the war had spread from the Sunni Triangle. From what he was hearing, the Kiowa pilots flying up there were taking a beating.

"Mosul is the next Fallujah," he told Ann.

"Stay away from Mosul, then," his mother advised.

"I'll be going to Mosul next month."

———

The most prominent landmark that George could see circling over Mosul was the ruins of the ancient walled city of Nineveh, on the eastern bank of the Tigris River. The massive stone and mud brick gates of the Assyrian capital stood as a constant reminder that the animosities playing out below were as ancient as man itself. A review of his Bible reinforced George's belief that this place was cursed. Nineveh had been the wonder of the ancient world and its fall the theme of the prophets. It was here that Jonah prophesied in the Hebrew Bible against the city's inhabitants "for their great wickedness." Now, twenty-five hundred years later, the words of another Old Testament prophet Zephaniah still seemed to apply to the violent crush of humanity George could see below him: "He will stretch out his hand against the north and destroy Assyria, and will make Nineveh a desolation and dry waste like a wilderness."

There had once been hope for Mosul. In the months after the 2003 invasion, Iraq's third-largest city had been a bastion of relative stability and a point of pride for American generals when Baghdad and other cities were being looted and the insurgency was gaining strength in the Sunni Triangle. Now, more than two years later, Mosul's fault lines were fully exposed. It was considered Iraq's deadliest city, where a lethal mix of Iraqi insurgents and Islamic terrorists was waging war on the U.S.-led coalition and, increasingly, the Iraqi people.

American reinforcements were locked in a desperate struggle against at least three different groups mounting suicide attacks, planting roadside bombs, and ambushing U.S. troops from their hideouts in Mosul's labyrinth of concrete apartment blocks, mosques, and garbage-strewn streets. First, there were the holdouts from the toppled regime. More than a third of Saddam Hussein's officers were Sunnis from Mosul, and considerable Army infrastructure was left to draw upon, including weapons stockpiles. Mosul was also now the headquarters of the outlawed Baath Party that had run Iraq under Saddam and still clung to the hope of restoring the party to power through a guerrilla war. It was in Mosul where Saddam's two sons had been tracked down and killed by U.S. troops. The Sunni population, living mostly in the western part of the city, had largely been implanted there by Saddam Hussein and was helping to stir the cauldron.

At the same time, the city had become a base of operations for terrorists inspired by al-Qaeda who had fled the Sunni Triangle or slipped in from neighboring Syria to recruit from a population suffering from unemployment as high as 75 percent. Yet still another well-armed foe was the Shia Muslim militias that intelligence reports suggested were financed and armed by neighboring Iran.

In this environment, Kiowas were particularly vulnerable. The previous September a Kiowa had been shot down by a surface-to-air missile, several more had been hit by RPGs, and a number of pilots were wounded or killed when they struck electrical wires. There had also been a host of crashes due to mechanical problems.

George, darting in and out of Mosul's neighborhoods to come to the aid of ground troops, was regularly shot at as he watched the flashes of IEDs exploding in the streets below.

———

On a sweltering morning in early August, George and his co-pilot, Joey Moorhouse, were sitting side by side in the cramped cockpit of their Kiowa flying low over the Tigris River through Mosul. Their mission for the next few hours was to be on standby to provide air cover for ground units conducting operations in the sprawling population center. Strapped to the right leg of George's flight suit was a "knee board"—a tri-fold with a small notebook for making quick flight calculations and jotting down notes. Tucked inside was his good luck charm: a snapshot of him and his mom taken a few years earlier during a birthday dinner at Bud and Alley's, a seaside restaurant in the Florida Panhandle that was one of their favorites.

The pilots were winding their way north, following the greenish-blue waters of the Tigris, when an urgent message came over the radio. An American patrol in the al-Yarmouk neighborhood in the western part of the city had been fired on near the main traffic circle, and at least one soldier had been shot. Two men fled the scene in a black Opel sedan and were being chased through the cluttered streets by heavily armored 4x4 troop carriers from the First Battalion of the Twenty-Fourth Infantry Division. George quickly punched in their reported position and headed for the scene.

Within a few minutes, visible through the cockpit glass up ahead were the clouds of dust being kicked up by the Americans' eight-wheeled Strykers. George spoke into the headset to Lieutenant Colonel Michael "Erik" Kurilla, the senior officer on the scene, who was riding in one of the armored vehicles. George reported that he had the sedan in sight, and Kurilla ordered him to stick with it.

The Kiowa was flying at top speed, but the sedan was outrunning George and his co-pilot on the straightaways. They were able to catch up only when the car slowed down to turn onto another street or into an alley.

"It's going about 105 miles per hour," George estimated.

Kurilla radioed back with orders to use force to stop it.

George had to make a decision fast. He could open up with the

Kiowa's .50-caliber cannons and disable the car, possibly killing the two men inside. But he didn't know exactly who they were. All that was known was that they had been standing next to the car with the hood open in the traffic circle when automatic weapons were fired at the American patrol. When U.S. soldiers approached, the two men fled. George darted his eyes around the area. Several blind alleys branched off from the main roadway, which was lined with low-slung homes and shops. If he used heavy firepower, civilians might be injured or killed. Besides, if the men were in fact insurgents, they were worth more alive than dead. The Strykers were closing in, and if the men could be captured they might provide valuable intelligence about other insurgents in the area.

George instructed his co-pilot to take control of the chopper and swoop low over the car. As the Kiowa was flying about fifty feet off the ground, George turned his body ninety degrees into the swirling dust curling up into the open side of the cockpit. He planted his right foot on the floor, bent his left knee, and braced the heel against the seat. He carefully raised his M4 carbine with his left arm and took aim at the speeding car below.

Bang, bang, bang. George pulled the trigger. The three quick bursts struck the sedan, shattering the rear window. The car careened left and right, but the driver kept control—and his foot on the gas.

George instructed Joey to try to fly beyond it, circle back around, and come in over the top. Carefully, and after some difficulty, they maneuvered the Kiowa into position. George steadied his weapon and fired three more shots directly into the hood of the car. The car came to a sudden stop at an intersection next to a row of run-down market stalls.

As the Kiowa hovered, George craned his neck to see what the passengers would do next, steadying his weapon so it was pointed at the roof of the car. The seconds ticked slowly by as George, sweat dripping down his cheeks and his heart beating loudly, watched for any movement. The driver, wearing a traditional long white frock with his head partially covered, finally opened his door and gingerly started to get out. As he stood up, he turned his body toward the car but kept his arms hidden under the roof—a sign for George that he was shielding a weapon and intended to take aim at the helicopter. Training one eye on the passenger-side door, which was still shut, George decided not to take any chances. He fired off a few more rounds at the hood, hoping to draw out the driver and force him to make a move. At that very moment the driver, wielding an AK-47, and the passenger scrambled from the car and into the adjacent stalls.

The Strykers arrived on the scene, and what happened next, George thought later, was eerily reminiscent of the episode burned in his brain of his grandfather's last moments in Vietnam.

————

Lieutenant Colonel Kurilla, who had given George orders to fire on the car, was a towering figure who took special care of his troops and always led from the front. In his body armor and wraparound shades, the tall and well-built thirty-nine-year-old Army Ranger from Minnesota commanded a unique physical authority. But he was also known for a softer side. He praised his men for showing restraint when civilians were nearby and kept a list of phone numbers so he could personally call the families when one of his troopers was killed or wounded so they wouldn't hear it from someone who wasn't there.

Kurilla sprinted out of the lead Stryker and headed after the insurgents into the stalls. Following behind him were a fresh-faced lieutenant and an Army specialist, both with little combat experience, along with a former Green Beret turned war correspondent named Michael Yon, who had been covering the war up close for more than a year.

While Kurilla was still in mid-stride, a burst of machine gun fire erupted from one of the corner stalls. He somersaulted to the ground and fired back with his M4. A few seconds later, while he was still firing, he slumped over on the ground a few yards from one of the outer walls.

"I'm hit three times!" Kurilla called. "I'm shot three times!"

The spray of gunfire had shattered both legs and burrowed into an arm. Bullets were still striking off the ground all around him.

Circling overhead, George heard the rat-a-tat-tat of the gunshots over the radio. But with the noise of the rotors and the dust clouds, he couldn't quite make out the commotion in the courtyard in front of the market. Crouched nearby the wounded Kurilla were the pair of soldiers riding in his vehicle and the unarmed Yon. Kurilla couldn't move, but he shouted orders at the soldiers to go in after the shooters. They hesitated. He ordered them into the market again, but they didn't move. Then Yon started yelling for them to throw a grenade. Finally, a few moments later, Kurilla's top NCO, Command Sergeant Major Robert Prosser, rushed up and ran straight into the shop just as one of the shooters lunged forward firing a pistol at Kurilla. Prosser shot the man at least three times at point-blank range even as he was hit in the leg. Seconds later, American reinforcements entered the market, and the second gunman surrendered.

George, still circling above the scene, heard over the net that Kurilla was shot and another soldier wounded; both needed to be evacuated as soon as possible. He got back on the radio to headquarters to make sure the evacuation mission was already under way.

As they returned to base and the adrenaline began to dissipate, George's mind raced. Was he to blame for this? Should he have handled the situation differently and just blown up the car? Maybe he was too careful this time. Might the commanding officer die because of his actions?

He was relieved to learn later that both men would survive. But when he was given a citation for his role that day, he felt he didn't deserve it. This was not what he had trained for. He was trained to scout enemy positions and support ground troops in battle with an opposing Army. Instead, he was being awarded a medal for chasing pickups and sedans down crowded city streets.

George desperately needed to rationalize what he was doing and why. After the Mosul chase, he got in the habit of circling the half a dozen neighborhoods in the southeast section of the city that he knew were minority Christian communities. The sight of statues of Jesus Christ atop some of the churches, visible through his cockpit glass, was comforting to him. At least he felt some connection to the people down there, who would often come out and wave at his helicopter.

"At least I'm protecting them," he thought.

He confided to Scott he felt there was little worth fighting for.

"There are three reasons to breathe here," George told him. "One is to wake up. I prefer to do that when I can. The second is lunch. And the third is of course dinner."

For the rest of the summer and into the fall, as he flew more long missions over Mosul, a recurring thought nagged at George.

"Why are we here? Why am I here? If I get killed, I'm gonna be really pissed."

PART THREE

For we are like olives: only when we are crushed

do we yield what is best in us.

The Talmud

CHAPTER SIX

MOVING UP THE LINE

Just after New Year's 1942, as the bodies of American sailors were still being pulled from the twisted metal that remained of the U.S. Pacific Fleet in Pearl Harbor, Japanese warplanes were headed for another port, this one virtually unknown to the outside world. On January 4, 1942, while Ryan was still in flight training in Jacksonville, Japanese air forces began pummeling Rabaul, on the northernmost tip of New Britain Island.

The garrison of Australian troops on the lightly populated Gazelle Peninsula, about nine hundred strong, were the only thing standing between the Japanese and the large island of New Guinea, situated just to Australia's north. Under the cover of darkness, on the night of January 23, five thousand Japanese soldiers went ashore at Blanche Bay. The Australian defenders were quickly overrun. Within hours, most of them had been captured, tortured, and beheaded. As for the rest, the Australian commander ordered a full withdrawal, "every man for himself." Few survived to tell the harrowing tale.

In the ensuing weeks, tens of thousands of Japanese troops, dozens of warships, and, eventually, a large air force descended on Rabaul, with its deep port—known as the "Pearl of the Pacific"—surrounded by volcanoes and a natural defense of high rocky cliffs that straddled the strategic Solomon and Bismarck seas. It would soon host one of the largest concentrations of Imperial forces outside Japan.

The New Guinea campaign had begun. It would last more than three years, nearly the entire duration of the war, in one of the most treacherous places on earth, where thousands of American and Australian fighting men would be swallowed up by a forbidding jungle that literally reached the clouds.

On February 3, 1942, as Ryan was flying in formation on a three-hour training flight off the Florida coast six thousand miles away, Japanese bombs fell for the first time on Port Moresby, Australia's dusty colonial capital and the largest city on the main island of New Guinea. The Japanese were now within range of Australian soil. Later that month, in a demonstration of what might be next, the Japanese bombed Darwin, on Australia's northern coast, killing 250 people and destroying nearly a dozen warships and two dozen aircraft.

Panic spread like wildfire Down Under, where Australians had watched with foreboding as Japan's mockingly named "Greater East Asia Co-prosperity Zone" stretched from Hong Kong to Malaya, Burma, Singapore, Guam, Java, the Dutch East Indies, and now Rabaul—nearly one-sixth of the earth's surface—leaving devastation in its wake. By May, the Japanese had seized all the major coastal towns on New Guinea and the nearby northern and eastern islands.

Australia was nearly defenseless. Twelve thousand militia members, the under-trained home guard, made up its only sizable security force. In 1940 it had sent most of its air, land, and sea forces to fight alongside England against Germany and the Axis powers in North Africa, Greece, and the Middle East. The Australians' fortunes now depended on the Americans. "Our resources here are very limited. It is in your power to meet the situation," Prime Minister John Curtin wrote to President Roosevelt.

American resources, however, would prove scarce as well, as the war in Europe was given higher priority. On February 17, the U.S. Army chief of staff, George Marshall, ordered to Australia the Forty-First Infantry Division, a unit of National Guardsmen from Idaho, Montana, Oregon, North Dakota, and Washington. Their job was to hold the line pending reinforcements, if and when they became available. Soon afterward, the Thirty-Second Infantry Division, mostly members of National Guard units from Michigan and Wisconsin, was also ordered to Australia.

But before the Americans could complete a crash training course in Australia, the Imperial Japanese Army was on a high ridge of the Owen Stanley Range, overlooking Port Moresby, just across the Tasman Sea from Australian territory. The newly arrived Allied commander in the Southwest Pacific, General Douglas MacArthur, paced back and forth on the long porch of his Port Moresby headquarters. He appealed to the Joint Chiefs of Staff in Washington for more ground, air, and naval forces to beat back the Japanese advance—to no avail. He had little choice but to order the ill-prepared American units into combat.

Their mission was to traverse the Kokoda Track through the Owen Stanley Range and beat the Japanese back to New Guinea's northern coast. The trail is sixty miles long, but only passable on foot, and winds near the 7,185-foot peak of Mount Bellamy. It is among the most "geographically disturbed" places on the planet, where there is virtually no flat land and no roads—just goat trails. There was no direct route to get anywhere. If you trekked a thousand feet up into the rain forest, the topography would often descend six hundred feet before climbing another one thousand. With no roads or railways through the nearly impassable terrain, supply lines were simply native tracks cut through the jungle, little more than narrow footpaths that quickly turned into knee-deep mud in downpours that turned streams into rivers. In short, the terrain made a mockery of conventional military deployments. Covering two miles in a day was considered a rousing success.

At first, the Allies didn't only fear the Japanese, who were quickly earning a reputation for ruthless brutality matched only by the Nazis. The barefoot natives, decorated with exotic tattoos, shell necklaces, and colorful skirts, grinned at them through teeth stained a deep red from chewing betel nut, the local narcotic, as they leaned on their twelve-foot spears. Some GIs, hearing stories of cannibalism, remembered thinking the natives were eyeing them for dinner.

New Guinea's intricate web of tribal societies, the GIs learned, was governed by a combination of myth, magic, and sorcery. The natives had a deep fear of the mountains, where they believed evil spirits roamed the darkness. By and large, though, they were eager to help the Americans and Australians as carriers and scouts, for they had already experienced firsthand the depravity of the Japanese invaders. "They were totally on our side because of the Japanese cruelty whenever they had contact with them," recalled Sergeant Major Arthur May of the Third Air Task Force, whose job was to build makeshift airfields for the U.S. Army Air Forces.

At best, the American-led ground campaign on New Guinea in 1942 and early 1943 could be called a stalemate. The Forty-First and Thirty-Second Divisions suffered heavy casualties before reinforcements could arrive. Nearly 25 percent of the Forty-First was killed, wounded, or succumbed to tropical disease. The Thirty-Second, woefully short of medical supplies, had it far worse. Of the 9,825 men who went into combat, a full 66 percent fell ill. Added to those killed and wounded in action, the total casualty count for the division was 9,956. Accounting for replacements, that was actually more than the division's entire official battle strength.

In command of the Japanese fortress at Rabaul was Admiral Isoroku Yamamoto, considered one of the most brilliant Japanese naval officers. Yamamoto, standing on the bridge of his flagship, also knew his enemy all too well. After graduating from the Japanese naval academy, he was seriously injured in the Japanese war with Russia in 1905. He came to America in 1919 to study at Harvard University, where he learned English and recommended Carl Sandburg's three-volume biography of Abraham Lincoln to his friends. He drank scotch, smoked cigars, and became an accomplished poker player.

He also traveled to the heartland—including Chicago and Detroit—where he saw firsthand America's industrial might. "It is a mistake to regard the Americans as luxury loving and weak," he wrote upon his return, after he changed his military specialty from gunnery to aviation. "I can tell you that they are full of spirit, adventure, fight, and justice." On the eve of World War II, Yamamoto was the only member of the Japanese high command to recommend against the attack on Pearl Harbor. In 1940 he told the Japanese prime minister: "If we are ordered to go to war with America, then I can guarantee to put up a tough fight for the first six months, but I have absolutely no confidence about what would happen if it went on for two or three years."

By the end of 1942 the Japanese forces on New Guinea were no longer an imminent threat to Australia, but their heavily entrenched positions at the military fortress at Rabaul presented a main obstacle to MacArthur's grand strategy to move across the Central Pacific, retake the Philippines, and ultimately defeat Japan. Rabaul was Tokyo's lifeline in the Southwest Pacific, but the Allied command concluded it could not be taken outright. Every Allied warplane—Army, Navy, and

Marine Corps—that MacArthur and his commanders could muster would be needed to isolate the Japanese forces there.

"Tanks and artillery can be reserved for the battlefields of Europe and Africa," remarked General George Kenney, commander of the U.S. Fifth Air Force from 1942 to 1945. "The artillery in this theater flies."

———

"Got two letters from you Friday and did enjoy them. And by the way, who is the one to keep up the morale of this family? I'm the Mother, and here it is, you are keeping us all going."

Grace's letter to Ryan was mailed from Charleston on Monday morning, November 8, 1943, via the Fleet Post Office in San Francisco. It was filled with the news of home he was so desperate for. His sister Uranie had "covered herself with glory" when she presented at a local medical conference the previous Thursday, Grace told him. She was even more of a hit at the banquet afterward at the Francis Marion Hotel.

"She did look very pretty in a white dress with large red flowers and a bright red coat with her white earrings," Grace gushed. "All of her professors remarked that she looked so pretty and wanted to know why she didn't come to class with something on like that—maybe then they could keep awake!"

Ryan's military checks were arriving all right, Grace reported, and relayed that she had shipped him a month's supply of Vimms, the vitamins advertised in storefronts and magazines as "a great thing for you—and a great thing for wartime America." Santa would also soon be bringing Ryan the mirror he requested. "Maybe he will appear in a hula skirt," his mother teased. "Will try for the socks," she added, "but don't know where I'm going to get all wool ones."

As Grace's letter made its way to Ryan, the Hell's Angels were waiting on Samoa for the USS *Pocomoke*, a seaplane tender, to take them to the advance base at Efate. Their next stop was in the New Hebrides, a chain of forty primeval islands to the southwest of Samoa and three hundred miles south of the ferocious battle taking place between the Allies and Japan for control of the approaches to New Guinea. Ryan's flying would soon be getting more intense, and he expected to be in the cockpit for longer stretches of time as the squadron moved closer to the battle zone. Even in the tropics it could get cold up there at twenty thousand feet—thus the urgent request to Grace for warm socks.

When the squadron crossed the 180th meridian in the *Pocomoke*, all hands were inducted into the Domain of the Golden Dragon, a Navy tradition for "crossing the line" into the "silent mysteries of the Far East." On November 20, the Hell's Angels arrived on the fiddle-shaped island of Efate and took up quarters next to Quoin Hill Airfield, the 6,080-foot runway built by the Seabees on high ground on the northeast corner of the island. It, too, was made of coral, which engineers had discovered was extremely useful for runways and roads when laid down in layers, wet down with salt water or freshwater, and then rolled until the coral hardened almost to the thickness of concrete.

Efate, code-named Truculence, was approximately twenty-five miles by sixteen miles and even more primitive than Samoa. The Foreign Policy Association, perhaps relying on a bit of hyperbole, informed Americans in a twenty-five-cent pamphlet at the time that the island and its neighbors in the New Hebrides group were "not far removed from the days when white traders came in for ebony and sandalwood and were glad to get away without being cooked and eaten by the ferocious natives."

What Efate did have was two excellent harbors. The previous year, vast compounds of military supplies, tank farms for fuel storage, and vital repair facilities were built almost overnight to support the Americans' unfolding strategy in the South and Southwest Pacific. Here the squadron would wait—how long Major Overend didn't quite know—for another Corsair unit to complete its combat tour so the Hell's Angels could inherit its planes. The days went by, and they made the most of it, holding a three-day softball series between the officers and the enlisted men that ended in favor of the enlisted men, three games to two, on Thanksgiving Day, November 25. The holiday spirit proved to be too much for some in the unit, though: two corporals in the ground crew were confined to the brig for five days for being AWOL all Thanksgiving Day.

During the downtime, Ryan, puffing on a tobacco pipe, went for long strolls down to the beach, passing some tents of the younger pilots, where he often stopped to give them a few words of encouragement. Some would complain to their senior officer about their living conditions, to which the perennially optimistic Captain McCown would lecture: "Do you know what it would cost to go to a beach resort like this?"

Some of the pilots got word of an Englishman who ran a trading post on the island and had a warehouse filled with cheap brandy and gin from the Australian distillers Tolley, Scott & Tolley—at two dollars a bottle. Several of them commandeered a car and stocked up. They were building up quite a stash. They also still had the Teacher's Highland Cream scotch whiskey they had purchased before their sea voyage back in San Diego.

Ships docking in Efate also brought Australian beer. The Hell's Angels soon devised a handy way of getting it cold without the benefit of an icebox: cans wrapped in towels were stuffed into one of the gun bays in one of the few available Corsair's wings, flown up to twenty thousand feet, and delivered nice and frosty for the evening. One night they got an even rarer treat when a Navy vessel filled with nurses passed through and they got to dance to Glenn Miller records at a hastily scheduled dance at the makeshift Officers' Club.

After nearly a week of mostly sitting on their hands, the members of the squadron finally inherited what their official war diary described as "battle scarred, old, and worn out" Corsairs. The pilots were split into two wings. Each wing was to rotate days flying, ensuring pilots had one day off for every day they flew missions. Ryan didn't have to wait long. On November 27 he had to sprint to his assigned fighter plane when the air raid sirens on Efate started blaring and the squadron scrambled into the air to avoid a feared Japanese air attack that never came. Two days later the squadron's mechanical problems returned to haunt them. On the morning of November 29, Lieutenant Norman, who was almost killed when his Corsair flipped over coming into Atlanta at the beginning of September, crash-landed in the water after the engine started belching thick black smoke and the propeller stopped turning. Half a century later, the few tourist shops on the island, later known as Vanuatu, sold a postcard showing Norman's Corsair, with coral growing around the wing, still sitting in the lagoon. If that wasn't enough to rattle them, later that day two other pilots had a midair collision that resulted in a second plane being declared a total loss. They considered themselves exceedingly lucky that no one was seriously hurt.

Over the next week, Ryan logged more hours in the cockpit with gunnery practice and a series of training exercises to further hone his fighter tactics. On other days, he flew cover missions over Efate or provided air protection for Navy battle groups operating in the area.

Efate was in striking distance of the battle zone, which lay three hundred miles to the north in the Solomon Islands. A double chain of craggy, disease-ridden islands about nine hundred miles long and covered in coconut plantations, sweltering jungles, and mist-hung peaks, the Solomons lay to the east of New Guinea and spread south and eastward into the shipping lanes between the United States and Australia. The Japanese had moved into the area in early 1942 when their top naval officers concluded that a broad area would have to be occupied to secure the air and naval forces at Rabaul and on the main island of New Guinea. Encountering little resistance, Japanese forces developed a series of outlying bases in the Solomons to cover the approaches to the fortress at Rabaul.

By the fall of 1943, just as Ryan and the Hell's Angels arrived in the Pacific, the Allies' noose was tightening. Relentless attacks from B-25s and other heavy bombers of the Army Air Forces were pummeling the Japanese airfields from bases on the south and east coast of New Guinea, while dive-bombers and attack planes operating off the decks of Navy aircraft carriers were steadily whittling away at Japan's naval strength. By November, however, there were still nearly 100,000 Japanese troops at Rabaul. They blocked any Allied advance along the north coast of New Guinea toward the Philippines, a cornerstone of General MacArthur's strategy. Thus, every move the Allies were making in the region was geared toward subduing the Japanese garrison at Rabaul. But before they could do that, they had to clear the way, which meant wresting from the Japanese control of the Solomons—beginning with the bloody fighting on the island of Guadalcanal, on the southern end of the Solomons.

Another step, approved by the high command back in July 1943, was to capture territory farther up the Solomon chain suitable for air bases that would permit fighters and light bombers to reach Rabaul and return. Having fighters within range of Rabaul was considered especially critical because they could protect the large, lumbering bomber planes that were carrying tons of firepower but were highly vulnerable to Japanese fighters and the anti-aircraft artillery guns that ringed the heavily defended Japanese stronghold. Allied planners trained their attention on the island of Bougainville, which lay only a few hundred miles from Rabaul.

Bougainville, code-named Frigidaire, was the largest of the Solomon Islands at 125 miles long and 48 miles wide. Two active volcanoes, ten-thousand-foot Mount Balbi and eight-thousand-foot Mount Bagana, blanketed the island in steam and smoke. On the northern and southern ends the Japanese were dug in at a series of air and naval bases; according to Allied intelligence estimates, there were nearly sixty thousand forces in all. An Allied foothold on Bougainville, it was agreed, would not only put more air forces in range to strike at Rabaul but also allow aircraft to avoid some of the Japanese strongholds elsewhere in the Solomon chain and the empire's naval forces operating in surrounding waters. The need to seize territory on Bougainville suitable for airstrips was only reinforced when in August the Joint Chiefs of Staff recommended bypassing Rabaul rather than attempting to seize it with a costly invasion. In fact, the necessity of subduing Rabaul was now greater than ever. As the famed war correspondent Robert Sherrod put it, "By-passing an island obviates the necessity of landing on it, but also imposes the responsibility for keeping it knocked out." The Allies had to make sure that Rabaul was kept out of commission for the rest of the strategy to defeat Japan to succeed. Flying from air bases in Bougainville was how the Allies hoped to land the knockout punch.

As the Hell's Angels were heading for Samoa in late September, the plan was put in motion. The submarine USS *Guardfish* landed a small detachment of Marines about ten miles northwest of the fishhook-shaped Cape Torokina—code-named Azalea—on Bougainville's southwestern coast. They waded through the heavy surf of Empress Augusta Bay to reconnoiter a coastal plain about seven square miles framed by forbidding swamps and isolated from the rest of the jungle island by a spine of volcanic mountains. After they took soil samples and found relatively few Japanese defenders, it was decided that Torokina would be assaulted by Marines on November 1 and an airstrip hastily built to strike Rabaul.

———

By December, Ryan found himself eating at the "training table," enjoying rare chow like steak and hollandaise sauce.

"To be fattened up," he told Grace.

He and his fellow pilots also began memorizing the geography of the Solomon Islands—especially "the Slot."

A strip of open water about 350 miles long and 70 miles wide, the Slot stretched from the island of Guadalcanal in the south to Bougainville in the north. In between lay the Russell Islands and the New Georgia group. The pilots knew their lives might depend on being able to recognize the thickly forested islands and atolls on either side of the Slot. Heavy concentrations of Japanese forces and air forces were spread throughout, and if a pilot had to make a forced landing on land or in the water, he wanted to make sure to avoid them.

The especially inhospitable climate—and inhospitable natives—were two reasons the islands remained largely unoccupied by Europeans at the outbreak of World War II. In a theater of war that had no shortage of challenging climates and terrain, the Solomons stood out as hardship duty. The writer Jack London, who traveled there earlier in the century, remarked, "If I were king, the worst punishment I could inflict on my enemies would be to banish them to the Solomons."

On the fifth of the month Ryan got his first taste of the Solomons when he was ordered, along with a fellow captain and five lieutenants, to ferry the first of what would be several batches of Corsairs up to Guadalcanal.

Code-named Cactus, Guadalcanal had been the scene of one of the bloodiest struggles of the war against the Japanese. Ryan knew from the newsreels and newspaper dispatches about the living hell the island had been for so many of his fellow Marines. Marines first waded ashore in August 1942 on both the main island and the smaller, adjacent Tulagi. The Japanese poured in thousands of crack troops from Rabaul and other bases in the northern Solomons to beat back the Allied advance. A series of sea battles for control of the surrounding waters ensued, and a stretch of open water about twenty miles wide between Guadalcanal and the small island of Florida earned the grim name Iron Bottom Sound. At the same time, Navy, Army,

Marine, and New Zealand combat planes fought the Japanese to a standstill in the skies. But by the first anniversary of Pearl Harbor at the end of 1942, the Japanese Imperial General Headquarters had ordered its forces to evacuate the island.

Now, with Guadalcanal firmly in Allied control and the Japanese forced farther back up the Solomons, Ryan was awestruck by the landscape he saw out of his cockpit, scenes of paradise reminiscent of the adventure tales and motion pictures that he so loved.

"We saw an awful lot of water—and an awful lot of cloud formations," he wrote to Grace. "The cloud formations in the southwest Pacific are many, very large, and very striking—if not beautiful."

He was particularly taken by the sunrises and sunsets on Guadalcanal, where he spent a few days before returning to the Hell's Angels on Efate. But he couldn't fully appreciate them. They were also a reminder of what else was waiting just beyond the horizon to the north and west.

"The sunrise we saw on Guadalcanal always looked so much like the Japanese emblem that I didn't like to look at it."

The ferry hops turned out to be almost the only time in the cockpit he and his fellow pilots got for most of December. Their hand-me-down Corsairs were soon grounded due to a continued lack of spare parts. First it was due to inadequate fuel supplies, then night flying was suspended because "the crash boat is not equipped with search lights," and finally all flight operations were suspended on December 9 as they awaited a new shipment of fuel diaphragms. Early December also saw three more accidents. That was after one of their planes flipped over upon landing at Quoin Hill on Efate, another cartwheeled during a night landing, while a third was forced to ditch in the water. Thankfully, there were no major injuries.

Ryan, still ebullient about the simple pleasures in life, was crowing about a care package that included a subscription to *Newsweek* magazine.

"Back in the States, I never let a Friday afternoon go by that I didn't buy a *Time*, *Newsweek*, *Collier's*, *Life*, and *Saturday Evening Post*—to read them on Sunday," he wrote to Grace in December. "Needless to say, all the stuff you sent comes in awful handy."

He also received a V-mail from his sister Claudia alerting him that the whole gang was planning to be home in Charleston for Christmas and expressing how she wished her big brother could be there. Ryan, too, longed to be with them—just like last Christmas—but he had more important things to do.

"Great stuff," he told Grace. "You ought to have a swell time. We ought to have a swell time here too. I'm afraid there won't be too much 'Peace on earth' or 'good will toward men,' but there will definitely be no dearth of fireworks."

He closed the letter by thanking his mother for the ID bracelet she shipped to him: "I'm glad you sent it. I needed some sort of a 'good luck charm' with me, and this is just the thing. Thanks a lot."

———

On Christmas Eve, the Hell's Angels' gear, half of the pilots, and all the support personnel—and some of the booze—were loaded onto three DC-3s for the short trip to the combat zone and an island named Vella Lavella. The rest of the pilots, including Ryan, ferried their battered planes, along with more booze wrapped in towels and blankets and stuffed into the Corsairs' middle gun bays. Their next island home, code-named Dogeared, lay less than a hundred miles from Bougainville. Hilly, thickly forested, and about twenty-six miles long, Vella Lavella had been evacuated by the small Japanese garrison when the Allies came ashore in the middle of August on the south side of the Barakoma River on the island's southeast end.

It was a choppy flight, and when Ryan and the others backed their aircraft into revetments, some of them were leaking. But it wasn't hydraulic fluid, as the mechanics first suspected. It was broken bottles of brandy and gin—the Tolley, Scott & Tolley scooped up at the trading post on Efate. One of the senior officers went up and down the line and collected what was left, and it was mixed together in a concoction that was soon designated Jolly Tolley.

Word quickly spread across the base that a new squadron had arrived with Christmas spirits. As the Hell's Angels were settling into their tents, a commotion ensued as rowdy members of another squadron barreled into their camp, knocking over some of the tents. It was the legendary Major Gregory "Pappy" Boyington and his rabble-rousing Black Sheep Squadron. The boisterous Boyington had apparently already tracked down his old friend Major Overend and broken into the Hell's Angels' stash of scotch whiskey that had arrived with their footlockers aboard the DC-3s. Soon both the Teacher's Highland Cream they had saved from San Diego and the Jolly Tolley flowed liberally at the impromptu Christmas party on Vella Lavella. There were feats of arm wrestling, poker games, singing, and even a few drunken injuries that required some patching up by Doc Wolfe.

The next day, Christmas, they enjoyed turkey dinner with all the fixings and even real butter. But the respite didn't last long. While they were receiving an intelligence briefing beneath a thatch of palm trees, the air raid sirens started blaring, sending them scrambling into the nearest bunker. They also knew that on the twenty-seventh, after a few "familiarization hops" around the island, eight of Ryan's fellow pilots in the squadron were scheduled to fly their first combat mission to Rabaul. One of them buckled under the pressure of it all, shaking like a leaf on Doc Wolfe's cot, muttering that he couldn't hack it. Major Overend soon agreed and instructed him to turn in his wings. The skipper put him in charge of packing the parachutes. There was no time to court-martial him. Perhaps Overend couldn't blame him.

A few hundred miles away, an Army Air Corps F-5 Lightning from the Seventeenth Photographic Reconnaissance Squadron was flying at thirty-five thousand feet over the northernmost tip of New Britain Island. Fitted with K-17 aerial cameras in the nose, the aircraft made several passes over the Japanese airdromes surrounding Rabaul. The specialized cameras, manufactured by the Fairchild Aerial Camera Corporation, relied on a series of exchangeable Bausch & Lomb Metrogon lenses with focal lengths up to two feet long. The cameras' shutters clicked automatically, capturing images of the airfields and surrounding ground installations that the Japanese had carved out of the jungle. They also snapped photographs of Simpson Harbor, dotted with Japanese warships and supply barges, and the surrounding waters leading into St. George's Channel.

Within a few hours, the film was developed, and photo interpreters determined that at the Vunakanau Airdrome, built on a plateau about a thousand feet above sea level and surrounded by coconut plantations about eleven miles south of Rabaul, the Japanese had cleared a series of trails snaking deep into the jungle where dozens of aircraft were parked in revetments to shield them from Allied bombing raids. The trained eye could make out numerous Japanese fighters and bombers nestled beneath the jungle canopy, some with the "meatballs" painted on the tips of their wings. Images of other Japanese airfields ringing Rabaul, with names like Tobera and Lakunai, showed runways pockmarked with craters from recent U.S. bombings but still in operation. Despite the relentless pounding by Allied aircraft for nearly two years, the Japanese installations ringing Rabaul still posed a powerful threat.

The film was soon turned into charts, maps, and pilot navigation strips by a team of enlisted technicians working in a makeshift photo lab. They considered their work a sacred trust, as their commander had recently reminded them:

> Your maps will guide men, planes, and ships along their way forward. . . . The foot soldier will carry your maps along his march. He will unfold his map at night somewhere, maybe in a muddy ditch, and hold up a match to it. He will fold it up again and go forward along a jungle trail, which you located on photographs many months ago. . . . You topographers, whose fingers grow stiff and tired from drawing in precise and fine detail, must keep on. Look at the little strip maps you are making for pilots to carry with them on each mission. They need these to find their way to the enemy and back home.

The day after Christmas, Ryan flew a cover mission for a Navy task force steaming past Vella Lavella, another "chore" hop that consisted of flying from dawn to dusk, "getting the rear part of your anatomy well acquainted with a hard parachute during the four hour stretches." It was an uneventful foray, as Ryan dutifully recorded in his flight log, with no sign of enemy planes.

———

Ryan awoke in his tent in the predawn darkness of January 3 and crawled out of his mosquito net. There was no time for a shower or a shave. Sitting on the edge of his cot, he groggily pulled on his flight suit and shook his boots out on the sand floor, in case any poisonous centipedes had crawled in overnight. He grabbed his gear and slogged through the towering banyan trees to a larger tent that served as the chow hall, where he joined dozens of other newly arrived fighter pilots at the hastily built base at Torokina on Bougainville Island. After a typical breakfast of a few cups of coffee, a slice of bread, and a can of beans, they climbed into the back of olive-colored trucks, called carryalls, for the bumpy ride along freshly bulldozed jungle paths to the nearby airstrip.

When Ryan and the Hell's Angels were moved to Torokina, on New Year's Day aboard a DC-3 transport plane, they learned first-hand the precarious nature of the Allies' strategy in the South Pacific. Cape Torokina, situated on the southwestern tip of Bougainville, was seized after the Third Marine Division waded ashore on November 1 under unrelenting fire from Japan's Twenty-Third Infantry Regiment and Sixth Artillery, which had been in position for more than a year and had constructed an intricate network of bunkers and pillboxes. Bougainville, covered in swamps, thick jungles, and volcanoes and swarming with as many as sixty thousand Japanese troops, held little attraction for the Allies. The Americans had come for only one reason: to take control of a seven-mile-wide, pie-shaped slice of jungle poking into Empress Augusta Bay, where they could quickly construct a fighter and bomber strip to launch attacks against Rabaul. The invasion plan for Cape Torokina called for leaving the rest of the disease-ridden island to the Japanese and relying on air attacks to keep the enemy forces brooding just on the other side of Mount Bagana occupied.

When Ryan arrived, Japanese bombs were still striking Torokina almost daily, and artillery barrages were a constant threat. The Hell's Angels had spent their first night curled up in foxholes between their tents after an approaching "Washing Machine Charlie"—a Japanese floatplane with clanking engines—set off the air raid siren before tossing para-frags—bomblets with a small parachute—out over the beachhead. At least one member of the squadron had already been injured by shrapnel from a Japanese artillery round that screamed toward their positions from the nearby jungle. The pipeline the Americans constructed to supply fuel to the airfield was severed no fewer than eighteen times.

The living conditions were also among the most meager yet. The Marines, sailors, and soldiers, living four to a tent or in foxholes drenched in tropical rain, had to contend with cramps, diarrhea, vomiting, and malaria. The makeshift hospital ward was "rather like an excavated basement before the foundation is built," and the operating room was a "rectangular hole in the ground covered by a tent." The chow, too, was a constant source of complaint. There were virtually no fresh vegetables, meat, eggs, or milk, and bread was scarce. Rations usually consisted of oatmeal and powdered eggs for breakfast, and the menu for other meals wasn't any more appealing: sausage loaf, better known as "sliced horse cock," and creamed dried beef on toast, or "shit on a shingle." The New Zealand mutton that was flown in was universally hated, so Spam and Vienna sausages became staples.

They tried to make the most of the primitive setting. While fatigues were the most common uniform, they were permitted to wear whatever they wanted to contend with the sweltering heat. Some got into the habit of walking stark naked along the busy paths of the base to bathe in a stream, sometimes catching a lift on the running board of a truck. There was virtually no chance of running into a woman. In fact, the only white woman they knew on Torokina was a nude woman tattooed to the chest of Private Albert Harron of Toledo, Ohio, who had been a taxicab driver before the war. A few special touches helped to make the place look and feel a little civilized. Wooden signs were posted on the muddy tracks that served as roads—"15 mph for Trucks," "20 mph for Jeeps," and "No Parking." Tacked to the buildings that housed the Thirty-Seventh Army Division were gag signs like "Bougainville Grill," "Empress Augusta Tea Room," and the "Torokina Trocadero."

Now, one by one, Ryan and his fellow pilots filed into their command post, a large, rectangular bunker bracketed by coconut logs that had been gouged into the beach on the southeast side of the airstrip. In the distance, through the early morning mist, they could just make out the rows of makeshift white crosses marking the final resting places of scores of Marines and soldiers who had died seizing the beachhead from the Japanese weeks earlier. Some were the freshly dug graves of those killed in one of the almost daily ambushes by Japanese troops along the American perimeter just three miles inland.

Nearly ninety officers huddled in the gloom for the preflight briefing. The day's mission would be a "fighter sweep" over the Japanese-held redoubt at Rabaul, a little over two hundred miles away. The objective was to "destroy enemy aircraft by aggressive offensive action." It was Ryan's first combat mission, and he was assigned as the flight leader.

Ryan had few illusions about the dangers awaiting him across the Solomon Sea. He was raw with grief and disbelief that Zombie Blount had failed to return from a mission the day before. Zombie was the feisty former boxing champ from the University of Mississippi whom he had become fast friends with back in the States when they both joined the new squadron. Zombie now marked the squadron's first combat loss. He was last seen spiraling downward from about twelve thousand feet over Simpson Harbor after twelve Hell's Angels were attacked by at least thirty Japanese Zeros that emerged out of the north from the nearby island of New Ireland. Zombie's cot had been swiftly removed from his tent upon orders from the skipper, Major Overend, that same afternoon. He thought it better for morale not to have an empty rack staring at his pilots through the night when they were headed to the same place in hours themselves.

Today would be Ryan's turn. He would be going up against the fortress that terrified a million Allied fighting men. Thousands of enemy troops were concealed in a maze of tunnels that had been dynamited into the rocky cliffs. Some of Japan's most experienced fighter pilots, including members of the 204th Fighter Group, awaited them on five nearby airfields. The entire area bristled with anti-aircraft guns, the so-called ack-acks, high-caliber explosives that lit up the sky with their tracers, flying up in sheets so heavy, some pilots reported, you could step out of your cockpit and walk on them.

Ryan and his fellow pilots would also have to cross more than two hundred miles of the Solomon Sea and complete the nerve-racking journey back to base—all in the single-engine Corsair, with its now almost legendary mechanical problems. Even a minor malfunction and they could find themselves clinging to their life vests—their trusty Mae Wests—and floating in their inflatable rubber raft. Landing back on their airstrip, meanwhile, was dicier than usual. On one side of Pima One, as the new fighter strip was called, was a swamp and on the other a tangled web of thick palm trees. On the approach for landing, the trees had been cut down, but the stumps were sticking up. At least one Corsair had already struck them and burst into flames.

In the dim light of the command post, a few colonels stepped in front of a series of maps to brief the pilots on their mission. The "fighter sweep" was a tactic first employed by the Americans a few months earlier. Instead of escorting large bomber planes to protect them from being shot down by Japanese fighters during their raids— one of the primary missions of fighter planes—the pilots would force their Japanese counterparts into the air and "mix it up." It was little more than picking a fight in the skies, designed to inflict as many losses of Japanese aircraft as possible. Today, with Ryan in the lead, the mission called for forty-eight Marine Corps Corsairs from several squadrons.

Many of the pilots, standing shoulder to shoulder in the bunker, had a hard time hearing. Others strained to get a good look at the maps at the front of the room. They were told that two Catalina flying boats were on alert off Torokina to fish out any pilots downed at sea, and they were instructed to radio "Dane Base" if they got into trouble. One of the so-called Dumbos, so named for the seaplane's floppy-looking wings, would come looking for them and, if they were lucky enough, pull them in through the gun ports. If they went down or bailed out close enough to Torokina, they might also have a chance of being picked up by one of the Navy patrol boats that were tied up on small Piruata Island in Empress Augusta Bay just off the airstrip. They were to avoid, at all costs, coming down on Japanese-held New Britain, where their chances of being rescued were exceedingly slim. They would be on their own, their only hope of survival to find some friendly natives and hide out in the jungle, or locate a river or stream and follow it to the coast. They would have a better chance if they could reach New Ireland across the channel. If they could evade the Japanese there, they were told to find a village near the Weilan River where a friendly native named Boski would help them. But they should be extra careful to look out for cannibals. New Ireland was still notorious for them. A water landing was by far their best option, because they could deploy their lifeboat, shoot their signal flares, and possibly be spotted by the rescue plane, which would have at least several fighter escorts. A successful rescue, however, would depend on how accurate their fellow pilots were in reporting their last position. Time would also be of the essence, as the currents and unpredictable weather could quickly carry them off. If the Dumbos couldn't find them, the Japanese might. By now all the pilots had memorized the little ditty penned by a fellow Corsair pilot, titled "In a Rowboat at Rabaul":

If the engine conks out now,
We'll come down from forty thou'
And we'll end up in a rowboat at Rabaul,
In a rowboat at Rabaul.

We'll be throwing in the towel,
'Cause they'll never send a Dumbo 'way out here.
We'll be prisoners of war
And we'll stay through forty-four
Getting drunk on *sake* and New Britain Beer.

But they all knew better. Being captured at Rabaul almost certainly meant torture and death. Japanese soldiers were known to take target practice with their bayonets on captured pilots' chests before beheading them. If the Americans were taken to a prisoner-of-war camp, they would likely die in captivity. Some pilots, relying on humor and tall tales to help cope with the jitters, joked that if you got hit or were experiencing engine trouble over Rabaul, you might as well land on one of the Japanese airfields and sprint right to the commander's tent—just to get it all over with.

Just as the mission briefing was about to wrap up, another officer stepped in front of the group of pilots. He was "chubby" and "yellow-skinned," apparently suffering from the tropical skin disease that had become known as the crud. The image did not instill confidence. But the dour mood quickly brightened after a few whispers and murmurs passed through the packed bunker. The man standing before them was Pappy Boyington, perhaps the most famous Marine fighter pilot of the war.

Boyington now had twenty-five Japanese planes to his credit, four of them over Rabaul in the previous week alone. He was just four days away from being shipped back to the States. He and his famed Black Sheep deserved the rest: they had lost six pilots in the last ten days. Pappy had recently been asked by one of the greener pilots what strategy he recommended for going toe-to-toe with Japanese fighter pilots over Rabaul. He replied that "there is no such thing as strategy in fighting up there. Gambler's guts would be better to describe what a fighter pilot needs. It's like street fighting. If you hit the other guy first, and hit him hard, you'll probably strike the last blow. That he'll hit you back harder than you hit him is the chance you have to take."

Boyington had pioneered the fighter sweep, and his willingness to egg on the Japanese to come up and fight was already legendary. One such tale was well known among the ranks of Marine fliers at Toro-kina. It turned out that one of the radio operators at Rabaul, Chikaki Honda, had grown up in Hawaii, where he was known as Edward and played baseball at McKinley High School before attending college in his parents' homeland of Japan. After Pearl Harbor, Honda forfeited his American citizenship, joined the Imperial Japanese Navy, and by the summer of 1943 was stationed in Rabaul. On a fighter sweep three weeks earlier, Boyington eyed between thirty and forty Japanese fighters lined up on the reddish-brown dirt airstrip at the Lakunai Airdrome, on the north shore of Simpson Harbor.

"Come on up and fight," Pappy shouted over the radio.

"Come on down, sucker," Honda responded.

So Boyington did, dropping to ten thousand feet and spraying the airfield with nine hundred rounds.

Now Ryan and the other pilots crowded into the bunker were told that Boyington would also be going on the mission with them. His presence stiffened their spines. After Boyington delivered a pep talk, the pilots were given their altitude assignments and mission folders containing smaller maps for their journey. The group then broke up, and the pilots scampered out into the dawn to their planes, which had been pulled out of their revetments and lined up, nose to tail, on the perforated steel plates known as Marsden Matting that served as the runway, which was now streaked with mud and still wet from the previous night's rain.

At the front of the snaking line of Corsairs were Ryan and eight other pilots from the Hell's Angels, followed by aircraft from three other squadrons, including Boyington's Black Sheep. As gas trucks topped off their tanks, in the distance they heard the faint volleys of gunfire being exchanged between the Army's Thirty-Seventh Division and the Japanese troops just outside the Torokina base perimeter. At 6:50 a.m. sharp, Ryan was given the signal and pushed the throttle forward. One by one the line of planes roared down the runway, from east to west, and into the air. The expanding swarm climbed in a wide arc over Empress Augusta Bay, bearing a heading that took them up the coast of Bougainville to the northwest. Below them, shielded by the thick jungle, Japanese coast watchers were likely already radioing to Rabaul that they were coming.

——

At five thousand feet, the Hell's Angels rendezvoused with Boyington's squadron and the rest of the fighter sweep. By 7:10 a.m., all forty-eight planes were on course for the 214-mile journey to Rabaul. When they reached about ten thousand feet, they engaged the "Low Blower," the supercharger that pushed more oxygen into the engine, and then continued to climb through several layers of thick clouds. At about eighteen thousand feet they turned on the "High Blower," the supercharger that fed the maximum amount of air into the engine's eighteen cylinders. To their right they passed the island of Buka, located across a narrow strait directly northwest of Bougainville where the Japanese had several airstrips. They soon left the Solomon chain behind them and were plotting their course due west across the Solomon Sea. Below them was a mixture of shallow water dotted with large coral reefs, and some of the deepest waters on earth, including the yawning New Britain Trench, which reached depths of more than thirty thousand feet. A number of the pilots pulled out of the formation temporarily to fire their six .50-caliber Browning machine guns, a precaution that some found reassuring, the *chug-chug-chug* of the quick bursts and the curving tracers giving them a little extra confidence. Soon the entire formation cruised between twenty thousand feet and thirty thousand feet under a bright sun and blue skies with nearly unlimited visibility. Ryan and his squadron mates flew in a tight group at about twenty-four thousand feet, the hum of engines and the whir of the propellers carrying them south of Cape St. George, on the lower tip of New Ireland, up St. George's Channel, over New Britain's Cape Gazelle, a headland smothered by jungle, toward Rabaul.

At 8:15 a.m., they arrived over Simpson Harbor, and almost immediately the sky lit up with ack-acks, the deafening *chuk chuk* of the aerial cannons reverberating across the sky and bursting a few thousand feet below them in an orderly pattern. Down below, at the Lakunai Airdrome, they saw the dust being kicked up from enemy aircraft taking off from the airfield. The American formation circled Simpson Harbor, waiting for the Japanese planes to come up to meet them. As they were coming around for a second loop over the harbor, eight Kawasaki Ki-61 fighter jets, designated by the Allies as "Tonys," headed straight for them with their brown markings and orange "meatballs" emblazoned on their fuselages.

The American and Japanese fighters scattered across the sky in swirling dogfights, their hurtling planes diving and climbing in mortal combat. At about twelve thousand feet, Lieutenant Richard "Cosmo" Marsh, who had joined the Hell's Angels as a replacement pilot in San Diego, hit one of the Tonys in the right wing with his .50-caliber guns. Trailing smoke, the plane careened down to the right and out of sight. Lieutenant J. M. Lambdin was flying at seventeen thousand feet when he attacked a lone Zero that had come up to challenge them, striking it in the forward section and causing it to nose over and plunge toward the earth in a trail of thick smoke.

The fracas quickly subsided as the Japanese planes scampered away and the Hell's Angels began heading back to base. Then, about twenty miles down St. George's Channel, Lieutenant Marsh was again jumped by a Tony on his tail. He turned, got into position, and fired a short burst directly into the fuselage behind the cockpit, sending the Japanese plane spiraling down toward the water.

Everyone was accounted for as the Hell's Angels headed for home with three kills. They landed at Torokina and quickly assembled in the ready room to recount the mission for the intelligence officer. The other squadrons had also seen their share of action on the fighter sweep. In all, seventy Zeros faced off against the forty-eight Corsairs, along with at least several enemy Tonys. Boyington's Black Sheep Squadron also claimed several kills, but what they soon learned shocked them all: Boyington and his wingman, George Ashmun, had not returned from the mission. Boyington and Ashmun had last been seen dropping down to a few thousand feet above the water as Japanese fighters were coming up to meet them.

There was no shortage of volunteers that afternoon to escort the Dumbos in their search for any sign of the Marines' most famous fighter ace. By 1:35 p.m., Ryan was back in the air leading seven Hell's Angels to escort one of the Dumbos to Rabaul in search of the lost pilots. Another volunteer to search for Pappy was Lieutenant Eugene

"Vic" Smith of Ohio. The search for the downed pilots went on for hours. At one point Ryan's division reported what appeared to be a pilot afloat in the channel, but rain squalls made visibility exceedingly poor. Finally, they had to give up, and it was almost dark by the time the full search party "pancaked" back on the Torokina airstrip.

The loss of ole Pappy cast a pall over the pilots stationed at Torokina. The news that the rabble-rousing ace was missing sent shock waves throughout the Marine Corps. One of his fellow Corsair pilots remarked: "If the Japs had been able to get Gregory Boyington—the man, above all men, who knew what to expect from a Jap in a fight— then what was the chance for the rest of us, who were rank amateurs by comparison?"

———

The Hell's Angels' first missions, as one among their ranks put it, "brought some reality and experience where guesses and dreams had been." In their bunks at night back on Torokina, they breathlessly recounted spying the dreaded "meatballs"; the rapid hit-and-run tactics of aerial dogfights; the puffs of ack-ack fire; and the large bursts of white phosphorus from shells the Japanese pilots sometimes released in an effort to break up and confuse their formations. The pilots in the squadron recounted strafing Japanese barges in the surrounding waters or shooting up enemy airfields, Pappy Boyington–style, when they could get low enough. It was all certainly exhilarating. But they also now knew that the storybook life of a fighter pilot was just that— fiction. The real glory, as they quickly grew to appreciate during those first few days in combat, lay in "efficiency and a long life."

Though they had been in combat for only a week, the Hell's Angels were already exacting a heavy price on the Japanese air forces stationed around Rabaul, slowly gaining a ruthless reputation on both sides. On January 9, Ryan and his wingman, Lieutenant Robert See of San Francisco, were circling over a group of eighteen U.S. Navy torpedo bombers high above Rabaul, on the lookout for enemy planes, when they spotted three Zeros below. Making several passes, Ryan and the younger See, who had drawn the squadron's first enemy blood, riddled the Japanese planes with long bursts of their .50-caliber guns, leaving billowing black smoke in their wake.

They also waged constant battle with nature and machine. On

a bomber escort to Rabaul a few days later, Ryan had to circle for more than an hour on the outskirts of St. George's Channel and link back up with the bombers upon their return because he discovered his cockpit was missing the CO_2 bottles designed to "blow down" the landing gear if the hydraulic power was lost. Indeed, on numerous flights headed to Rabaul, pilots had to turn back to Torokina due to fuel leaks, engine trouble, or jammed guns. There was also the unpredictable weather. One minute there could be nearly infinite visibility, the next so many black clouds they blotted out the sun. On several occasions Ryan and his fellow Hell's Angels were bedeviled by heavy tropical fronts that scattered them to outlying bases in the Solomons with barely enough fuel to land. They topped off their fuel tanks and hopped their way back to their crowded, muddy tents at Torokina.

It wasn't just the Japanese—and their planes—that took a beating those first few weeks in the war zone. The day after Ryan's maiden combat mission, on January 4, another one of his fellow captains, Harvey Carter, was lost on a fighter sweep over Rabaul, becoming the squadron's second casualty after Zombie Blount. Carter, who "wore a mustache and carried himself with the air of an Englishman," had been commissioned in Saskatchewan, Canada, before joining the squadron in San Diego. He had a reputation as a skilled pilot who as a Navy flight instructor in New Orleans was known for flying loops around a bridge over the Mississippi River. He was last seen flying at about twenty-one thousand feet over the southern edge of Simpson Harbor after his division of four Corsairs was attacked by a dozen Zeros. A Dumbo rescue plane, escorted by sixteen Corsairs, failed to locate him, and he was reported missing in action.

Then, a week later, Major Harold Jacobs, the squadron's operations officer and one of the most experienced pilots, clipped another plane while coming in for a landing on Torokina, shearing off nearly the entire tail section of his Corsair. The rest of the aircraft hit the water just off the airstrip "at a terrific rate of speed, exploded, and submerged immediately."

Jacobs's death marked the third Hell's Angel to be lost in ten days and was a particularly fierce blow to morale. Jacobs was the only one of the three they knew for sure was killed; the fate of the others no one could say with any certainty, though the men were becoming all too familiar with the grim possibilities.

The loss of their comrades and the constant danger they faced drew Ryan and his fellow pilots into an ever-tighter circle. They needed one another more each day—up in the skies, certainly, to fend off the enemy, but also back on the ground in their bunks as they waged an internal struggle, mostly using the weapons of humor and tall tales of girls back home, to keep at bay the ever-present fear of a violent death. Their fates were weaving together like the innumerable strands of rope that ultimately become one thick and strong cord. Their skipper, Major Overend, tried to put it into words at the time in a letter to the grieving mother of one of his lost pilots.

"It is impossible to explain to one who does not fly how closely we live and comfort each other," he wrote. "All of us live very close to death and accept it because we are doing a job we love to do and at the same time we know and can see that we *are* making great progress toward the day when those we love at home can live in peace and security again."

Overend decided to hold a short memorial service for Jacobs, gathering the squadron on the beach just off the airstrip to say a few prayers. It was a rare instance of collective reflection, and he didn't let it last too long. The skipper didn't need his men thinking too much about their own mortality.

———

By the middle of January the Hell's Angels had been in combat two weeks, and Ryan was flying combat missions to Rabaul every other day. On January 13, it was another bomber escort, but the fighter formation failed to rendezvous with the bombers and was forced to turn back. The next day, January 14, was a Friday—and Ryan's twenty-seventh birthday. He marked the milestone at the Torokina camp with the other pilots who also had the day off, including the three pilots he was regularly flying with in his four-plane division.

There was his wingman, the young Californian Bob See, who could now boast several downed Japanese planes; Roger Brindos, the dark-haired card shark with movie-star good looks from Minnesota whom just about everyone now owed money; and Brindos's wingman, the quiet and unassuming Bob Marshall from Amite, Louisiana, the small town whose name meant both "friendship" and "young."

The twenty-one-year-old See, a lanky kid with a cat-ate-the-canary grin, had graduated in 1939 from Balboa High School in San Francisco's working-class Mission Terrace district. An only child, he was already proving to be one of the best pilots in the squadron and well on his way to becoming an ace.

Brindos, whose parents owned a hotel on London Road in Duluth overlooking Lake Superior, had quit Duluth Junior College and enlisted in the Navy a few months after Pearl Harbor. Brindos was the only one of the four who was married. Waiting back in Minnesota was his new bride, Patricia, who had been among the wives who piled into a red convertible for the cross-country journey to bid them all farewell in San Diego at the end of September.

But Ryan had a special rapport with the red-haired Marshall, even though Ryan was five years older. Like Ryan, Marshall studied engineering—at Louisiana State University—and had been captivated by airplanes ever since he was a kid. He also loved Edgar Allan Poe, naming his Corsair "The Raven" after one his poems. Ryan and Marshall also shared an affinity for motorcycles.

Ryan spent much of his birthday tarrying in his tent and taking it easy. He huddled with some of the other pilots for their now almost daily ritual of tuning in to Tokyo Rose, the English-speaking Japanese propaganda broadcaster who constantly harassed the Allies, vowing that MacArthur would be captured in a month. They were eager to hear any news about their lost comrades who might have been captured.

In the afternoon Ryan and the others reported for the daily intelligence briefing near the airstrip to learn about the next day's assignment. They were informed they would once again be flying cover for Army Air Corps bombers attacking one of the Japanese airfields near Rabaul. Ryan opened his mission folder to analyze the maps and flight charts that would guide them.

One location, as its code name, Sordid, suggested, filled him with almost as much contempt as Rabaul. The volcanic island of Buka sat directly to the northwest of the larger Bougainville, across a narrow strait less than a mile wide. He had been able to see it from the right side of his cockpit on his first mission to Rabaul a dozen days earlier. The island, about thirty miles long and eleven miles wide, straddled the northwesterly flight path across the Solomon Sea from Torokina to Rabaul. On both sides of the Buka Passage were concentrations of Japanese troops, along with two airfields and a seaplane base. Buka was also home to native tribes that supported the Japanese—and helped them hunt for downed airmen in the nearby waters and jungles.

Just before noon the next day, January 15, Ryan strapped into the "birdcage" of his assigned plane, a battle-worn Corsair stamped with the tail number 17448. After proceeding through the preflight checklist, he reached underneath his seat to inventory his survival gear—life raft, signal flares, emergency rations—and then set out once again across the expanse of the Solomon Sea. But yet again, after little more than an hour in the air, the mission was called back—this time due to a heavy weather system cloaking the northern tip of New Britain and the airfields around Rabaul. Frustrated at being denied another chance to do his part, he was eager to press the fight. As the leader of the four-plane division, Ryan took the initiative on the return journey to Torokina and decided to do a low-level reconnaissance of one of the enemy-held airdromes on Buka. He hoped to use the element of surprise to detect any Japanese supply vessels in the area or ground installations that could be attacked. Along with his wingman, Lieutenant See, he descended toward the western entrance to the Buka Passage and soon spotted activity on one of the airfields. See took the lead and made the first pass, unloading his cannons and shooting up the airfield and surrounding structures. Ryan, trailing close behind, unleashed a second round of strafing fire just as a symphony of tracers began to light up the sky. Within seconds, sheets of withering anti-aircraft rounds were exploding all around him. Engulfed by the deafening sound of the shells detonating outside the cockpit, Ryan tightened his grip on the controls, shifted his feet on the rudder pedals, and pulled up in an arc to dodge the incoming fire and get out of the range of the Japanese gun emplacements. Almost immediately he noticed something was wrong. There was a series of abnormal hissing and popping sounds. Ryan examined his cockpit gauges, but they told him what he already sensed. The aircraft had taken fire, and he was in serious trouble. Ryan's heart pounded as he fought to maintain control. He struggled to fly the plane as far away from the Japanese base as possible. The Torokina strip, he guessed, was at least fifty miles away, and as the seconds ticked by, it became more and more apparent that the plane was too badly damaged to make it back. There was little time to think. In virtually every direction were concentrations of Japanese troops—on Buka and across the narrow passage on Bougainville. Enemy patrol boats were also probably plying the surrounding straits. The brilliant green jungles and crystal blue waters of the Solomon Sea below—the scenery Ryan had thought so beautiful and so forbidding—were growing larger and larger through the Plexiglas of the cockpit as the riddled plane steadily lost altitude. Ryan was going down fast.

Ryan was trained to slide the canopy open with the yellow lever to his right before ditching in the sea, but when his plane violently splashed into the water, he barely had time to unhook his harness and scramble out before going down with it. All he had with him was what he was wearing, including the Mae West life vest wrapped around his neck and an automatic pistol strapped to his body. The rubber life raft and survival packet beneath the pilot seat were dislodged in the jolting water landing, and there simply wasn't time to locate them. Before Ryan fully realized what it meant, the aircraft disappeared beneath the waves.

Although his plane had been badly damaged from taking antiaircraft fire, Ryan had managed to keep it level and fly southwest of the opening to the Buka Passage, reaching the open sea before going down. He ditched in an area dotted with coral reefs. Some of them, nearly a mile wide, lay just beneath the surface, especially at low tide, and were visible from the air. After slipping into the clear blue water, Ryan located one of the reefs and was relieved to discover that if he stood on his tiptoes with his chin up, he could keep his mouth above the waves. It was now about 2:30 in the afternoon, and the scorching sun beat down on his head. He struggled to keep his wits as his mind sought to grasp what had happened and his survival instincts began to kick in. Without a rubber raft, he had little choice but to wait on the coral outcropping in the hopes that a Dumbo had been dispatched to search for him. He saw in the distance that he was still awfully close to the passage flowing between the islands of Buka and Bougainville. The area was crawling with Japanese and hostile natives. Swimming ashore was out of the question. But in his adrenaline-infused state of mind, Ryan also started to think through what he might do if the rescue plane couldn't locate him. There was no way of knowing if his wingman had seen where he went down. It had been pretty hairy back there, and Bob See might not have made it. As he tried to keep calm,

Ryan's racing mind was interrupted by distinct ripples in the water just a few yards away. In an instant, blind curiosity turned to a nearly paralyzing fear when he realized what it was: a shark.

The shark circled, inching closer with each pass. It didn't appear to be very large. But it also didn't seem to be afraid of the strange and bigger creature that had violently arrived in its placid undersea domain, with the sound of crashing metal and screeching cables and gallons of leaking fuel and hydraulic fluid. Ryan whirled around trying to keep watch on it and suddenly felt the shark nudge him from behind, knocking him off the reef. He kicked and scrambled to regain his footing, scanning frantically in the water around him. The shark did it again, once more poking his nose into Ryan's behind. The chilling little game continued for several more rounds—until Ryan's very unwelcome visitor apparently tired of it and swam off.

As the minutes slowly ticked by, Ryan tried to calculate his chances of being rescued. Nightfall was approaching, and once the sun set, any rescue effort—if there even was one—would be called off. He didn't think he could last very long stranded and exposed in shark-infested waters. If he did make it through the night, he might be spotted, but more likely by the dreaded Japanese. He recalled from his flight charts that there were small, mostly deserted islands near the entrance to Buka Passage and off the northwest coast of Bougainville—in the direction of Torokina. He wasn't sure how far, but he had to try. Ryan made a fateful decision. He started swimming.

————

One of the islands, it turned out, was about six miles from where he ditched—and he almost made it. Ryan swam for more than four hours, taking brief rests with the aid of his Mae West. But by 7:00 p.m., exhausted, suffering from shock and exposure—and with daylight fading—Ryan was still two miles away. He was also forty-seven miles to the northwest of Cape Torokina. It didn't look like he was going to make it. But in a stroke of good fortune, he was spotted by a Navy PT boat plying the Bougainville coast for a nighttime patrol in search of Japanese vessels.

After being picked up by the PT crew, Ryan was returned to the squadron the next morning. His aircraft, of course, was designated a total loss. Under pilot injuries, the single-page report said simply,

"Safe." Ryan was checked out by the docs and then "insisted that he resume his place in the squadron and not lose a day's flying time," his skipper reported. Ryan's only complaint, apparently, was that his toes were sore—from straining to keep his head above water on the reef.

When he finally got back to his bunk, he recounted his little adventure for his fellow pilots, who were thrilled to see him safe and sound, and eager to hear every detail. They especially relished his retelling of the encounter with the shark. Ryan later lay awake on his cot reflecting silently about what he had been through. He gained a new appreciation for how in the final analysis it was cold and merciless mathematical odds—not flight experience, but luck—that governed their fates. He had been given another chance this time, and he knew what he must do with it. Ryan took out some blank sheets of writing paper. He neatly printed the date on the top right of one of them, "Jan 16, 1943"—he apparently had yet to overcome the habit, which for many usually takes several weeks to break after New Year's, of writing the calendar year that just came to a close instead of the new one.

"Dear Ma," he began in his flowing cursive, and the words just kept coming:

> Cuss it all—if somebody doesn't get on the ball pretty soon and bring us some mail in here, I'm going to start my own private little war. Still we haven't gotten any mail except that batch last week in which I didn't even get a letter from home. Of course there is nothing you or I can do about it except wait and hope. I'll wait and you hope!
>
> In spite of the reputation the Oriental has for a "dead-pan," I've decided they have nothing on the American way of hiding emotions and feelings. It seems to be our nationwide credo to hide all emotion, softness, or human feeling really, under a tough outer shell. This, I've also decided, is all to the good—but it can be carried to too great a degree. Maybe you remember the line of The Fool's Prayer that went something like "The word we had not thought to say, Who knows how grandly it had rung?"
>
> At this stage of the game, I don't really think I need to express my unlimited appreciation for everything you've done for me (and Uranie and Claudie), the way you brought us up, the ideals that

you instilled in us, the channels through which you guided our thoughts, the desire you gave us for clean living, clean speech, clean thoughts, the abilities that you gave us and then encouraged until they came through. I don't really think I need to express my admiration for you in these things. The time at least 22 years ago when you all forgot your keys to the old house and pushed me through the front room window to let you in. "You've got it to do," you told me. I always remembered—now more than ever. "You've got it to do." It must be that you know (and if I sound stuffy, you don't really have to read all this) that "All that I am and all that I hope to be, I owe to my Angel Mother" (Angel, in this case, being a term of endearment). But—even if I am sure you know all this—I satisfy myself by putting it in writing.

As you've guessed, there was an action, an incident, that has inspired this. I'll tell you about it in the future of non-censored letters. I had a thrilling time. At the same time, don't be alarmed. At the time of this writing, it is something that is past and that I'm back safely from—much better off and a lot wiser than I was.

I'll never worry about being in good shape again. Boy I'm in good shape!! Remember the five miles swim from the Cooper Bridge to the Ashley Bridge? Drop in the bucket, they were. A mere drop in the bucket!

—and while I think of it, thanks for making me at home in the salt water and a good (enough) swimmer.

Yers Trooly,
Capt. M. R. McCown

CHAPTER SEVEN

A NEW PATH

George fidgeted in the passenger seat as the pickup wound its way up to a bluff high over the Pacific Ocean and was waved through the gate by Marine guards onto Camp H. M. Smith. In front of him stood the majestic-looking headquarters of the U.S. Pacific Command with its multi-inclined roof, reminiscent of East Asian architecture. Surrounded by tall, thin Cook pines and beds of tropical flowers, the perch offered a breathtaking view of the gleaming waters of Pearl Harbor and Honolulu beyond.

George arrived in Hawaii a few days after Christmas 2005. Captain Grover Harms, a chiseled thirty-two-year-old West Point graduate, had volunteered to be his guide and offered him his spare bedroom while he got settled. George met a few of the other captains he would be serving with but hadn't officially reported for duty, nor did he have a chance yet to meet his new boss. Harms had already warned him about what to expect from their commander, and George now felt a little anxious to meet him.

Harms led George across the main parking lot toward a large box-like white structure of concrete surrounded by fence and barbed wire. This was the home of Detachment 4, the largest field unit of the Joint POW/MIA Accounting Command, or JPAC—and George's new assignment. On a patch of grass just outside the entrance, a group of noisy soldiers were grilling hamburgers and steaks next to an outdoor pavilion lined with picnic tables and vending machines. Harms pointed out Lieutenant Colonel James Hanson IV, the detachment commander, among the throng of soldiers enjoying a rare holiday season "organization day."

Hanson was hard to miss. Tall and in top physical shape, the forty-two-year-old infantry officer and Army Ranger from California had a shock of blond hair and deep tan that gave him the look of a world-class surfer. But he was anything but laid-back. The son of an Army officer who was also married to one, Hanson was previously chief of staff for a brigade of 5,000 paratroopers in Afghanistan and before that commanded 570 soldiers in Iraq. Now he oversaw 150 personnel from all branches of the military, including eighteen recovery teams, three investigation teams, and three sections of linguists. He was in charge of planning nearly a hundred missions each year worldwide in the search for missing soldiers from previous conflicts.

Always in high-speed motion, Hanson had a vibrant, excitable personality that demanded much of the men and women under his command. He wasn't afraid to let them know how much—often at a high decibel level and in salty language. He counseled his team leaders: "Don't be offended by my sometimes explosive, dramatic, and theatrical feedback. . . . Understand my technique: it trains the masses rather than the individual."

George stepped through the throng milling around the charcoal grills and over to Hanson.

"Sir, Captain George Eyster," he said, saluting. "I am your new team leader."

The first thing Hanson noticed was the insignia of an Army Ranger on George's fatigues. He was expecting an aviator and was intrigued that his new officer was also wearing the coveted Ranger tab.

"You're a Ranger, I see."

The extra attention always made George feel a little uncomfortable, and he shifted his stance slightly before clumsily recounting how he transferred out of the infantry to become a helicopter pilot.

"Do I make you nervous?" Hanson interjected.

"No, sir," George replied as confidently as he could.

Hanson held his gaze for a few extra moments before shaking his hand.

"Welcome to Det. 4."

———

At the far end of a vast runway at Hickam Air Force Base, beneath the deafening whine of jumbo jets, Mamala Bay Drive winds past Hope Street, a narrow lane that disappears into the thick brush. Just beyond it, facing the aquamarine waters of a lagoon, is a cluster of buildings that look like little more than storage sheds and trailers. The largest—a one-story beige structure with dark trim and a sloping roof—is designated simply Building 45. Its purpose is evident only by the black-and-white flag emblazoned with the image of a bowed head set against barbed wire and a guard tower, with the phrase "You Are Not Forgotten."

The first time George arrived at the JPAC headquarters, a short drive from Detachment 4 on Camp Smith, he didn't really know what to expect. At first glance, Building 45 contained the drab-looking offices, cubicles, and conference rooms he had seen on every other military base. There were the leadership offices housing the commander, a one-star general, and the command's top civilian. Only when he was escorted to the other side of the building, where visitors were required to sign in and out, did he realize he was in a wholly different setting.

Down a windowless corridor with more offices, display cases lining several of the walls were arranged with some of the personal effects recovered in the search for the MIAs over the decades. There was a tattered wallet with a faded photograph of a special gal; a small pocketknife; a letter that a soldier folded inside his helmet; a pair of twisted wire-rimmed glasses; a pocket Bible; a rusty, dented canteen.

The hallway led to a series of large, glass-enclosed clean rooms set off from the main office spaces. Here, in the most geographically isolated spot on the planet, was the Central Identification Laboratory, one of the largest forensic skeletal laboratories in the world, totaling 11,500 square feet. Above the main entryway hung a bank of clocks depicting the local time in Hawaii as well as in Washington, D.C., Vietnam, Thailand, and South Korea.

In the glass-enclosed clean room, laid out neatly on more than a dozen examination tables, were human bones. Some were merely fragments, others aligned into skeletons. Nearby lay bits of clothing, helmets, boots, and other artifacts, everything carefully tagged or placed in evidence bags. Anthropologists and technicians in white coats moved gingerly around the specimen tables, conferring in hushed tones. Along one side of the main lab space were a series of workstations with high-powered microscopes. On the other was a smaller interior room marked "X-ray." A separate glass enclosure was the autopsy room, where full-scale computer models of the human skull were created using just a few shards of bone. At the rear of the laboratory complex, where the rumble of jet engines was even more pronounced, was a set of double doors that opened onto the apron of the air base's busy runway. That was where remains recovered on far-flung battlefields were unloaded by lab staff—day or night—from the cargo hold of arriving military aircraft.

The words painted above the laboratory lent expression to the subdued, almost funereal atmosphere, where lab staff liked to say every day was Memorial Day.

"We write no last chapters. We close no books. We put away no final memories," the words of President Ronald Reagan reminded them. George was especially struck by another quotation, for both its powerful message and its relatively obscure source, President Calvin Coolidge: "A nation that forgets its defenders will be itself forgotten."

———

JPAC kept records on more than eighty thousand soldiers, sailors, airmen, and Marines listed as missing in action. The vast majority were lost in World War II, followed by Korea and Vietnam. The lab was also trying to untangle a thicket of unsolved cases in the form of almost a thousand boxes of unidentified remains either turned over by foreign governments or recovered in remote corners of the globe. In an effort to capitalize on cutting-edge advances in technology, the lab had recently begun disinterring some of the eight hundred unknown soldiers from the Korean War who were buried just a few miles away in the so-called Punch Bowl, the National Memorial Cemetery of the Pacific. To assist in its efforts, the JPAC lab was building one of the largest DNA databases in the world, collecting genetic material from the families of the missing—that is, when they could be found or came forward. Working closely with the Armed Forces Institute of Pathology based in Washington, JPAC's lab was pushing the limits of forensic science, even searching for ways to extract the more elusive nuclear DNA, which comes from both parents, as opposed to the more commonly analyzed version known as mitochondrial, which is passed down from the mother. It was research driven by the uniqueness of the mission, where remains were often commingled. An estimated 8 percent of Caucasians share mitochondrial DNA that is too similar to positively separate one from the other; in effect, they are genetic cousins. The challenge was confronted when trying to identify soldiers buried together on the battlefield or bomber crews that crashed—especially in the 1940s and 1950s, when most units consisted of all white men. Nuclear DNA might be especially useful in Korean War cases because of the 1973 fire that destroyed many of the personnel records from that conflict—including dental records. By the time George arrived in late 2005, JPAC was identifying roughly eighty missing soldiers a year, on average more than one per week.

Outside the main headquarters building and the lab, much of JPAC's work took place in nearly a dozen trailer-like buildings situated across the parking lot from Building 45, where in a rabbit warren of cubicles there were offices designated for operations, intelligence, and public relations—and where the mood was decidedly brighter than the somber atmosphere of the lab. That is where George met some of the command's more colorful characters.

Military personnel assigned to the command usually spent just a few years before moving on to another assignment. So the continuity flowed from a handful of ex-soldiers whose nearly religious belief in the MIA mission led them to stay on as civilian employees after leaving the service. One of them was Bob Maves, a small and sinewy ex-soldier with wire-rimmed glasses and a ruddy complexion who bustled about the complex planning new missions with the energy of a man half his age. His cluttered corner office in one of the trailers often more closely resembled a college dorm room than a military planning cell, with cases of beer from his many travels since joining JPAC more than a decade earlier stacked in one corner and two caged guinea pigs in the other. Gregarious and salty-tongued, Maves was also the command's unofficial social planner. Behind his office trailer, hidden behind a clutch of palm trees, he was overseeing the construction of "the sanctuary," an outdoor watering hole of bamboo, fish ponds, and secondhand furniture—a perennial work in progress fashioned from donations and surplus lumber where, after long hours, the JPAC staff could relax with a few cold ones.

Behind Maves's outgoing exterior was a laser-like recall of the case numbers and pertinent details of scores of cases the command had worked to close over the years. His singular focus was evident by the POW/MIA flag covering the wall above his cluttered desk and the copies of two names etched on the Vietnam Veterans Memorial in Washington clipped to his file cabinet. For many veterans of JPAC like Maves, the Vietnam War was their touchstone, their generation's call to arms. It was also when the search for missing soldiers began in earnest.

Families and veterans' groups concerned that some of their loved ones might still be alive and in captivity led to the establishment of organizations like the National League of POW/MIA Families. Indeed, it was the wife of a missing soldier from the Vietnam War, a young woman named Mary Hoff, who came up with the idea of the POW/MIA flag that would quickly become a national emblem. It is the only flag other than the Stars and Stripes to fly over the White House.

A milestone came in 1973, during the American withdrawal from Vietnam, with the creation of the Central Identification Laboratory in Samae San, Thailand. The lab, which fell under the command of the Army, was responsible for searching for and identifying the remains of the estimated 2,489 service members missing across Vietnam and neighboring Laos and Cambodia. In 1976, when the lab was moved to Hawaii, the effort consisted of merely twenty-nine military personnel and thirteen civilians.

But the Communist victories in Vietnam, Laos, and Cambodia in 1975 virtually halted U.S. recovery efforts in the region. In the decade after the war Vietnam returned a few remains of missing Americans, but it wasn't until 1988 that John Vessey, a retired U.S. Army general, convinced the Vietnamese to allow the United States to actively search for remains throughout the country. The government in Laos slowly opened up beginning in the mid-1980s, while the ruling Khmer Rouge in Cambodia didn't give search teams access until the 1990s. The effort to account for the missing in Southeast Asia, as men like Maves knew all too well, was often stymied in other ways. In the 1980s the most common tip about a possible MIA in Southeast Asia came in the form of what became known as "dog tag" reports—nearly four thousand of them on individual soldiers. In most of the cases, residents of Vietnam claimed to possess the remains of American service members and provided as proof their dog tags, data copied from a dog tag, or other personal identification documents. About 90 percent of the reports, however, turned out to involve soldiers who had served in the war but returned home safely. Another 6 percent had been killed in combat and their bodies recovered. That left only 4 percent that actually involved a potential MIA. "Years of investigation and analysis have shown that the dog tag reports have been instigated by elements of Vietnam's government in an effort to influence and exploit the POW/MIA issue," a Department of Defense report concluded in 1990. "Nevertheless, each report is carefully analyzed to determine its validity."

Over a few cold beers and clouds of cigar smoke in Maves's sanctuary, the discussion often turned to plans to return for more of their missing comrades in Southeast Asia. Soldiers' remains that had already been recovered but were still in the lab awaiting identification—some of them for years—were given special attention. Maves and his merry band did not use their names, of course, not until the lab could make a final determination. But as they gestured across the parking lot in the direction of the lab, the pending case numbers were uttered as if they were proper nouns, merely old friends who would be sprung any day now to return to their families. All it would take was one more mission to collect additional evidence at the crash site where they died or on the remote battlefield where they had fallen.

Long before the Vietnam War, the U.S. military sought to account for its losses on the battlefield and to search for those left behind when the guns fell silent. Though it was haphazard, some officers in the Revolutionary War filed reports on the number of soldiers both killed in battle and missing. Pressed by soldiers' families, Congress passed a law in 1846 directing the secretary of war to compile the names and hometowns of soldiers missing from battles in the Mexican War. During the American Civil War, from 1861 to 1865, the government actively sought to identify and bury its war dead in registered graves. After the Spanish-American War, in 1898, U.S. service members who had been buried in battlefield cemeteries overseas were systematically disinterred and returned for permanent burial in the United States. During World War I, the Graves Registration Service was established to recover and identify American war dead.

But countless soldiers were buried where they fell, and the U.S. military's ability to account for them was bound by the limits of technology and the lack of information on their whereabouts. That began to change dramatically in World War II, the first high-tech war that introduced radar and other modern navigation aids that helped to pinpoint where some troops fell. At the end of the war, Graves Registration teams traveled to far-flung battlefields in Europe and Asia to recover remains and try to locate crash sites. They also gathered clues about the possible whereabouts of those who might have been captured alive and held in prisoner-of-war camps.

Technological advances in forensic science, transportation, and communications steadily made the recovery and identification of missing American soldiers more practical. New technologies could extract DNA from the smallest shards of bone. Fresh clues about the possible whereabouts of lost soldiers and missing fliers from as far back as World War II began reaching the military as never before. Opportunities also opened for the first time on battlefields that had seemingly been closed off forever. Like high up in the Himalayas, where a critical air route during World War II known as "the Hump" doomed more than thirteen hundred American fliers to icy graves on the roof of the world in China, India, and Burma. For the first time in 1994, an American recovery team crossed a Himalayan glacier on horseback to retrieve the remains of two U.S. airmen who were literally frozen in time.

Tips came in from farmers plowing their fields, from construction crews digging new foundations in European cities and towns, and by word of mouth. Before long, there were more MIA cases than ever before that had a real prospect of being resolved, even in places that didn't see fighting during the war, like the jungles of South America. Early in World War II, American bombers headed for bases in North Africa could cross the Atlantic from the eastern tip of Brazil without having to stop to refuel, and some of them crashed on the first leg from the States to airfields in Brazil, where new information was emerging about potential crash sites. In rare cases, the MIA effort reached back before World War II. Even though the U.S. military did not actively search for missing soldiers from World War I, several remains from that conflict were identified, and by the time George arrived, anthropologists had spent years trying, as yet unsuccessfully, to identify the remains of two sailors recovered from the USS *Monitor*, an ironclad sunk during the Civil War.

Changing global politics also gave the search for the missing a boost. Beginning in the 1980s, even hostile nations such as North Korea began turning over remains from the Korean War and permitted a limited number of American recovery teams to investigate in the country. By the 1990s, with the end of the Cold War, the Iron Curtain was pulled back to reveal new records of U.S. service members and intelligence agents captured and imprisoned in the gulags of Siberia. The United States and Russia set up a commission on the MIA issue in 1992, and investigators began interviewing prison guards and reviewing newly opened Soviet files.

When George arrived for duty, JPAC had grown to four hundred personnel. A growing focus of the command was on the eastern part of New Guinea and the series of adjacent islands in the Solomon and Bismarck Seas. More U.S. warplanes were missing in New Guinea than any place on earth; some of the most sustained air combat had taken place there between the Allied powers and Japan during World War II, and nearly two thousand Americans were swallowed by the forbidding jungle.

In those first few days of his JPAC orientation, George was jolted by an overriding thought: In every other assignment he was expected to be an instrument of destruction, to be prepared to inflict as much damage as possible on America's enemies. This place was about putting things back together.

———

George's orientation program at Detachment 4 began with a one-on-one session with the commander himself. In early January, Colonel Hanson summoned George to his office up on Camp Smith to discuss what he expected of him and what George, in turn, should expect of the men and women he would be leading in the field.

George would be relied upon to build his own recovery teams and plan and execute all of their functions in the field, Hanson told him. That meant he would have to be intimately familiar with all the key tasks required of an MIA recovery operation. Like all officers in the military, he was also expected to develop the noncommissioned officers and other enlisted troops under his command—to counsel them and, if necessary, show them how to accomplish their jobs. Physical training was considered a key requirement, and George was expected to ensure both he and his team were in top physical shape, which meant PT both in Hawaii and when they were deployed.

"Everyone on our team must be in top condition to endure the stresses of the mission," Hanson told his new team leader.

But George's paramount duty would be the safety of his soldiers. His job was to minimize the dangers inherent in the search for MIAs. The JPAC handbook warned that many recovery sites presented a host of hazards, from unexploded bombs left over from distant battles to treacherous terrain like the side of a mountain. Personnel were reminded whenever they showed up at JPAC headquarters of the potential dangers of the job. A memorial outside Building 45 was erected to the seven members of a recovery team who were killed in April 2001 in Quang Binh Province, Vietnam, when the Russian-built Mi-17 helicopter they hired crashed in the jungle. Some of the veterans at JPAC also still talked about the recovery team that had been held hostage in the Philippines in the 1980s.

"Nothing we do is worth risking a life or crippling an individual," Hanson told George.

They also talked about George's financial responsibilities as a team leader. The entire command had an annual budget of about fifty million dollars. By Pentagon standards that wasn't much. It had to cover the headquarters and the lab, as well as four field detachments and their far-flung operations. George was expected to make the best use of taxpayer dollars in the field. For example, if he was contracting with a local helicopter pilot for transportation or compensating locals for damage to their property or crops, he had to keep expenses to a minimum.

"Plan and prepare to maintain low costs," Hanson instructed.

George must also never lose sight of the bigger picture, his superiors instilled in him, and he had a responsibility to ensure his younger troops didn't either. They had all been entrusted with a special honor to do the hard work necessary to give their comrades-in-arms a long-overdue homecoming. Day after day George and his team would be living in some of the most spartan conditions of their military careers and be required to do hard labor in stifling heat or bitter cold. They could all too easily overlook what they were there for. It would be George's job to make sure they never forgot why they were doing this.

George would be putting it all into action sooner than he thought. Hanson informed him that Detachment 4 was down a recovery team leader for an upcoming mission. He was counting on George to take over. There was little time to prepare. In fact, the operations order from the general had been issued weeks before George had even arrived in Hawaii, and the departure date was quickly approaching.

"You're going to Laos."

———

As Grover Harms's houseguest, George spent a lot of time his first month with his fellow team leader. Harms, a member of the Army's Quartermaster Corps specializing in supply and logistics, was the son of a Korean War vet and a Japanese mother. He had a habit of wearing a Superman T-shirt on recovery missions. Grover had learned the universal S struck up an immediate kinship with the locals in far-flung nations.

When Harms first heard that a new team leader was arriving directly from a tour in Iraq, he offered his spare room in part because his tour in Hawaii was winding down and he was soon headed to Iraq for the first time. He was eager to learn more about George's experience. He would share JPAC, he thought, and George could share Iraq.

Harms lived in a three-bedroom house just a few miles from the command in the suburb of Aiea, situated on a ridgeline overlooking the shores of Pearl Harbor. He showed George where to grocery shop, how to find the Navy Exchange at the end of Bougainville Drive, and how to get around the cluster of military installations in the area.

They quickly hit it off. Both in their early thirties and single, they were interested in meeting women and took excursions to some of Honolulu's hot spots, swapping out their uniforms for polo shirts and shorts to soak up some of the island's beachfront bars, dance spots, and restaurants in Waikiki Beach, Honolulu's central tourist district. In between talk of sports and girls, the discussion often turned to George's experience in the war. At first, he was reserved about his views. George barely knew Harms and was just beginning a new assignment, where Harms was an experienced hand whom the boss relied on. But over time George opened up. Harms detected a sharp bitterness in his new housemate about his chosen profession. George seemed to have few, if any, positive memories of his experience "down range," and it soon became clear that he was pretty disillusioned about the war. George told him bluntly that he simply couldn't grasp what all the sacrifice was for. While he sounded genuinely grateful to be doing something so unique like JPAC, George was clearly down on the Army. Any remaining doubts about George's view were removed when he confided that he thought this would be his last assignment.

George's closest friend and confidante remained his mother, Ann, whom he often spoke to by cell phone several times a day.

———

The most crucial member of George's first recovery mission was the laboratory anthropologist assigned to oversee the excavation in Laos. Though only in his mid-thirties, the bespectacled Dr. Derek Benedix had salt-and-pepper hair and a graying beard that made him look older. Benedix joined the laboratory staff in 2001 after completing a postgraduate fellowship at JPAC. By early 2006 he had already participated in more than a dozen MIA recoveries in Europe and Asia. In the aftermath of the Asian tsunami in late 2004, he was dispatched to Thailand to help the U.S. State Department identify victims' remains. As George's team anthropologist, Benedix would be calling a lot of the shots once the dig began, using his scientific expertise to determine where they should excavate and the overall pace and direction of the fieldwork.

At his first opportunity George phoned Benedix down at the lab on Hickam and introduced himself.

"Hey, I'm brand-new here," George said. "Can I come talk to you?"

It was an unusual gesture in Benedix's experience. No fresh team leader had ever reached out like that. Benedix traditionally met a new leader only after he was assigned to a recovery and the Detachment 4 commander convened a briefing for the senior members of the team. In truth, the relationship between the scientists working in the JPAC lab and the military officers who led the recovery missions wasn't always smooth. They came from nearly opposite cultures—on one side a rigid chain of command that brooked little dissent and on the other an environment that encouraged questioning orthodoxy and asking tough questions.

When George and Benedix got together, over a cup of coffee in the small library across the hall from the lab, they immediately developed a rapport that was unique in Benedix's more than four years at JPAC. George was eager to learn as much as possible from Benedix about the lab's work, and Benedix could immediately see that George had special leadership qualities.

George quickly saw that behind Benedix's professional exterior was a barely hidden mischievous streak and a full-blown sense of wanderlust. Benedix, who was fondly called *"el mono"* by those who worked with him for his love of monkeys, exuded an infectious energy for the work JPAC was undertaking.

To his surprise George even found himself opening up a little to his new colleague about where he was coming from.

"I have seen some crazy stuff," he told Benedix of his recent tour in Iraq, "and I am ready for something different."

————

New recovery team leaders at JPAC commonly led their first mission to Laos, where the hard-line Communist government strictly controlled the search for the nearly six hundred American military personnel reported missing in the jungles along the border with Vietnam. The host government insisted on controlling as much of the process as possible, dictating every movement by JPAC personnel. The American teams were chaperoned by Laotian officials during their stay and instructed where they could search and for how long. The government also determined the amount of compensation for local landowners and payment for local workers hired to assist in any excavations. The lack of independence translated into fewer responsibilities and fewer variables for the team leader, making it a good training ground for fresh team leaders. But rarely did anyone get assigned a recovery team so soon. George only had several weeks to prepare.

In one key measure, JPAC's field detachments were no different from other military organizations: the more experienced sergeants and petty officers handled virtually all the day-to-day tasks of running operations, and the smart officers took their cues from them. George came to rely on one of them in particular, Sergeant Kili Baldeagle, a thirty-year-old combat engineer with a muscular build, close-cropped dark hair, and a large tattoo on his left bicep of a Lakota Indian symbol with a medicine wheel in the middle. Baldeagle was a graduate of the Army's elite Sapper training course for combat engineers, where he had perfected a host of skills from mountaineering to spotting booby traps by noticing subtle differences in terrain. He also had a reputation for being able to solve some of the most intractable problems in the field with virtually no tools or supplies, earning him the nickname The Architect.

Under the tutelage of Baldeagle and others, George received a crash course in the mission tasks, beginning with how to operate the communications equipment to keep in daily, even hourly, contact with higher headquarters and the outside world and to send encrypted data, including video. The recovery team might need to consult with specialists back at the laboratory about possible evidence, need new instructions from top-level JPAC officials, or require help in the event of an emergency. One day George was taken down the hill from Detachment 4 on Camp Smith to the parade ground overlooking Pearl Harbor to run through the equipment.

At its most basic, the search for missing Americans requires a lot of digging in the ground. That means sifting through mound after mound of earth looking for signs of human remains. One of George's early requirements was to attend "bone-screening training," held outside Building 45, where he learned the difference between "wet screening" and "dry screening."

The preferred way of sifting for evidence is through fine mesh screens attached to wooden trays a few feet long and a few feet wide. With the screen hanging at chest level, one person can stand on each end and break up the dirt, work it through his or her fingers, and push it through the screen, leaving behind anything larger than a tiny pebble. Rows of such screens would be set up at the upcoming excavation. Ideally, George was told, there would be a nearby water supply that could be piped through hoses to wet the dirt and loosen up the hard clumps before washing it through the screens—reducing the chances of missing something such as a small tooth or a tiny bone fragment. Lack of a nearby water source would make a thorough excavation more difficult.

Then, in late January, George was called down to Building 45 for a chat with JPAC's top commander. Brigadier General Michael Flowers, who like George was both a Ranger and a Kiowa pilot, was eager to meet his newly arrived captain. He also recognized his name.

Flowers, a barrel-chested African-American whose father had been a career Army sergeant, had been selected to run JPAC the year before in part because of his experience dealing with foreign government officials in places as diverse as Egypt and Kosovo. He had also served in Grenada and Operation Desert Storm—and had once worked closely with George's father planning a large-scale training exercise.

The general greeted George warmly and told him how sorry he was to hear about his father's untimely death.

"It was a tragedy your dad passed away so young," he told him.

Flowers, whose job often required sensitive negotiations in places where the command was operating, impressed upon George the importance of doing everything possible to strengthen JPAC's relationships where it was searching for lost military personnel. The assistance from hosts, he stressed, spelled the difference between the success and the failure of a mission. The general, in his slow, methodical voice, also wanted to make sure George understood something else as he prepared to lead young soldiers in some very difficult conditions.

"It is one thing to just go out there and dig holes in the ground," Flowers explained. "It is another thing to understand who we are looking for and what happened. It makes it a lot more personal and gives you a lot more motivation."

———

George was ready to get up to speed on the Laos case file. It was called a "last known alive" case, which meant it involved a missing American who was believed to have survived initial contact with the enemy and either radioed his position or was seen by a fellow soldier before all communication was lost. In the immediate aftermath of the Vietnam War, there were hundreds of such cases, further fueling the belief that some Americans might have survived and been taken prisoner.

He reviewed the details in the file, stamped with the case number 1535, which was compiled by JPAC's history section, a jumbled set of cubicles and file cabinets in a secure room a few steps from the lab.

The missing pilot's name was Benjamin Franklin Danielson, captain, U.S. Air Force. George was mesmerized by the story of what happened to him—and how for three days after he was lost, a herculean effort was made to locate him, at terrific cost.

Captain Ben Danielson and Lieutenant Woodrow Bergeron Jr. had taken off from Cam Ranh Air Base in South Vietnam in their F-4C Phantom, call sign Boxer 22, at 9:00 a.m. on December 5, 1969. Their mission, along with another Phantom crew, was to drop Mk-36 antipersonnel mines along the Ho Chi Minh Trail, which was alive with southbound traffic and heavy concentrations of enemy troops. The first jet made its run over the target, but when Boxer 22 released its weapons, it was hit by anti-aircraft cannons positioned in one of the towering limestone formations known as "karsts" that dotted the landscape. With seconds to spare before the plane crashed and exploded, both pilot and navigator ejected.

Bergeron, whose helmet was blown off in the windblast, descended earthward in the face of machine gun fire and came down safely on the river's edge, which was shielded by a twenty-foot-high embankment behind him that led to the karst formation a few hundred yards farther east. Danielson's parachute got snarled on a forty-foot-high tree on the opposite side of the river, just seventy feet away from Bergeron, and he came down in a Vietcong work area with an outhouse and well-worn paths leading to the river. Bergeron could hear small-arms fire coming from the nearby jungle.

Within a few minutes the two men were in radio contact with each other and sent distress signals. Their Mayday call and the homing beepers outfitted on their parachutes were picked up by an HC-130 search-and-rescue plane flying about sixty miles to the west, and several rescue helicopters were quickly scrambled to the scene from across the border in South Vietnam. The two fliers were continuing to report their position when two American attack aircraft arrived simultaneously at about 11:00 a.m. Twenty minutes later, more helicopters and fighter jets arrived. The rescue operation had begun. American aircraft fired rockets to beat back the enemy from the river and struck at the larger enemy guns to the north and in the direction of the limestone tower. But the enemy anti-aircraft guns on both sides of the river fired with greater intensity, and it became clear there were more enemy troops and weaponry in the surrounding jungle than the rescue force first realized. Rescue aircraft flying down the valley were caught in the cross fire. Especially nettlesome was a large-caliber machine gun located in a cave at the foot of the karst about three hundred yards behind Bergeron.

After about an hour, the ground fire died down enough to try to make a pickup. The rescuers went for Danielson first because the terrain was flatter and there seemed to be more enemy forces on his side of the river. The first try almost got to him, but the helicopter was driven away by ground fire. Another chopper made a rescue attempt and was driven away. As friendly aircraft continued to drop bombs and antipersonnel mines on the surrounding jungle, several more attempts were made to reach Danielson. They all failed. In one, a helicopter was hit in the rotor blades and had to return to base. In another, disaster struck. A para–rescue jumper, a young airman first class named David M. Davison, was hit by ground fire and killed.

By daybreak the rescue effort had begun again, and contact was made with Bergeron but not with Danielson. An hour later, Bergeron reported that he had heard excited voices across the river, a long burst of automatic weapons fire, and then a scream that sounded as if it came from Danielson. For the next five hours the Americans strafed and bombed the valley, with direction from Bergeron, who was using a compass and his best guess to pinpoint the enemy positions. The Americans dropped riot-control agents into the surrounding trees and built a wall of smoke on both sides of the river with special-purpose munitions—a pillar that looked from five thousand feet like a Texas sandstorm and was even detected by a satellite passing overhead.

But it wasn't until the third day, after hundreds of sorties, that the valley became eerily quiet. One of the rescuers remarked of the enemy forces that "they were all either dead or had given up." It was then that Bergeron was finally hoisted up to one of the helicopters and returned to safety. Ben Danielson was never heard from again.

Now, nearly four decades later, JPAC had new information strongly suggesting that Danielson was killed by the Vietnamese near where he had last been reported—including a bone fragment turned over to JPAC that was a DNA match with relatives, a set of dog tags recovered nearby, and the testimony of a former North Vietnamese anti-aircraft gunner. But George's recovery team would need to be larger than most, Dr. Benedix explained, because the site of the potential burial covered a large swath of territory and was littered with hundreds of unexploded bombs dropped by American jets during the war. George would need eighteen soldiers, as well as local workers.

He set about identifying the right mix of personnel. Detachment 4's watchword for building recovery teams was "task organized," meaning each member's skills needed to match the unique characteristics of the recovery site. The considerations ranged from the number of potential MIAs they would be searching for to the geography and the surrounding environment. Striking the right balance could spell the difference between success and failure.

"The teams are this organization's main effort," Colonel Hanson impressed upon his new recovery team leader.

One major challenge would be unexploded ordnance. A number of locals in the area had been maimed or killed by some of the thousands of small leftover bombs that had been dropped on Communist forces during the war. The JPAC team would therefore need several explosive-ordnance specialists to detect and dispose of any potentially dangerous material. George also identified a life-support specialist, a soldier steeped in the knowledge of what an F-4 Phantom pilot would be wearing at the time Danielson went down, along with any equipment he might have had with him when he ejected from his disabled fighter, such as signal flares, a survival kit, or a life jacket. This knowledge would be of paramount importance to correctly identify any evidence they might uncover and where to focus the excavation. After consulting with Dr. Benedix and some of Detachment 4's more experienced members, George determined that the team would also need a supply sergeant, a medic, four communications specialists, a Lao linguist, and a photographer to chronicle the excavation.

George soon discovered that personnel shortages were as acute at JPAC as in the rest of the military, which was fighting two wars in Iraq and Afghanistan. To round out the recovery teams, JPAC often had to request "augmentees" from other commands for temporary duty. Medics were especially in high demand, as were explosives experts, engineers, and soldiers with mountaineering experience or, for underwater recoveries, Navy divers. Meanwhile, additional enlisted soldiers would be needed as recovery specialists, the glorified description of what were more commonly referred to as diggers—the personnel whose main job would be to wield shovels, picks, trowels, and ultimately their hands to remove thousands of pounds of earth and carefully sift it through the "wet screens" that George planned to set up at the recovery site, which was near a riverbed. In the first week of February, George submitted his "manning matrix," setting forth the assignments of his key team members.

The long hours of preparations continued. A risk assessment of the recovery site had to be completed. All equipment that would be needed—from communications gear to medical supplies—had to be identified and cargo manifests submitted. Case folders had to be prepared and regular updates provided to the commanding general and senior JPAC staff. Meanwhile, all team personnel had to be prepped on their responsibilities, while orders had to be prepared for each of them, and their immunizations and passport information all brought up to date. George's days were filled with a host of tasks that weren't all that different from previous assignments that required him to plan operations. But there were constant reminders that this would be different, such as when he had to make preparations for a possible repatriation ceremony in Laos if they recovered the remains of Captain Danielson.

He was still waiting for all the augmentees from other military commands to complete his team when he unexpectedly got pulled into Colonel Hanson's office. A highly sensitive issue had come up about the mission, he was told. They were both needed down at the headquarters on Hickam. When they arrived at Building 45, George was informed that JPAC was going to be doing something it never had before. It would give his mission higher profile and likely draw media attention, he was told. It would also put greater pressure on him to make sure everything was handled with the most extreme care. George was dumbfounded when he heard what it was. Ben Danielson's son—a thirty-eight-year-old Navy officer who had been a year old when his father went missing—would be part of the recovery team.

"But is he going to be emotional?" was George's first reaction.

Further complicating matters, in his view, was the fact that the son of the MIA was a lieutenant commander in the Navy. He was higher ranking than George. "How is this gonna work?" George thought.

He felt a little better when he learned that the son's participation in the recovery was approved only after he agreed—even insisted—

that he receive no special treatment. Still, George's unease about bringing a family member along lingered when he saw the reactions of Dr. Benedix, Sergeant Baldeagle, and others with far more experience. JPAC just doesn't do that, they told him gravely. Too many potential variables the command couldn't control.

On February 27, 2006, the team's augmentees reported for duty, including Commander Brian Danielson. Tall and lanky, Danielson had served four tours over Iraq as a navigator in the twin-engine prowler that was first introduced during the Vietnam War to jam enemy radars. When George met him for the first time, he almost immediately felt better about the situation. Danielson was a garrulous guy whose wisecracking demeanor quickly endeared him to George and other members of the team. He also seemed genuinely grateful for the unique opportunity he was being given and maintained that he was committed to working hard like every other team member and doing as he was told. He again promised to take orders from George and not cause any problems. He just wanted to bring his father home. George did, too, now more than he ever anticipated.

Even so, George was keenly aware that Brian's presence would make his job harder. For one, Brian apparently had some of his own ideas about where JPAC should be searching, which injected more angst into the mission planning. He had done a ton of research on his own about his father's case and had brought along stacks of research on where his father was lost, including maps and interviews with some of the men his father served with. George got the feeling Brian Danielson knew more about the case than JPAC, and he was worried about how he would maintain control of the recovery.

George was also disappointed that Sergeant Baldeagle, who had quickly become his right hand, was needed for other duties and would not be going on the mission. But the team's departure was now approaching, and it made little sense to fret about it. Over the next few days the team augmentees received communications and bone-screening training, a flurry of briefings on Lao culture, and a slew of vaccinations, including for Japanese encephalitis, rabies, and typhoid. Anyone who had a history of heatstroke or heat exhaustion was disqualified.

On March 2, the full recovery team gathered in the Hickam Memorial Theater for a pre-deployment briefing, where George also assigned some of the younger soldiers to research what happened during the Vietnam War in the area of Laos where they would be working so they could report back to the team. He wanted to instill in them the gravity of what they would be doing.

"You are going to Laos," he told them. "There is an opportunity to drink beer and get into trouble, but we will be there for a very honorable reason."

The following morning, March 3, 2006, the team members packed their supply chests, known as tough boxes, with flashlights, leather gloves, mosquito nets, two pairs of boots each, eye protection, sleeping bags, and various other types of personal gear. They brought them down to the yard behind JPAC headquarters to be loaded onto pallets for storage in the belly of a C-17 transport plane. George was also issued six thousand dollars in cash.

———

On the morning of March 7, 2006, a white Mi-17 helicopter shuddered as it lifted off from the grounds of a vacant two-story guesthouse in the remote village of Boualapha in Khammouan Province in central Laos. The aging Russian aircraft and its crew had been contracted by JPAC from a private company to ferry George's recovery team to a remote valley a few dozen miles away at a place called Ban Phanop. George rode in a separate chopper, a smaller red-and-white AS350, along with a Laotian government official assigned as the team's minder.

The choppers soon banked north into the Truong Son mountain range and climbed high over the jagged outcroppings of rock poking out of the dense jungle. From a distance George thought the mountains looked like menacing teeth.

Stretching for more than six hundred miles through what is now Vietnam, Laos, Cambodia, and Thailand, the Truong Son range was steeped in myth. According to local legend, the terrain's tortuous shape was carved when giants of yore carrying massive stones from peak to peak stumbled and fell, their heavy loads crashing down with them. It also had a history of resistance to outsiders; as early as the year 722, the Vietnamese erected a citadel along its spine to resist the Chinese invaders of the Tang dynasty. To the outside world, the Truong Son range was better known as the Ho Chi Minh Trail.

At the base of the stone formations snaked a forest of thick tree roots, long wooden vines, bamboo thickets, and hidden culverts and rivers—a perfect setting for transporting food, supplies, and weapons for a guerrilla army. For centuries the mountain range was traversed only on foot with the aid of bushwhackers or pickaxes. But after World War II, the Marxist revolutionary leader Ho Chi Minh in Vietnam realized its strategic importance as a supply line for a long resistance war. By 1959 the trail was lengthened and widened so that a battalion of six hundred men carrying weapons and medicines on their backs could march more than a dozen miles in a day, almost without detection. By 1964 a system of roads had been completed through the valleys and mountains of Truong Son; one of them, just wide enough for a single truck, meandered for more than a thousand miles through perennial forests from North Vietnam, into Laos and Cambodia, ending in the combat zone in South Vietnam. Along the portions that crossed through thinner foliage, rocks were tied to branches to bend them and conceal the supply convoys. If the trail ran through a fully exposed area like a streambed, watchmen were posted to warn truck drivers with gunshots that the swirls of dust from their tires might assist enemy planes overhead seeking to strike them.

That is exactly what Brian Danielson's father had been trying to do when he was piloting his F-4 Phantom on the morning of December 5, 1969, in what the Americans had come to call the "War Against Trucks."

As the deafening whir of the rotor blades carried them to their destination, George's mind raced. There were dozens of tasks to put in motion when they touched down. They would have to use metal detectors to find any unexploded bombs; clear the jungle around the coordinates where the lost pilot had been reported buried; rope off a network of grids to guide the excavation; build screening stations; and establish emergency evacuation routes, just to name a few. When the excavation began, George would take cues from Dr. Benedix, but he was responsible for the welfare of the entire team and about eighty locals who had been hired to help in the search. He had memorized the laundry list of potential hazards they faced, both natural and man-made. There were cobras, bamboo vipers, bats, and a host of other variations of unwelcome wildlife to contend with in Laos. But his greatest worry was what the intelligence briefings informed him were more than twenty different kinds of UXO, or unexploded ordnance, dotting the search area. The valley where Captain Benjamin Franklin Danielson was last heard from thirty-six years earlier was literally a minefield, littered with countless bomblets that had been dropped by American jets during the war. Even with the passage of more than three decades, the high percentage of duds could go off at any time. The team's explosives-disposal specialists, George knew, would be working nearly nonstop.

Something else was also weighing heavily on everyone's mind. It was not expressed in conversation, nor was it mentioned in any of the reams of reports on the case saved on George's laptop. It was visible only by the glances the team stole at Brian Danielson. His mere presence instilled a deep sense of purpose in what they were doing. Everyone, from JPAC rookie to veteran, felt a halcyon-like awareness of what had happened here and why they had come all this way after so many years. Usually, recovery teams got to see how their efforts made a difference long after their work was done, in the photographs of families finally granted some measure of closure with the return of a long-lost loved one. For the first time in JPAC's history, a loved one was here with them. Even the most seasoned members of George's team, who had been on numerous recoveries, were seized by the feeling that they had a personal stake in this one. Like George's team linguist, Sergeant First Class Sengchanh "Sammy" Vilaysane. Sammy, who came to the United States from Laos when he was ten and served nearly twenty years in the U.S. Army, felt a particularly strong emotional attachment to what they were doing. As they neared the recovery site, he tried to imagine what was going through the mind of the determined-looking Navy officer strapped in a few feet away who had come searching for the father he never knew. Dr. Benedix, who had been on more than a dozen recoveries, had never felt such immediacy or so much pressure to succeed.

George was awed by the amount of effort being made, all these years later, for a single fighter pilot and his family. JPAC had literally occupied the village of Boualapha and erected tents on the grounds around it, even hiring a contractor who set up a mess tent to feed the team each morning and night. It had moved in a whole support network from the city of Savannakhet, where JPAC had a warehouse, and ferried loads of supplies by helicopter to the recovery site itself deep in the jungle.

"This is more than just a cool thing to do," George thought of his new assignment.

Somewhere out ahead of them in the jungle below, Brian Danielson's father had probably been captured and killed and then buried in a makeshift grave. George was determined to do everything he could to try to bring him home.

The helicopters passed over a ridge, about ten miles south of Mu Gia Pass, a key terminus where the Ho Chi Minh Trail had entered Laos from North Vietnam, and the aircraft descended swiftly toward the valley floor. The first thing George noticed as the pilots prepared to set the choppers down beside a small river was the huge columns of limestone hundreds of feet high, the karst formations that he had read about in the MIA file and, he knew, had probably spelled Ben Danielson's doom that day nearly forty years before. The second thing George noticed was that the narrow valley, which was about two miles long and half a mile wide, was dotted with dozens of circular indentations. The landscape, he thought, looked as if someone had taken a golf ball and flattened it. The round depressions on the valley floor, he was told, were from the thousands of baseball-sized munitions that U.S. jets had dropped in the valley during the Vietnam War. Most were now filled with water and used by local villagers to raise fish.

Fifteen minutes after George's team took off from the base camp, the pair of helicopters set down a few miles southeast of the village of Ban Phanop. Dozens of villagers were waiting nearby, most of them chain-smoking young men wearing traditional baggy pants, shirts with large sleeves, and sandals, jostling to get a look at the American visitors. George, his linguist Sammy Vilaysane, and their Laotian escort went out to greet them as the rest of the team unloaded their personal gear and the helicopters got airborne again for the return trip to their base camp.

The site selected for the search was a patch of jungle on the western perimeter of the valley, where JPAC investigators concluded it was most likely the small shard of bone and dog tag matching Ben Danielson had turned up. George and his coterie were led to the area, where he directed the team to begin preparing the site for Dr. Benedix. The immediate task was to clear the area of foliage and expose the bare earth. As a soldier carefully scanned the area with a metal detector for any aircraft wreckage or explosives, others hacked away trees, ripped up shrubs, and cut down bamboo. A separate group set up a screening station, a medical tent, and a communications post and constructed a rest area out of bamboo. Dr. Benedix, clutching a pen and notebook, took detailed notes about the terrain and inspected and tested the dirt, which he could see was hard and claylike, typical of Southeast Asia, and contained a high level of acidity—not ideal when looking for bones that have been out in the elements for almost forty years. He also began organizing his scientific equipment and plotting a three-dimensional map of the area on his laptop. Everyone—Americans and Laotians—shared in the backbreaking labor in the stifling tropical heat. Water breaks were ordered every sixty minutes to prevent dehydration, and insect repellent was applied to ward off bugs. The Americans all wore gloves. George, who had spent his share of hot summer days in the wilds of northern Georgia on a forestry crew, was no stranger to hard work and did his part, while Brian Danielson lived up to his end of the bargain, following orders as if he were the lowest-ranked soldier on the team.

Before the team left Hawaii, Captain Jeremy Taylor, another new arrival to JPAC who was attached as George's assistant team leader, inquired of the bomb-disposal specialists whether they should all turn off their radios at the recovery site. He knew all too well from his tour in Iraq that radio signals could set off bombs with a magnetic trigger. These leftover bombs were much different, they told him, and that wouldn't be necessary. But soon after the team arrived in Laos, one of its bomb techs, after removing a rocket found on the recovery site and placing it in a special bunker a safe distance away, returned ashen-faced. The weapon had a magnetic trigger on it, he was surprised to learn. From then on they maintained radio silence to ensure a transmission signal didn't blow the mission to bits.

Later, Benedix and a team member were digging in one of the depressions alongside an embankment taking soil samples when the young soldier noticed a few small deep holes in the dirt. "Hey, doc, what's with the holes?" he asked. "I got a bad feeling."

Just then a bamboo viper slithered out, sending them scrambling. The team members then watched in awe as a Lao boy, no older than eight, jumped in the ditch, grabbed the poisonous snake, and snapped its neck, all in one swift motion. About an hour later they all smelled the enticing aroma of a barbecue and were told the locals had cooked the snake for an afternoon snack.

It took several days to prepare the recovery site for the scientific excavation. Dr. Benedix plotted an area of a hundred square meters and then ordered it roped off in grids of four meters square. Then the painstaking work began. Each Lao worker was closely supervised as the Americans and locals dug in the hard clay from morning until late afternoon, grid by grid, sifting every ounce of earth through the screens in a highly choreographed process designed to leave no stone—or, in this case, bone—unturned. Anything that did not appear to be naturally of the forest, even a cigarette butt, was set aside for inspection by Dr. Benedix, who closely monitored every aspect of the excavation, from the digging to the operation of the bucket lines delivering earth to the screening station that had been constructed nearby. They dug and sifted, methodically if slowly clearing each grid. Every part of George's body ached. Every ligament was sore; every muscle throbbed. So far they weren't finding any sign of Ben Danielson.

But even in the monotonous hours of backbreaking work, George was struck over and over again by the thought that here he was, with the kid who had been a year old when his father was shot down in the Vietnam War, standing on the very ground, looking for his remains.

"How lucky I am to be a witness to this," he thought.

After each day in the field the team was ferried back to the concrete slab of a guesthouse with no electricity or running water in the village of Boualapha. The team members tried to make the best of their measly living conditions. They spent their few precious hours of rest listening to music, watching movies, or playing video games. On their few days off, they passed the time playing cards and competing to see who could cook up the most imaginative snacks with the canned goods and prepared dinners they had stuffed in their rucksacks. One day they got a visit from the American ambassador to Laos and for the special occasion slaughtered a pig and had a Lao-style barbecue. Some of the more experienced members also teased the unmarried augmentees about how the villagers were choosing a Lao wife for all of them. They ribbed George about the pretty young girl hired to work at the recovery site who wouldn't let any other locals work at the screens with him. One night, with the help of a portable generator and an old TV set their hosts rustled up, the team was able to pick up a television broadcast of—of all things—*Lifestyles of the Rich and Famous*. Brian Danielson had them all in stitches with his off-color commentary, delivered in his best impression of the British host, Robin Leach.

Despite the primitive living conditions and the daily drudgery, George grew to admire the simple life of the locals, whose lack of medical care was heartbreaking. He was also drawn to their superstitions—especially those that revolved around the little girl with the liquid blue eyes whom they all treated so reverently. The story went that her mother died in childbirth and her father mysteriously died shortly later. She lived by herself for weeks deep in the jungle, the villagers told them, until they took her in. The Americans all wanted to have their picture taken with her. The entire team also took pride when the medic was able to extract a large piece of metal embedded in the ring finger of another local girl.

———

About midway through the mission, the recovery team was invited by their hosts to a dinner in their honor. They gorged themselves on water buffalo, pigs, and chickens at a candlelit feast beneath wide banyan trees. Before long, most of the team retired for the evening, and George, Brian Danielson, Dr. Benedix, and a few others remained behind with the locals. They soon lost count of the number of toasts over rice wine, known locally as Lao Lao, and the bottles of Johnnie Walker Black that Danielson had hidden in his trunk. Before long, they were all in a festive mood, and Dr. Benedix, who had packed along his guitar, provided some entertainment. It turned into a pretty raucous gathering. At one point, in their deepening stupor, George and Dr. Benedix had a fierce argument over the name of the Cambodian currency. Later, in an ill-advised effort to impress his hosts, Benedix smashed his guitar in a fit.

Soon the revelry died down, and as the rest of the team slept on their floor mats on the concrete slabs of the guesthouse, the conversation turned to more serious—and more personal—subjects. They spoke of the long odds that they would bring Brian's father home after all these years. Even if they were digging in the right place, Dr. Benedix warned, making a positive ID of any remains would be more difficult here than in other countries. The high acid content of the soil in Laos caused bones to erode more quickly. The chances of extracting usable DNA were greater even in places where remains were sitting in the jungle far longer. George and Dr. Benedix also listened intently as Commander Danielson quietly answered their questions about his family.

Brian Danielson had grown up an only child on a farm in Kenyon, Minnesota, where his parents were high school sweethearts. He was a year old when his father was reported missing and had no memories of him. But he grew up surrounded by his father's legend and those who knew and loved him. His father's unknown fate cast a long shadow. Brian's mother, Mary, had been instrumental in the creation of the National League of POW/MIA Families, an early advocacy group established during the Vietnam War to lobby the U.S. government for more answers about what happened to the Americans whose fate remained a mystery. Danielson recounted the ups and downs over the years, the deep frustration that more should be done to find out what happened to his father. The early years were especially difficult for his mother, when the American government did not even acknowledge that the U.S. military had been fighting in Laos. There were lingering doubts about whether the Danielson family was told the whole story. The early years of the POW/MIA movement were synonymous with a deep distrust toward the American government. After the war Mary Danielson's hopes steadily faded when no evidence emerged that her husband was among the pilots taken prisoner by the Vietnamese Communists. Ben Danielson was officially declared dead in 1976.

As he grew up, Brian Danielson told them, he struggled with how to bring dignity to his father's memory while not letting the unanswered questions control him. In the close-knit world of POW/MIA families, he had seen how other families were consumed by the lack of closure. He determined as a young man that he could best honor his father by living up to his example, which led him to be a military flier.

Danielson also told George and Benedix about how a string of new clues and other bits of information fueled the family's hopes that they might someday bring his father home. When he was in college, in 1991, an intriguing piece of information reached the family. A pistol said to belong to his father was discovered on display in a war museum in Vietnam, along with a painting of the battle that ensued when American forces tried to rescue him after he was shot down. The clue suggested Ben Danielson might have been captured, and it only added to the family's questions and desire to learn more. Then, in 2003, a bone fragment and his father's dog tags were turned in to the MIA command. The bone matched the DNA of Brian's grandmother. The case, which had lain dormant for years, was reopened. In 2005, a JPAC investigation team was taken to a location where a former North Vietnamese anti-aircraft gunner had reported seeing an American pilot on the ground that day.

But even as they were searching for his father's remains at that very location, Brian Danielson told them he feared they were looking in the wrong place. Other sources, including a self-published book written by a retired American general based on interviews with locals and photographs from the attempted rescue of his father, suggested Ben Danielson had been killed nearly a mile and a half away, closer to the riverbank. JPAC's own data also raised questions. The former North Vietnamese gunner had said the American jet had come in from the west, whereas the records suggested the bombing run had been on a north-south heading. The Vietnamese source also reported seeing an orange or red parachute when Ben Danielson's was white.

As he heard Brian Danielson's story under the brilliant starlight, George, too, found himself thinking about his family ties here. Perhaps it was the booze or having so unexpectedly found himself on the Ho Chi Minh Trail not far from where his grandfather was killed. He began to pour forth some of the powerful feelings that had been coursing through him since he was handed this mission. George told Danielson and Benedix about his family. He recounted Grandpa George's death in neighboring Vietnam. Danielson and Benedix were mesmerized as he then recounted how he had watched footage of it as a kid. They could both sense what a burden it had been for George to carry the Eyster name. They could also see how earnestly he was trying to do it justice. By the time the three of them tried to sleep off the Lao Lao for a few hours, George was more determined than ever to find Brian's father's remains. It nagged at him that they might be missing their opportunity.

————

The recovery team worked ten days at a stretch in the valley where Brian Danielson's father was last reported alive before taking a day of rest. The effort went on for nearly a month, and they didn't find anything. That is, except for hundreds of unexploded bombs left over from the war that had to be carefully removed and destroyed in a special pit. All day they could hear the controlled detonations in the distance by the bomb-disposal techs. One day they learned that just a few miles to the south of where they were searching, two local kids had been killed when one of the leftover weapons exploded—apparently, George was informed by the Lao escort, not an uncommon occurrence in these parts.

As the long days blended together in a sweaty, muscle-aching blur, they were all growing more and more frustrated. Even Brian Danielson found it harder and harder to get up each morning and set out for another day in the grueling heat. The lack of success only deepened George's feeling that this was a wild-goose chase. For starters, he knew they were making an educated guess about where Ben Danielson's remains might have been buried. The information was based on the testimony from participants nearly four decades after the fact. Memories fade, and some of the new information they had was muddled and confusing. They could also never be sure that their hosts were being fully straight with them. The commander of JPAC's detachment in Laos had warned George when he arrived: "Don't believe the first thing the Laotians say." The government of Laos had been known to take advantage of JPAC's single-minded objective in order to reap the financial benefits that its work in the country bestowed on the local economy.

As the excavation neared its close, with no sign of the missing pilot, it only gnawed at George more that they might be blowing their big chance to give Brian Danielson and his mom some closure. They might be digging in the wrong place. George's desire to order his team to the other location Brian had mentioned grew stronger. But when he broached the idea with higher-ups, he got in some hot water. He was told in no uncertain terms that he was to stick to the JPAC recovery plan. A lot of work had gone into planning the mission, and they were searching in the location that the command determined was most promising based on the information at its disposal.

But near the end of the dig George let one of the hired choppers ferry Danielson up to the location where he suspected his father had been buried so he could lay a memorial wreath. It was March 31, 2006—what would have been Benjamin Franklin Danielson's sixty-third birthday.

———

George returned to Hawaii in early April deeply disappointed that they had not succeeded in bringing Brian Danielson's father home. But he was also emboldened by the experience and eager to hear what might be in store for his next mission.

"That was an amazing experience," he told his mother, describing Laos and the new connection to the MIA community he felt after getting to know firsthand the need for closure that hung over families like the Danielsons. One recurring thought he had was that their experience was even worse than that of Grandma Harriet and his own father, who at least knew what had happened to Grandpa George.

As Brian Danielson prepared to return from Hawaii to his Navy unit in California, George and Dr. Benedix got together with him one last time at the oceanfront Sea Breeze restaurant on Hickam to bid him good-bye. Danielson expressed deep appreciation to both of them—and to JPAC. Knowing that his father had not been forgotten—and seeing firsthand the military's efforts to locate the missing—brought some measure of closure for him and his mother, he told them.

George found some solace in those words, along with the fact that JPAC wasn't giving up hope, either. The Danielson case would remain open. If nothing else, George reflected, his team's painstaking excavation ruled out at least one place where Ben Danielson might have been buried. It was just like in the intelligence business, he thought, where knowing where the enemy isn't can be just as important as knowing where he is. If they were ever going to find Brian's father, JPAC needed to confirm or deny the information it had about his possible fate. One day, he liked to believe, Brian and his mother, Mary, might know the answers to those questions that had burned for forty years: What had been Ben Danielson's ultimate fate? Did the government tell them everything it knew? Perhaps they might have a chance to bury Brian's father in Kenyon, Minnesota.

The promise to never leave a man behind wasn't simply a slogan, George was learning. JPAC's motto, scrawled on official documents and attached to the signature block of many of the command's e-mail addresses, in both Hawaiian and English, made a lot more sense now: *"E Huli Ho'i Lakou Ika Home!"* "Until They Are Home!"

———

Despite his intentions, George did not end up living on a boat in Hawaii. It proved too expensive to buy one large enough on the mainland and have it shipped out, while purchasing one on Oahu didn't seem to make much sense, either, considering he'd have to sell it in a couple of years. Instead, he had his small fishing boat shipped from Florida and on weekends set out from Grover Harms's extra bedroom to hunt for an apartment.

After a few months he settled on a gated community in Ewa Beach, to the west along the island's south coast, not too far from JPAC but distant enough that he could get away from most of the hustle and bustle. There, on Iroquois Avenue, a quiet palm tree–lined street that ran along the beach past a park and a coffee shop, his patio opened up directly onto the surf, just the bucolic setting he had looked forward to during his Iraq tour.

But the job of MIA recovery team leader meant precious little time for rest and relaxation, let alone opportunities to find what he wanted most: a nice girl to settle down with. By the end of April, after only a few weeks back on the island, George and Dr. Benedix boarded another military cargo plane with a new recovery team bound for Laos—this time with Sergeant Kili Baldeagle as his top NCO.

Their mission was to complete the excavation of a crash site where four crew members in a UH-1 helicopter had been shot down during the Vietnam War. JPAC previously recovered remains from the location, and the team's job was to make sure no evidence had been missed. Their living quarters in the Ta-Oy district of southern Laos were even more spartan than the drab guesthouse in Boualapha. They huddled in two-person Denver tents erected on slabs of concrete and survived mostly on rice and noodles cooked in a hot pot and canned beans and soups they packed in their rucksacks. At the recovery site itself George felt a surreal connection to the missing crew they were searching for. UH-1s had been the Army's workhorses in Vietnam, his father had flown them in the Persian Gulf War, and they were still in service even now. As an Army helicopter pilot, he could recognize many of the pieces of wreckage that his team was pulling out of the ground, including a metal chain from the tail rotor that was also used on the Kiowa and looked new enough to be fitted to one of the choppers he flew. The team worked quickly, and Dr. Benedix determined the excavation was complete in just over half of the thirty days allotted. But again, to George's abiding frustration, no more remains were found.

However, George discovered that he drew unexpected inspiration from Sergeant Baldeagle. They seemed to work seamlessly together organizing the recovery team's daily tasks. Both men were paratroopers and Rangers who had served in the Eighty-Second Airborne Division. It also helped that they were both chowhounds. Baldeagle was the first to break bread with the locals, while George, too, would try most anything. They dined on chicken feet and water buffalo tartar, although George drew the line at congealed pig's blood. They were kindred spirits in other ways, as they soon learned over heaps of chicken and rice. While they were rooted in very different cultures, they were both the progeny of long warrior traditions.

Baldeagle's father, Davy, who was now in his eighties and still living on the reservation in South Dakota where he was chief of the Lakota tribe, had parachuted into France on D-day during World War II. Davy was tutored as a boy by Kili's great-grandfather White Bull, a revered Lakota warrior said to excel in all the cardinal virtues of the Hunkpapa—or "head of the circle"—especially bravery. White Bull, who lived nearly a century before he died in 1947, had galloped into battle to defend tribal land in the 1860s and 1870s with a breech-loaded rifle and whip. He fought alongside his uncle, the great leader and warrior Sitting Bull, and his boyhood friend Crazy Horse, one of the most iconic Native Americans, who was later honored with a U.S. postage stamp. Though Baldeagle's great-grandfather denied it to his death, it was the same fearless White Bull, after riding through a hail of gunfire and having his horse shot out from under him, who was credited with killing Major General George Custer at the Battle of the Little Bighorn in June 1876—better known as Custer's Last Stand.

Like the Eysters, the Baldeagles had bestowed a warrior ethos and tradition of military service through the generations. George and Kili both had close relatives who served in World War II, Korea, Vietnam, and the first Gulf War, while three of Baldeagle's brothers were also soldiers and one of his sisters was an Army officer. But as they compared notes, it was clear that the traditions affected George and Kili quite differently. Baldeagle spoke animatedly about his Lakota warrior traditions. The spirits of his long-dead ancestors seemed to burn within him, and he was empowered by them, literally channeling them in his Lakota worship ceremonies. George's experience was very different, he confided. He told Baldeagle that he often felt his father didn't think he was capable enough to make the military a career and spoke of how he often felt weighed down by the burden of his name and his ancestry.

George longed for a tighter connection, a more meaningful affinity, with those who came before him—to draw strength from them, as Kili did from his ancestors. Baldeagle crystallized for George how much further he had to go.

———

After George's team completed the excavation of the helicopter crash—and with two weeks left to go in the mission—the commander of JPAC's Detachment 3, headquartered in Viangchan, handed George a new mission, one usually reserved for more experienced personnel.

He was to take a small group and locate half a dozen remote sites that might be ripe for future recoveries of MIAs. It was an unusual move. Such a task was usually reserved for the command's specially trained investigation teams, not recovery leaders. But JPAC wasn't going to waste the extra personnel, and the contract for the helicopter was already inked. George's job was to survey six isolated locations that had not been investigated by Americans in years. He would have little information to go on other than a few rough coordinates and a brief description of what JPAC's history section believed happened there. His best chance of a successful survey, he was told, was to identify a local elder who might be able to point them to a crash site or possible burial of American military personnel. He should expect any landing zones used by previous investigators to be overgrown and the map coordinates to be inexact or completely wrong, pinpointed before the advent of modern Global Positioning Systems.

George was given a crash course in how to conduct an investigation: Introduce yourself and your team to the village chief and explain why you are there. Remember you are not conducting an interrogation. Try to put the locals at ease. Ask permission to take photographs and be conscious of social customs. If possible, find witnesses to the crash or battle, or those who heard details of the incident from witnesses. Try to interview people individually if possible. Also, get as much of the story as possible so that another investigation team didn't have to return. One tip sheet on field investigations circulated around JPAC at the time instructed the interviewer to imagine he was going to write a screenplay about the incident. What blanks would have to be filled in to do that? Another tactic considered crucial to JPAC's mission was to ask about other incidents in the vicinity, not simply to focus on the particular loss and disposition of the Americans involved. Witnesses often had information about other burial sites or prisoner-of-war camps.

George's investigation team consisted of a soft-spoken Laotian government official, Sergeant Baldeagle, and a Navy lieutenant and medical doctor named Andy Baldwin. Dr. Baldwin, an Adonis-looking triathlete who also happened to be a Navy diver, had been assigned to JPAC to provide humanitarian aid to the native population. Baldwin, who was later featured on the reality television show *The Bachelor*, was attached to George's hastily created investigation team because it needed a medic but also because he would be able to keep up with two Army Rangers like George and Baldeagle. Then there was the pilot for Lao Westcoast Helicopter, which had been hired by the detachment in Laos. George knew him merely as Little Andy. Only in his twenties, Andy had been flying since he was a teenager herding cattle on his family's mutton farm in New Zealand.

Early one morning in May they boarded the small AS350 helicopter and headed deep into the interior, armed with the list of possible MIA sites—each designated with a four-digit case number—as well as a stack of maps, radio equipment, a GPS, a camera, some medical supplies and rations, and a bunch of machetes and chain saws. None of them anticipated how physically demanding it would be or the surreal quality of some of the people they would meet and the wild and unsettled landscape they would have to traverse. Nor did George expect it would be so dangerous.

To reach one of the first locations, they had to slog for several miles through rivers and streams. When he emerged, George's legs were covered in leeches. Dr. Baldwin painfully removed them, one by one, and then pulled a tool out of his backpack that looked like a soldering gun to burn the open wounds. When he was finished, George's pant legs were drenched in blood. At another location, they found the wreckage of a U.S. Navy helicopter near a ramshackle village of thatched-roof huts and rice paddies. From a distance the village appeared to be hanging precipitously off the side of a mountain. After Little Andy set the chopper down in a clearing, a throng of children rushed to greet them. The first thing George noticed was that they were all smoking cigarettes, including those who appeared little older than toddlers. As they got closer, he was struck by their physical features. Most of them were walleyed, their eyes set unnaturally apart, almost on opposite sides of their heads. Dr. Baldwin supposed it was the result of inbreeding; they probably rarely interacted with outsiders. How they came to have an ample supply of cigarettes was a whole different mystery. The Americans and their Lao guide were led on a short hike to the burned-out hulk of the Navy helicopter lying just outside the village. It had clearly been scavenged for metal, George could see, an ominous sign for a potential excavation. JPAC, he knew, treated every site like a crime scene. If pieces were moved, it would be far more difficult to know where to dig. George also noticed a crescent-shaped hole in the side of the helicopter, which struck him as odd.

The good news was that several of the more senior villagers maintained that no human remains had been removed from the wreckage since it crashed into the mountainside in a fiery fury nearly forty years before. George snapped photographs and recorded the grid coordinates on his GPS. He also wrote down the names and descriptions of some of the locals and made detailed notes of the surroundings, including what appeared to be several unexploded bombs. Before they departed, an older man identified as the village chief, who was stooped and graying around the temples, handed him a parting gift: a machete that George immediately understood had been cut out of the fuselage of the downed chopper, explaining the crescent-shaped hole in the side of the wreckage.

Each night after crisscrossing the Ho Chi Minh Trail in search of more clues, George and his small team returned to the base camp in Ta-Oy dirty, bloodied, and tired from hiking for miles through the mountains and traversing barbed thickets. He had barely enough energy to eat dinner before collapsing into a deep slumber in his tent. But after checking off another possible MIA site on his list, he rose the following dawn even more committed to reach every one, fueled by the knowledge that the information he was gathering might some-day allow JPAC to bring home another missing soldier.

———

George had one more possible MIA site in Laos to survey, and he suspected it would be the most difficult: on top of a mountain, no nearby village, literally in the middle of nowhere. Potentially mak-ing it even more challenging was that it was not an aircraft loss. It was another "last known alive" case, this one involving four Special Forces soldiers whose remote observation post had been overrun by the Vietcong. The suspected location of their last radio transmission, according to the little information he had, was about five thousand feet up on top of a small ridge just a few dozen yards across with steep inclines on all sides.

It was mid-morning as they approached what they thought was the right ridgeline, the helicopter's spinning rotor blades casting shad-ows on the valley floor below. When they got over the top, they saw there was nowhere to land. The ridge was covered with trees, some at least forty feet high, George guessed. Little Andy circled around to get another look, but there was virtually no open, flat ground. George quickly assessed the situation. What if Little Andy could bring the chopper in close enough to the side of the mountain and they hopped off the skids and hiked to the ridge? The perfectionist in him desper-ately wanted to be able to report back to the detachment commander in Viangchan that he had surveyed every site on the list. It was worth a try, he decided.

The most promising spot appeared to be about two thousand feet from the summit, where the mountainside was thick with beds of tall, swaying elephant grass, ideal for a soft landing if they could jump out, George thought. Little Andy maneuvered the bird at a slightly downward angle and as close as he could without striking the moun-tain with the rotors. George, sitting in the co-pilot's seat, was tense, sweat pouring down his face. He had watched with awe all week as Little Andy maneuvered the bird in and out of tight spaces. But now

George watched warily as the blades spun less than ten feet from the mountain in front of them. Andy was masterfully holding the aircraft steady, but as a helicopter pilot himself George knew they were in an extremely precarious position. A gust of wind could blow them into the mountain. He peered at the landscape below. It was impossible to tell how high the elephant grass was and how far of a jump it would be. Little Andy shouted that he thought he might be able to inch a bit closer, but not much. Just then, George glanced back to see Baldeagle heave one of the chain saws out the side door.

"What the fuck is he doing?" George thought. "I'm going to have to account for that."

Then, in a flash, Baldeagle jumped out after it. He disappeared with a whoosh into the tall grass below. George looked to see where he landed, but there was no sign of him. He felt a pang of nausea with the dawning realization that he might have just lost him. He recalled what Colonel Hanson had drilled into the recovery team leaders about how nothing JPAC did was worth losing a life. It would be his fault for taking too great a risk.

As George was nearing panic stage, he saw Baldeagle poke his head out of the grass and grin up at them with two thumbs up. They wasted no time. The rest of them threw out their chain saws, machetes, and rucksacks. As Little Andy hovered just feet from the mountainside, one by one they stepped off the helicopter into the swirling air kicked up by the rotors and landed on their feet in the tall grass. They quickly gathered up their gear as George recalculated their position. They soon began hacking away in the hopes of finding a path to higher ground.

It wasn't long before George realized how badly he'd misjudged what it would take to reach the top, if they could even get there on foot at all. They ran into obstacle after obstacle, slashing away at the thick and thorny brush in search of a way upward. The Lao guide, to the Americans' surprise, seemed the least encumbered by the imposing terrain, scurrying up the steep mountain. It was a lesson that George would remember later: if the locals say it is an hour hike, it is probably more like four hours for an outsider. The Lao guide's eyesight was also far better calibrated for the surroundings. He took the lead and pointed out a cobra and then a viper, two poisonous snakes lying in wait along their path. They got turned around several times and had to stop so George could check his GPS and consult an old map folded up in his pocket. At one point, they temporarily lost radio contact with Little Andy, who had flown back down the mountain to the valley floor to wait for them. George kept his wits, but as the hours dragged on, they all became increasingly worried they had made a big mistake. They were in the middle of nowhere and might not be able to get off this mountain in daylight. They also had little confidence they were even in the right place.

In the late afternoon, after hiking for more than five hours, they finally reached the ridge. The sun dipped lower on the western horizon, and nightfall quickly approached. They would still have to hack out a landing zone to get off the mountain, so they moved speedily to inspect the area for any sign that American troops might have met their fate on this nearly forgotten ground. As Baldeagle began making preparations for a landing zone, the rest of them fanned out across the ridge searching for clues. George hunted for any sign they were in the right location and soon stumbled upon an M16 magazine, rusted and weather-beaten.

"We must be on the right path," he concluded. "I don't think anybody locally has a twenty-round M16 magazine."

Soon they found spent rounds littering the ground nearby and, hidden beneath some tall trees, a series of indentations suggestive of shallow graves. George was immediately aware of the significance of what they had found. He imagined what might have happened on this godforsaken patch of earth before he was even born. He could picture four U.S. soldiers fleeing from a larger force of Vietcong, calling for help on the radio as they ran for their lives with virtually nowhere to turn. He wondered who they were, where they came from, and what loved ones they left behind. There was little time for such reflection, though. He snapped photographs of the suspected graves and scrawled detailed notes in his Army-issued green notebook. Their work here was done. They had freshened up another lead for JPAC. George then gazed out at the horizon to see the thickening and ominous rain clouds of an approaching tropical storm.

Under Baldeagle's direction, they worked feverishly to cut down trees and hack away the undergrowth so Andy could pick them up— George once again eternally grateful for those weary summers working for the forestry department in Georgia. Large trunks fell in every

As a toddler at Fort Carson, Colorado, George S. Eyster V (shown here with his father) was surrounded by the trappings of Army life. *Eyster family photo*

George and his mother, Ann, welcome "Big George" home from the 1991 Persian Gulf War. *Eyster family photo*

George, pictured in 1997 with his father and Grandma Harriet, on the day he was commissioned a second lieutenant in the U.S. Army. *Eyster family photo*

George's grandparents, George III and Harriet, are pictured with his great-grandfather, General Eyster. *Eyster family photo*

Lieutenant Colonel George S. Eyster III (Grandpa George) shortly before he was killed in Vietnam in 1966. *Eyster family photo*

(*Below*) Grandpa George is tended to by a medic near Cu Chi, South Vietnam, after being felled by a sniper's bullet—the image his grandson would see at the age of eleven. *Associated Press*

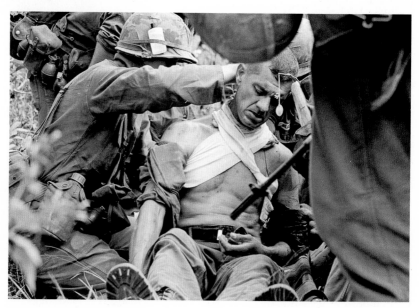

Ryan McCown as a young Navy reservist in the late 1930s before he enrolled in Georgia Tech and became a flight cadet. *John Almeida*

Jane McCown, Ryan's half-sister who was born while he was in the South Pacific, and their father, Marion Ryan McCown, Sr. *Mrs. Vance McCown*

(*Above*) Ryan's mother, Grace Aimar McCown. *John Almeida*

(*Below*) Helen Miller at the time she was dating Ryan McCown in wartime Charleston. *Helen Schiller*

Ryan and Helen in Charleston before he shipped out to the South Pacific. *Ellen McCown Schwab*

The Hell's Angels of VMF-321 in December 1943 on the island Vella Lavella. Ryan McCown is in the third row, second from right, in between Robert Marshall, who was reported missing on the same mission, and Richard "Cosmo" Marsh. Eugene "Vic" Smith is at bottom left. Roger Brindos, the third pilot lost with McCown, is at top right. *Marine Corps History Division*

A battered F4U Corsair, with its tell-tale gull-wing shape, taxis
on a makeshift runway in the South Pacific during World War II.
National Archives and Records Administration

A high-altitude reconnaissance photograph taken by the Army Air Corps
over Rabaul in December 1943. Japanese warships can be seen in Simpson
Harbor, and a Japanese airfield is visible middle right, below Mt. Tavurver.
National Archives and Records Administration

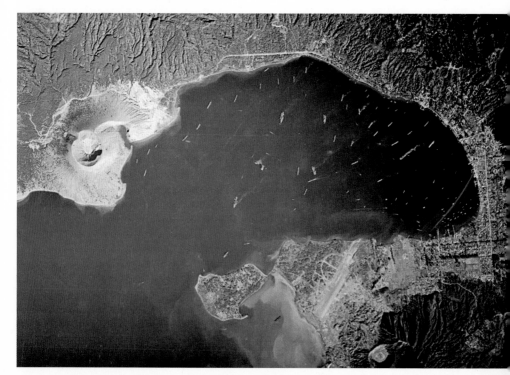

The original caption on this photo from January 18, 1944, reads: "Out of swamp and jungle muck, the Seabees carved this fighter strip on Cape Torokina Field, Bougainville." In the distance is Piruata Island in Empress Augusta Bay. *Marine Corps History Division*

Major Edmund F. Overend, commander of VMF-321, who along with Major Gregory "Pappy" Boyington had been a member of the American Volunteer Group, the so-called Flying Tigers, in Burma. *Marine Corps History Division*

The loss of the iconic Marine Corps fighter ace Pappy Boyington, shot down over Rabaul on Ryan McCown's first mission, deeply affected morale among the pilots on Torokina. Boyington was one of the few Allied pilots who survived the war after being taken prisoner at Rabaul. *National Archives and Records Administration*

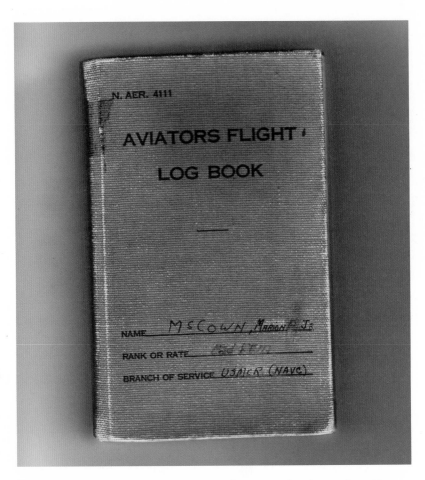

Ryan McCown's Aviator's Flight Log Book, returned to his mother, Grace, five years after he was reported MIA. The entry for January 20, 1944, (*facing page*) written by one of his fellow pilots, stated simply: "Missing in action, Rabaul area." *John Almeida*

January 1944

Date	Type of Machine	Number of Machine	Duration of Flight	Character of Flight	Pilot
1	F4U-1		2.0	J	Self
3	F4U-1		2.8		Self
3	F4U-1		2.1		Self
7	F4U-1	17435	2.4	J	Self
7	F4U-1	17517	2.8		Self
9	F4U-1	18173	3.7		Self
11	F4U-1	17489	4.0		Self
13	F4U-1	17798	2.7		Self
15	F4U-1	19489	3.3		Self
17	F4U-1	07517	4		Self
20	F4U-1	02402			Self

PASSENGERS	REMARKS
—	Patrol over Torokina.
—	Fighter Sweep over Rabaul.
—	Dumbo Escort. Cape St. George.
—	Local Patrol over Torokina No Contact
—	Escort B-24's to Rabaul
	Escort Bombers on Strike to Rabaul - Made contact
	Strike to Rabaul - No Contact
	Strike to Rabaul called back
	Crash landing at sea - Rescued by PT's Strike to Rabaul - No Contact -
	Forced to land early - Bad oil leaks & other defects
	Strike over Rabaul
	Missing in action, Rabaul area

I certify that the foregoing
flight record is correct.

.... USMC

MAG 31, 3rd MAW, FMF

APPROVED

V. B. Mangel Capt.

Total time to date,

16—18616

DATE		PILOT TIME	PASS. TIME	Total Flying Time
TOTAL FOR MONTH		57.0	—	57.0
Brought Forward		725.6	—	725.6
TOTAL TO DATE		782.6	—	782.6

16—18616   GPO

Then-Captain George S. Eyster V after a nighttime raid on a suspected insurgent safe house in Iraq in December 2004. Soon after this picture was taken, he fired warning shots at an Iraqi boy fleeing into the Tigris River after a powerful roadside bomb disabled an American tank.
Eyster family photo

Chief Warrant Officer Matt Lourey, one of George Eyster's squadron mates, was killed along with his co-pilot when his Kiowa was hit by a rocket-propelled grenade. Lourey's death deeply affected Eyster.
Senator Becky Lourey

Building 45, the headquarters of the Joint POW/MIA Acounting Command, Hickam Air Force Base, Hawaii, April 2011. *Bryan Bender*

The Central Identification Laboratory, Joint POW/MIA Accounting Command. *Department of Defense*

(Below) The Central Identification Laboratory relies on cutting-edge forensic technology to reconstruct bits of human remains in an effort to identify missing military personnel. *Department of Defense*

(*Above*) A JPAC recovery team in Vietnam searches for clues of missing Americans from the Vietnam War (2011).
Department of Defense

(*Right*) Sergeant Kili Baldeagle, who proved to be George Eyster's right-hand man at JPAC, is surrounded by locals during a recovery mission in Laos (2007).
Department of Defense

George Eyster and former Vietcong Major Nam Thuan, the commander of "those incredible men in the tunnels" who killed his grandfather in 1966, pose for a picture outside Thuan's home near Cu Chi in Vietnam in 2007. *Eyster family photo*

A view from Rabaul looking southeast over Simpson Harbor toward the active volcano of Mt. Tavurver, April 2008. *Bryan Bender*

One of the caves carved out of the cliffs surrounding Rabaul to shield Japanese troops and supplies from relentless Allied bombing, April 2008. *Kevin Baron*

Lieutenant Robert Thorpe, U.S. Army Air Corps, MIA. George Eyster had high hopes of recovering him on the remote island of Kairiru in 2007 until he learned that the grave reportedly containing Thorpe's remains had been exhumed and the bones burned by locals fearful of evil spirits. *Gil Thorpe*

The wreckage of Ryan McCown's Corsair is excavated by JPAC in the village of Vanakaur on New Britain Island, about fifteen miles south of Rabaul (April 2008). The Boston Globe *via Getty Images*

The remnants of the fuselage from McCown's Corsair, tail number 02402, sixty-four years after he was reported missing. *Kevin Baron*

The damaged ID tag belonging to Captain Marion Ryan McCown, Jr., given to an Australian helicopter pilot by villagers and mailed to JPAC in 2003, jumpstarting the stalled investigation of his MIA case. *Chad McNeeley*

Major George S. Eyster is welcomed home from a year-long tour in Afghanistan in 2010 by his girlfriend—now wife—Sandra Patricia. *Eyster family photo*

Hells' Angels Vic Smith and Cosmo Marsh in Washington, D.C., May 2012. In the fall of 2009, unaware that their missing comrade Ryan McCown had been recovered in New Guinea, they purchased a brick in his memory at the National Museum of the Marine Corps in Quantico, Virginia, Ryan's old base.
Bryan Bender

In January 2009, Helen Miller Schiller was escorted by a cadet from the Citadel at the funeral of Ryan McCown at the Unitarian Church of Charleston, more than six decades after she heard Ryan was missing in action.
The Boston Globe *via Getty Images*

A Marine hands a folded American flag to Ryan McCown's only surviving sibling, Jane McCown McKinney, at the Unitarian Church cemetery, where Ryan was laid to rest next to his mother, Grace.
The Boston Globe *via Getty Images*

direction as they carved out an area large enough for the chopper to touch down to scoop them up. They made swift progress but were filled with disquiet that they might be stranded. During one interval, when the whine of George's chain saw was silenced briefly as he moved from one tree to the next, the mountaintop was pierced by a strange sound that seemed to be coming from behind him. George couldn't place it at first. He then recognized the high falsetto tremors of a Native American chant, a tremolo created by the technique of rolling the tongue on the roof of the mouth or placing fingers over it to force out the notes. It reminded him of the Indian war whoops in the battle scenes of old Westerns. He turned to see Baldeagle, bent forward with his arms splayed out behind him, dancing and chanting, the high-pitched warbling carrying across the ridge and out over the remote valley. The hair stood up on George's neck and goose bumps traveled up his arms as he stood there, enraptured by the sight of his noncommissioned officer crying out to his ancestors high above the Ho Chi Minh Trail. Baldeagle chose a song written by a member of the Blackfeet Nation in Montana as a prayer for the salvation of the souls of American soldiers who never returned from battle. Chanting in a mix of English and his native Lakota, Baldeagle invoked the spirits both of his ancestors and of the missing Special Forces troops, in the hopes they would help the team get off the mountain and return safely to their comrades. "Soldier boy, soldier boy," he cried out, drawing out each refrain in a high-pitched chant. "They're home now, they're already home."

Just as quickly, Baldeagle returned to the task at hand. They were almost ready. As the rain began to pelt the ridge and the daylight narrowed to a reddish-orange sliver in the western sky, Little Andy attempted to touch down on the small landing area they had cleared. Almost as soon as the skids touched down, the chopper began to tilt dangerously to one side on a patch of uneven ground. He lifted off and looped around as Baldeagle struggled to stabilize the earthworks and logs he had arranged. Finally, George and his small team had just enough time to load their gear and hop on. As they headed back to camp, George glowed with pride. It had been a harrowing but moving experience. They had completed their task and took a major step on the long road to returning their lost comrades.

When he got back to Hawaii, he recommended in his final report from the mission to Colonel Hanson that other recovery team leaders be included in similar investigative work, "to maximize their professional expertise."

———

George reflected on how the work he was doing at JPAC was about as far removed from the wars in Iraq and Afghanistan as an Army officer could get. But as he told his mother when he was "on island," meaning back in Hawaii, he was still living and working amid Honolulu's cluster of military installations, where the current wars remained the focus of daily existence. Troops were constantly being deployed "down range." Others were returning physically or psychologically bruised and broken to Tripler Army Medical Center, the massive hospital complex on the slopes of Moanalua Ridge overlooking Honolulu. George would just as soon forget about the wars, but their enduring impact on the men and women he served with and their families was impossible to ignore. As he was coming to learn, being keenly aware of the emotional state of his team was also part of his job as a recovery leader. Colonel Hanson made clear when he arrived that tending to soldiers and their families was his responsibility.

"Spouses and children are an important part of our unit," Hanson counseled him, stressing that when it came to his team members, "you are on duty 24/7."

Many soldiers in Detachment 4, George soon learned, were struggling with their own experiences in Iraq or Afghanistan. More than a few sought his counsel about family or financial troubles caused or exacerbated by combat stress and the long periods away from girlfriends, spouses, and children. George served in the married Army, far more than during his father's generation, when most soldiers were single.

A steady stream of bad news also made it painfully clear the war in Iraq had gone from bad to worse since he'd left. In February, as George was planning his first mission to Laos, al-Qaeda terrorists blew up the golden-domed al-Askari Mosque, one of the holiest sites in Shia Islam, in the city of Samarra. It was a place where George had seen so much senseless violence. The brazen attack, by Sunni Muslim extremists, set in motion a cycle of violence that pulled the country into an all-out civil war. U.S. troop deaths spiked. Hundreds of Iraqi civilians were being found dead each month, many of them beheaded by death squads. By the fall of 2006, the unpopular war was cited as a main factor in the Democratic Party's sweep of the November congressional elections. The new year, 2007, was heralded by a particularly gloomy milestone: the three thousandth American soldier had been killed in the four-year-old war. As for Afghanistan, where the United States had less than a quarter of the combat troops, the war seemed to be forgotten altogether, with very little media coverage.

George's faith was further shaken by how apathetic the public appeared to be about the fighting overseas. The conflicts had cost trillions of dollars and had already ruined the lives of countless fellow soldiers. But the vast majority of average citizens were completely disconnected from the reality of military life and seemed to go about their business as if the country weren't at war at all. George saw the gulf firsthand in some of his interactions with old college friends. When the topic of Iraq came up at all, on Facebook or during rare get-togethers when he was on leave, the discussion often made him angry, as when one friend demanded, "When are you guys going to get out of there, George?"

George wanted to grab him by the shirt collar and shake him; his friend simply didn't get it. He should be answering that question. The military didn't just pick up and invade Iraq on a whim.

"You sent us there!" George wanted to shout at the top of his lungs. "When we come home is your decision!"

Despite his commitment to his work, it was still hard not to be depressed about the demands the Army continued to place on his personal life. He found precious little opportunity in Hawaii to try to set down the kinds of roots he hoped he would find after Iraq. He frequented his share of bars and nightclubs on the weekends to try to meet women but quickly tired of the scene. He had a few dates, but Waikiki Beach didn't seem like the place he was going to meet the type of girl he was looking for. As a single officer in his early thirties, he increasingly felt like the odd man out; most of his contemporaries were married and already had kids. With all the travel he was now doing, it seemed that for the next few years at least he would remain married to the Army.

On the rare occasions when he could get away from it all, George took advantage of the carefree existence that island life offered, slipping on a pair of flip-flops and board shorts and hitting the beach or going fishing on his boat—sometimes inviting other officers but often trolling alone. He also made several trips to the big island of Hawaii and to Maui to soak up the sun and relax by the surf. As he grew more familiar with his surroundings, he also became aware that in yet another way he hadn't expected he was following the path that other Eysters tread.

His father, he knew, spent some of his formative years in Honolulu when his grandfather was stationed at nearby Fort Shafter, which George passed on the expressway on the way into downtown Honolulu. Walking amid the throngs of tourists in Waikiki Beach, he recalled his father telling him about the only time he skipped school to go surfing there, inviting the wrath of his own father. It was on postcards from the tourist shops in Waikiki that George's grandfather sent updates to his son from the war in Vietnam; George still had a few of them in his collection of Eyster letters and heirlooms.

As he was learning in bits and pieces from Grandma Harriet and from the stash of family records, the Pacific region had been far more central to the Eysters' careers than he had realized, going as far back as the years after World War I, when his great-grandfather served in China and later as a battalion commander in the Twenty-First Infantry Division stationed at Schofield Barracks, a half-hour drive up H-1 on the northern side of Oahu. In the late 1940s, after he graduated from West Point, Grandpa George's first two assignments were in Manila, in the Philippines, and then in General MacArthur's headquarters in postwar Japan, where George's father was born. Among the faded black-and-white photographs in his collection of artifacts was one, taken in 1955, of his grandfather wearing shorts and a Hawaiian shirt relaxing with some fellow officers on Eniwetok Atoll in the Marshall Islands in the South Pacific, where they were observing an atomic bomb test. Retracing some of their steps now inevitably drew George to some of the historic military sites on Oahu.

George toured the monument at Pearl Harbor, where the sunken hulks of the USS *Arizona*, the USS *Utah*, and the USS *West Virginia* served as both memorials and tombs for the American sailors killed in the Japanese attack on December 7, 1941. He also made a special trip up to Puowaina Crater high above Honolulu, which James Michener had described in his novel *Hawaii*. It was now the 112-acre site of the National Memorial Cemetery of the Pacific, more commonly called the Punch Bowl for its shape. As he looked out over the flat head-stones lining the cemetery, many of them inscribed merely with the word "unknown," he took special notice of the black-and-white POW/MIA flags on the far side of the cemetery. There, on a series of concrete slabs known as the Courts of the Missing, were inscribed the names of 28,778 of the missing from Vietnam, Korea, and World War II. Only a fraction, he thought. But as he read some of the names of the men lining the high stone walls, he wondered if he might be the one to finally bring them home.

In late 2006, George received news that gave him even greater confidence that he just might. Local villagers in Laos, after hearing about the recent recovery operation he had led, turned over remains that were identified by the lab as belonging to Brian Danielson's father. In January 2007, thirty-eight years after he was last heard from over the radio, Captain Benjamin Franklin Danielson was laid to rest in the cemetery of the First Lutheran Church in Kenyon, Minnesota.

"This is our miracle," his widow, Mary, said at the funeral.

For his son, Brian, who had played such a major role in ensuring his father's case wasn't forgotten, the news of his father's recovery wiped away in an instant all the years of hopeless despair.

"My life will never be the same after this," he said.

————

The possibility that George might be sent to Vietnam had been a major inducement when he was first offered the Hawaii assignment. Just as he was beginning to feel he was getting a handle on his new job, he was granted his wish. In the late summer of 2006, Colonel Hanson assigned him to the first of what would be several missions to recover soldiers missing in Vietnam.

When he arrived in Hanoi, George swiftly struck up a genuine rapport with the Vietnamese Army officer who was assigned as his liaison by the Communist government. Approaching middle age, the bespectacled colonel had been too young to serve in the war but remembered it vividly from his childhood and the terrible price the Vietnamese people paid. His own family had suffered greatly. But if he felt any acrimony toward George and his soldiers, he didn't show it. His benevolent manner made the American team feel welcome, and George found a partnership rooted in mutual respect—as well as a common goal: to find missing Americans. George found he often wanted to spend more time talking with him in his broken English than with his own soldiers. When George told him one evening over a plate of fish and noodles that his grandfather had served in the war, the Vietnamese colonel peppered him with questions. His curiosity about his new American friend was only amplified when George later confided that his grandfather had been one of the highest-ranking American officers killed in the war. Eventually, George found himself telling him about it all: the photographs of his grandfather's final moments, the tunnels, and the book written about the battle. George's new Vietnamese friend made him promise to get him a copy one day.

The first recovery they organized together involved one of the largest in JPAC's recent experience. In the northwest province of Son La, deep inside what had been Communist North Vietnam, George's team was searching for the remains of the two-man crew from another F-4 Phantom jet. This one went down on a large tea plantation where aircraft wreckage was strewn across hundreds of square yards. The search required clearing away many acres of crops, which meant that George had to handle the sensitive negotiations with the landowners over compensation for the damage. Nowhere else in the Army, or the other branches of the military for that matter, were officers so far out on their own and acting so independently on behalf of the U.S. government.

"I better get this right," he thought. "Someone is going to have to cash this check."

After weeks digging on the plantation, keeping track of every plant, tree, and shrub they disturbed, the team could find no evidence of the missing airmen. It was a demoralizing experience that George was getting to know all too well.

He did, however, pick up a nickname from some of the locals: Tuy Lai. He was less than thrilled when he learned that roughly translated, it meant "short, fat white guy." His troops, of course, loved it and got their share of laughs at their commander's expense. But it only endeared him to them more. George eventually took it in stride and even grew to embrace it when it became clear that in Vietnam the description was considered a compliment; it suggested that because he was eating well, he was quite well off. It also explained why many of the Vietnamese women flocked around him at the recovery site. If he played his cards right, his soldiers ribbed him, maybe he would bring home a bride.

George returned to Hawaii disappointed by the outcome of the recovery effort but invigorated by his introduction to Vietnam. He was eager to get back and see more of the country. Following a brief leave, he returned in early 2007 to oversee the excavation of three additional MIA sites—two believed to be where American soldiers had been buried and another where a helicopter crewman was reported to have fallen to his death.

The months in Vietnam gave him a chance to absorb what he came to consider an enchantingly beautiful, if deeply scarred, land, one that had been the source of so much pain to his own family but also, in no small measure, made him who he was. He was also charmed by the Vietnamese people. In the north he visited the Vietnamese capital of Hanoi, where JPAC's Detachment 2 was headquartered. The museums there were filled with propaganda about the Communist victory over the American aggressors during the war. In the south he toured the vast citadel in the ancient city of Hue with its three towering ramparts, once the capital and so-called forbidden city of the Nguyen dynasty. Hue had also been a stronghold for the South Vietnamese Army fighting alongside the Americans. It had been a main target of the Tet Offensive of 1968, when the Communist North and its Vietcong guerrilla proxies struck a major psychological blow against the Americans. From Dong Nai Province in the south-central highlands to Khanh Hoa Province on the South China Sea coast, George took in as many of the sights and sounds and as much of the history of the country as he could. It was on one mission in Vietnam that his beloved camouflage Florida State Seminoles cap, and a bit of luck, helped him escape another potential disaster—and where, for the first time, his team found the remains of what were believed to be missing Americans.

They were living in a makeshift camp on a spur at the top of a nearly nine-thousand-foot mountain, which offered a breathtaking view of the countryside in all directions. But the perks abruptly stopped there. George and his team had to hike an hour each morning, snap on a harness, and rappel down to the recovery site and then hike back before dusk. The terrain where they were digging, adjacent to a waterfall and surrounded by rocky outcroppings, was so jagged and steep that a helicopter landing was out of the question. Baldeagle had to construct a rope bridge over a gully so they could bring in the proper equipment. Another constant danger was avalanches. Baldeagle fashioned a net with ropes and tarps to catch the massive rocks that rolled down the steep inclines into the recovery team's work area.

One day, as Baldeagle was relieving some of the pressure in the makeshift boulder net, a large rock slipped out and headed straight toward George, who was hunched over one of the excavation grids removing earth. Baldeagle shouted a warning. Just as George looked up, the tumbling mass of stone grazed his head, knocking him off his feet. When he emerged from his daze, he realized that some of the impact of the rock had been deflected by the ball cap, possibly preventing it from splitting open his forehead. He had a nasty bruise but considered himself lucky. After that he rarely took off his lucky cap.

Their luck held out a little longer. They were reaching the outer edge of the excavation site, having found no sign of the missing soldiers, when they had to remove a massive boulder to begin digging beneath it. There, a few feet below the surface, they discovered human teeth. Even with the advent of DNA, the lab still considered teeth the gold standard and the best way to identify missing soldiers. The enamel, which held up better than bone out in the elements, could be compared with detailed dental records kept on all military personnel beginning in World War II. Small bits of bone, meanwhile, might not be enough to extract usable DNA. But before George's team was finished, it appeared that the anthropologists back in Hawaii would have the luxury of both. Near where they found the teeth, they soon found numerous pieces of human bone; upon inspection, they appeared to be from a Caucasian.

Despite the somber nature of what they had found and the knowledge that the deceased probably died a violent death, George was ebullient at what they were on the cusp of achieving. The discovery was the culmination of the work of so many for so long: the diplomats whose frustrating negotiations with the Communist governments of Southeast Asia made the search possible; the military historians who painstakingly pieced together clues; the investigation teams that had come to Vietnam before him; the months and even years of planning back at JPAC; and the continual search for new scientific advances by the laboratory. But that wasn't enough. Without the ingenuity of

Baldeagle and the commitment of his young soldiers to brave the harsh conditions and physical danger, they would not be returning to the United States with the remains of what they believed was one of their lost comrades.

George was also burning with a new sense of purpose. When he first arrived at JPAC, he had been overwhelmed by the epic nature of the task. So many thousands were lost forever—sailors lost at sea, soldiers who disappeared without a trace on battlefields or in long-abandoned prisoner-of-war camps. JPAC's task would never be complete. But George now understood that wasn't the point. Each name that was crossed off the list, each soldier who was given a long-overdue homecoming, had a powerful significance. He was humbled that he had been given the chance to keep the promise and, in some small way, sustain a nation's commitment to its defenders—at a time when the bonds between those who were serving in uniform and their fellow citizens seemed to be fraying. George believed his mission was ensuring that the nation's commitment to its warriors was more than just words. Most Americans may have forgotten the fallen, but he was now the instrument through which the nation remembered.

The feeling of satisfaction was also deeply personal. George was writing a new chapter in the Eyster saga, one all his own.

——

In the middle of April 2007, at the end of a recovery mission, George settled his team into the Khach San De Nhat, a spacious tourist hotel with a cavernous glass-enclosed lobby in the Tan Binh district of Ho Chi Minh City, better known to Americans as Saigon. Before they returned to Hawaii, he hoped to experience some of the former capital of South Vietnam, where the American war effort had been centered. His soldiers would have a chance to go shopping and blow off some steam, but George also wanted to organize a "staff ride" so they could all learn a little more about the war. He was pleasantly surprised when his Vietnamese counterpart, the Army colonel, offered to set up a sightseeing tour for them. The day before their departure, the colonel arrived at the hotel early with a van and a driver. He didn't say where he was taking George and his soldiers.

George rode separately with the Vietnamese colonel as they made their way through heavy traffic out of the city and headed northwest into the countryside. Before long, George began to grow anxious. The colonel's repeated inquiries about his grandfather—George had finally given him a few copied pages from the book that depicted his grandfather's final battle—bordered on obsession. George now suspected that he was taking them to Cu Chi, where his grandfather was killed.

"Where are we going?" George finally asked.

His guide didn't have to say anything; his devilish grin said it all.

Cu Chi Province, about forty miles away, was at the end of the Ho Chi Minh Trail and had been the location where the Vietcong launched its operations against Saigon. The Vietcong had dug a network of tunnels estimated to snake 240 miles—some even crossing into Cambodia—that included hospital wards, dining facilities, and sleeping quarters. The entire area, which had been designated a "free fire zone" by the American command in South Vietnam, was the scene of some of the fiercest fighting of the Vietnam War. The tunnels were now a national landmark, heralded as a testament to the Communists' resolve and ultimate victory.

Traveling along Highway 1, George steeled himself. He had toyed with the idea ever since he was sent to Vietnam of making a pilgrimage to Cu Chi, but he wasn't psychologically prepared. Yet as they got closer to Cu Chi, his nervousness dissipated. A growing curiosity seized him. This was the place where Grandma Harriet, his father, and the whole Eyster clan had lost so much forty-one years earlier. He was to be their emissary in paying honor to the man who had meant so much to all of them. Soon he felt himself being pulled toward it.

At mid-morning they turned in to the dirt parking lot of the Cu Chi war museum. A rusted tank, helicopter, and other captured American war trophies were lined up in the courtyard, while posters beckoned visitors to "crawl through the tunnels that brought America to its knees." Vendors milled about hawking cheap souvenirs, including knockoffs of American GI dog tags. Inside the museum, which was adjacent to a shrine honoring the locals who died in the American bombardment of Cu Chi, George perused the small displays of photographs, guns, and other artifacts and viewed the Communist propaganda films about the war. His Vietnamese military guide followed close behind, explaining some of the collections to George and his soldiers through an interpreter. After about an hour they emerged into an extensive outdoor exhibit of reconstructions of some of the famous guerrilla tunnels and passageways. George lowered himself into one of the vertical crawl spaces, not much wider than himself, and pondered the miserable existence that the Vietcong guerrillas must have endured, living for months at a time in a claustrophobic, subterranean world.

He also thought about the heavy toll the tunnel fighters had exacted on his grandfather's troops and so many other American GIs. He had read and reread the bloody details of the fighting here so many times. How the tunnel fighters would lie in wait in the darkness of the shafts for an American soldier to enter, usually feetfirst, and by the dim light of the tunnel opening swiftly bayonet him in the groin or fire a few machine gun rounds into his stomach. How they would then retrieve the wounded American's flashlight, weapons, and grenades and slither back down the shaft through a trapdoor and disappear— until more Americans came to retrieve their mortally wounded comrade. What American soldiers confronted at Cu Chi made the war in Iraq look like child's play, he thought. But the destruction inflicted by the Americans across Vietnam was also unimaginable.

As he posed for a photograph in one of the shafts, George felt an eerie parallel to another image he had seen years before, right next to the one of his dying grandfather in the book on the Cu Chi tunnels. It was a photograph of one of the commanders of the Vietcong forces that ambushed his grandfather's battalion, poking his head out of a similar-looking shaft and peering back over his right shoulder.

The Vietnamese colonel interrupted George's reverie as if he knew what he was thinking.

"We shall go to the place."

———

George's grandfather was mortally wounded on a rubber plantation at a place called Trung Lap, about eight miles from the village of Cu Chi. Now George wordlessly wound his way along some of the very same paths that Grandpa George had trodden. His Vietnamese guide purposely walked several paces behind him. George glanced around him at the thick foliage. He raised his eyes toward the gnarled tree branches. He tried to imagine the hidden enemy bunkers and wondered where the sniper who felled his grandfather had nested.

George conjured the battle scene. Operation Crimp, as the incursion by his grandfather's Black Lions was known, had been an inferno.

"Riot gas drifted through the trees, burning where it touched a man's sweating skin," read the dispatch of the AP reporter who had been there. "Wounded writhed on the ground, looking grotesque in their black gas masks. . . . [D]eath lurked in the trees where the enemy snipers hid, and under the ground where their mines lay."

Now, on the very trail where his grandfather had been shot, George replayed in his mind those final moments when Grandpa George and his troops had proceeded carefully along the dusty path in search of the enemy.

"Cut the wires, don't pull them," the forty-two-year-old battalion commander had instructed one of his riflemen trying to disarm a claymore mine. Colonel Eyster then pulled out his map and conferred with the company commander. It was at that moment, standing where George now stood, that the crackle of gunfire pierced the trees. Colonel Eyster fell to the ground, his arms clutching his chest, and groaned in pain. A medic rushed to his aid and watched his eyes close, his skin turn gray. The medic lightly dressed the wound but privately concluded the bullet had entered his neck and lodged in a lung. Eyster probably didn't have much time. But as they waited for a chopper to extract him, the color began to return to the colonel's face, and his heart appeared to beat a little faster. Grandpa George lived long enough to utter those words that had been seared into George's consciousness.

"Before I go, I'd like to talk to the guy who controls those incredible men in the tunnels."

———

On the way back to Ho Chi Minh City, the car unexpectedly pulled off the main highway onto a one-lane paved road. George assumed his guide was stopping for a bathroom break or perhaps a cup of tea. They approached what appeared to be a small but modern-looking village. On the right side, set about thirty feet back from the road, was a row of simple but well-tended single-story brick dwellings with small gardens and open front porches. The vehicle stopped in front of one of them, and the Vietnamese colonel opened the door and got out. He motioned for his companions to follow. George and his translator, a

Vietnamese-American Army sergeant assigned to JPAC, hopped out and were led onto the small porch. They stepped through a sliding-glass partition covered in silk and entered the house. The Vietnamese colonel quickly disappeared through an archway covered in beaded curtains at the back of the house.

George was puzzled. They were standing in what looked like the main living space of a family home. "Was this the colonel's place?" he wondered. He scanned the small room. The immediate area was furnished with a few chairs and intricately carved cabinets, neatly decorated with houseplants and fresh flowers. The floor was covered with large square tiles and the walls painted pale blue. Toward the rear was a rectangular table covered in a green-and-white floral tablecloth set with a thermos and some kettles. A small electric fan circulated the stale, warm air. George also noticed various family heirlooms hanging on the walls, including several framed photographs. His gaze settled on one of them and then froze. It was the picture from the book *The Tunnels of Cu Chi*. The picture of the Vietcong major, poking his head out of one of the tunnels and glancing back over his right shoulder.

The Vietnamese colonel suddenly reappeared through the beaded curtains accompanied by an old woman in a print dress, her hair pulled back. She was carrying a tray of tea. She pointed to one of the chairs around the table and politely motioned for George and his translator to sit. She poured green tea into little porcelain cups. Then a slight elderly man, small even by Vietnamese standards, quietly entered from the kitchen in the back. He wore a white short-sleeved button-down shirt opened at the collar, dark slacks, and sandals. George looked at him intently. He studied the old man's face and then turned back to the picture on the wall. He drew in a quick breath. There was no doubt it was the same man—the legendary tunnel fighter at Cu Chi who had spent years fighting the Americans from his underground lair. The man who had commanded "those incredible men in the tunnels." This was his house. The old man sat across from George at the table.

Major Nam Thuan was thirty-three years old when George's grandfather came to Cu Chi. He had known war for much of his life. When he was a boy, his father fought the French invaders from the tunnel complex. He had played in them as a child. By the time the

Black Lions arrived, the American war had been raging for more than three years. Thuan had already been awarded several medals for his exploits as a member of the Vietcong. He was master of his subterranean domain, able to count the number of American armored personnel carriers by listening intently in the darkness to the rumble of their engines as they rolled by overhead. He became a guide for the regular North Vietnamese troops who used the tunnels to smuggle weapons through Cu Chi from the Ho Chi Minh Trail.

Thuan had lost count of the American GIs who were unlucky enough to be ordered into one of the shafts—flashlights announcing their arrivals—as he hid in the alcoves and crawl spaces barely large enough for a man.

One American tactic had always confounded him. Their concern for their dead and wounded defied the laws of war, in his view. Even though it meant placing other soldiers at risk—and allowed the enemy to regroup—the Americans almost always came back for their comrades. When they did, Nam Thuan often tossed one of their comrades' grenades at them, killing more.

As the long war dragged on, he was recruited to join the regular North Vietnamese Army and was eventually responsible for the defense of six hamlets. In 1973, as the Americans prepared to withdraw from Vietnam, he was a member of the district Communist Party committee when Vietcong and North Vietnamese troops wiped out forty-seven South Vietnamese military posts in a month.

Sitting across from George, he was now approaching the middle of his seventh decade, with deep lines etched in his tired-looking face and thinning gray hair. The two men looked at each other silently as they sipped tea for several minutes before George, still trembling and sweating, realized he should probably say something. He turned to his translator and relayed a greeting. Then George pulled from his pocket the photocopy of the page from the book depicting his wounded grandfather and slid it across the table. He tapped on the photograph and struggled to find words.

"You were the commander?" George asked. "My grandfather was the commander."

After George's words were relayed by the translator, the old man understood. His eyes widened and his mouth opened a bit in a sign of recognition.

George, meanwhile, noticed the Vietnamese colonel standing over them with a wide, mischievous grin on his face. He had set all this up without George's knowledge. That is why he wanted copies of the book.

George turned back to the diminutive man across from him. He had difficulty forming words. He clumsily recounted his grandfather's story—his family's story. The details stumbled out at first and then came in a torrent, until he felt a nudge from his translator. George had yet to pause long enough to give him a chance to relay what he was saying. He stopped so the young sergeant could catch up.

The old man stared intently at the blond American in the black polo shirt with the POW/MIA emblem on the arm, a symbol widely recognized in his own country. He said nothing. Finally, George repeated the words that his grandfather uttered before he was evacuated from the battlefield—those indelible words that would become his final, and unfulfilled, wish. George told of his grandfather's desire to meet the enemy commander—the same man who now, more than four decades later, was sitting across from his grandson.

"I'm here to do that part of it," George told him.

The old man grew visibly emotional.

"How is your family?" he asked George, almost pleading, wanting to know how many children George's grandfather had.

The last question got mistranslated as "Did your grandfather have any children that lived?" and for a brief moment the tense atmosphere was infused with a welcome dose of levity as George and his companions chuckled at the phrasing.

The man's question was repeated, accurately this time. "How many children did he have?"

George was still shaking a little, on edge about what he had been thrown into and nervous about where this was going. He blurted out that his grandfather had five children, though Grandma Harriet had only four—two boys and two girls, including his own father.

"Big family," the man responded. He seemed relieved by George's answer. The fact that George's grandfather had a big family—that his seed hadn't died out—was evidently important to him. So George repeated it.

"My grandmother is well," George added. "My grandmother had children, and everyone is happy."

George then asked the former Vietcong commander about his own family and what he did after the war. Nam Thuan told him he married after the Americans withdrew, had a child, and went into politics. George sensed the war had taken a toll on the old man's family as well, though he didn't say so.

George then suddenly realized that the man might think he hated him for what happened to his grandfather. He felt the need to let him know that it was all okay now.

"A big family in America," George said again. "The children of this man," he tapped on the photograph again, "we are happy and always together."

The old man now looked wistful, and for the first time he smiled. George's American translator, however, was on the verge of tears, the poignancy of the moment overtaking him. He had left Vietnam as a boy of twelve, he had told George, and along with his brother went to America, where he joined the Army. They were the only ones in their family who escaped the aftermath of the war.

The old man's wife watched them, shaking her head and rolling her eyes slightly, as if to say "you boys." George and Thuan sat and talked for a while longer, sipping green tea—two warriors, their kin once sworn enemies, now sharing their stories and their tears and making peace.

Before George bade good-bye to the man who commanded the troops who killed Grandpa George, the two of them stood for a photograph in the house's small patio, arm in arm.

CHAPTER EIGHT

MISSING

Corsairs soared in roaring flight
Noble arm first to fight
The foe was smitten by their might,
And our son,
His plane a mighty lance,
Flew high and fast,
By the seat of his pants
No stranger he to death, and so,
With blazing gun he strove against the foe.
He saw the great planes safe and homeward go.

But some must die,
But some must die—
Oh, God, not he!
Yet the brave must keep our nation free
Others pray on bended knee,
Others have, just as we,
Toy planes in attic hung
That their sons built when they were young.
Nostalgic memories of a day
Before their son was called away.

Woodson E. Marshall

On the late morning of January 20, 1944, under a deep blue sky dotted with puffy heaps of cotton-white clouds, eighteen B-25 Mitchell bombers from the Army Air Corps' Forty-Second Bombardment Group took off from a coral airstrip on the small island of Stirling in the Treasury Islands. The twin-engine planes, each carrying a crew of six men, eased into position in diamond-shaped formation and headed north, like a flock of menacing prehistoric birds. Their assigned mission was "to strike at minimum altitude Vunakanau Airdrome," about eleven miles south of Rabaul on New Britain's Gazelle Peninsula.

The bombers each carried a dozen "para-frags," small bombs weighing about twenty-four pounds and fitted with a parachute. Designed to break into small fragments upon detonation, they were developed primarily to be dropped in large numbers over Japanese airfields, where they could shred the aluminum of enemy aircraft parked in their revetments. But first the bombers had to rendezvous with the fighter escort that would protect them from the swarms of Japanese Zeros that might try to stop them. The bomber pilots tuned their radios to the frequency 6050 kilocycles and at exactly 12:15 p.m., flying at about one thousand feet, linked up with several dozen Marine and Army fighters over Torokina. Among them was Ryan, flying his newly assigned plane, tail number 02402, and the rest of his four-Corsair division. They were assigned to fly "top cover" above the bombers—the most likely position where enemy fighters might try to use the element of surprise to attack the formation.

The mammoth swarm of American aircraft—with the bombers flying at one thousand feet and fighters at two thousand feet—continued northwest from Torokina on a heading of 295 degrees. They flew in total radio silence. The hum of their propellers and the whine of their engines were the only things piercing the stillness of a bright Thursday afternoon in one of the remotest corners of the world.

Nearly ten thousand miles away, the War Department was preparing to officially open the nation's fourth war bond drive. "Every dollar invested in war bonds is an addition to our offensive power, a contribution to our future happiness and security," President Roosevelt told Americans as an army of five million volunteers was setting out across the country to solicit contributions from average citizens to help finance the war. In a welcome sign that all the effort was paying off, the Office of Civilian Defense announced the end of air raid alerts and blackouts in all but the coastal areas of the country. Also giving new hope that the rationing of goods might come to an end after all, the Aluminum Company of America unveiled plans to resume manufacturing tubes for toothpaste, pharmaceutical jellies, ointments, and shaving creams. There would be no further need to turn in old tubes when purchasing such items.

In Charleston, the Dock Street Theatre was showing *War Department Report* for the first time to the general public, advertising it as "an unusual motion picture telling a graphic story of what's going on in every battle zone." The Gloria Theater was playing *Guadalcanal Diary*. The *Post and Courier* published an interview with a veteran of the "Jolly Rogers" of the Fifth Air Force in New Guinea, who recounted the reports of mutilation and torture of American prisoners at the hands of the Japanese. "This is the roughest war since the Dark Ages," he concluded. A full-page ad in the newspaper made an appeal for war bonds: "When you go home tonight, think of a boy who never will."

When Ryan and the rest of the formation were fifty miles from Torokina, they switched off the radio transponders in their cockpits identifying them as Allied aircraft—to avoid alerting any Japanese radar installations of their presence. They continued on their course and, passing just south of Cape St. George on the lower tip of New Ireland, ran into a series of rain squalls before crossing over St. George's Channel and making landfall on New Britain just before 1:30 p.m.

Flying out ahead of the group, Ryan, his wingman, Bob See, and Lieutenants Brindos and Marshall began scissoring back and forth in a defensive maneuver at about four thousand feet, on the lookout for any enemy planes that might try to get over the tops of the bombers. The bombers would have to pass in close range of three other Japanese airfields en route to the main target at Vunakanau. Two of them were on the way in—Tobera, now about five miles out the right side of Ryan's cockpit, and Rapopo, a smaller field a little farther to the north on the shores of Blanche Bay. The bombers' attack route would also eventually take them near Keravat, another airstrip, on the far side of New Britain's Gazelle Peninsula, before they banked right and made a giant U-turn back toward Vunakanau, the airstrip situated on a plateau inside the ring of Japanese fortifications and hacked out of a coconut plantation.

A broken layer of thick white clouds hung over the peninsula, obscuring the view between the fighters providing top cover and the bombers, which were flying at about eight hundred feet along with another large group of fighters assigned to fly low cover. The cloud formations also made it more difficult for the pilots flying together to stay together. After completing the scissoring maneuver, Ryan was a little behind See when they both lost sight of Brindos and Marshall.

They were trained to continue on course and proceeded to sweep the skies out ahead of the bombers. Below, the bombers were descending to treetop level for the leg across the peninsula and around to the target. Ryan and See scanned the skies around them, but there was no sign of Brindos and Marshall. What they did see was forty Zeros from the Imperial Japanese Navy's feared 204th Fighter Group.

The sky lit up as Ryan and his wingman, joined by other fighter escorts, fended off the enemy planes, members of the same battle-hardened unit that had downed Pappy Boyington on Ryan's first combat mission just seventeen days earlier. Ryan and his fellow pilots were far outnumbered. Within moments a Zero was locked on Ryan's tail.

Ryan "poured the coals," pushing the engine to full torque to maneuver out of range of the Zero. Gripping tightly on the stick with his gloved hand, he pushed the rudder pedals all the way forward to keep the plane under control as the Corsair's powerful engine swiftly accelerated his rate of climb. Lieutenant See turned back in Ryan's direction, fired a short burst into the cockpit area of the Japanese fighter's fuselage, and it exploded at about five thousand feet.

Below, the bombers continued on their course through a nearly constant barrage of anti-aircraft fire from what appeared to be every atoll and ridge snaking through the jungle around the Japanese installations. Flying abreast in pairs, the B-25s crossed the Warangoi and Keravat Rivers before making a wide right turn and approaching the Vunakanau Airdrome in two waves from the northeast. More anti-aircraft fire flew up at them, while Japanese mortars burst just above the trees, giving off fine streamers like phosphorous bombs.

Above them the sky roiled with cannon fire and reverberated with explosions as the dogfights raged and the trails of smoke grew thicker. Bedlam, more than any strategy, reigned—the "gambler's guts" that Boyington had so memorably spoken of. The superior numbers of Japanese fighters tried to close in on the B-25s before they unleashed their ordnance on the target, and at least half a dozen got through only to be beaten back by the fighters and some of the B-25s' own gunners.

All the bombers reached the target at 1:40 p.m., where they scattered nearly all of the 216 para-frags along the Vunakanau runway, in the nearby personnel areas dotted with huts, and on some of the surrounding gun emplacements. All but one of the bombers made it out. As they were heading for the coast, one of the B-25s had its tail and then its right rudder blown off by anti-aircraft fire. The aircraft did a half roll, crashed into the trees, and exploded. The anti-aircraft fire didn't stop until the rest were nearly a mile out to sea.

"The fighter escort did an excellent job of protecting the formation," one of the Forty-Second's intelligence officers later wrote.

The furious effort to shield the bombers from the venerated 204th lasted all of about fifteen minutes, from roughly 1:30 p.m. to 1:45 p.m. But it came at grave cost for the Americans. Two unidentified fighters were reported making a water landing in St. George's Channel. A pilot was also seen parachuting over the water. A different plane, on fire and struggling to stay airborne, crashed into the sea. Another, this one positively identified as an F4U Corsair, flew through a phosphorous bomb, caught fire, and crashed near the target area, where another white parachute was also observed descending toward the ground. "One Corsair dove straight down, trailing a thin line of smoke, into the jungle," recorded a member of the Hell's Angels who was flying low cover for the bombers. Another three "unidentified flamers," meanwhile, were seen screaming out of the clouds before they crashed near the Tobera Airdrome. In all the confusion, no one was sure if they were American or Japanese. But the Japanese seemed to be everywhere, including half a dozen barges visible in the inlet below the mouth of the Warangoi, as well as thick concentrations of enemy troops all along the shores of the river and in Rabaul's Simpson Harbor.

Only one pilot from Ryan's division of four Corsairs returned to Torokina to tell their story. It was his wingman, Bob See. Marshall, Brindos, and McCown were missing.

Sixteen Corsairs were dispatched along with a Dumbo to try to search for signs of Ryan and his fellow missing pilots.

"The results were negative, unfortunately, and the next day's search failed to reveal anything further," reported Overend, the skipper.

But there were rumors, of course. One that made its way around the squadrons at Torokina was that Ryan had been hit near one of the Japanese airfields and was seen kicking up clouds of dust as he came in for a landing on the enemy runway. A few days later some of the Hell's Angels thought they had heard Tokyo Rose report McCown as a POW. They couldn't help but admire Mac. He had always been a stickler for the rules—if a bit naive—and their spirits were lifted just a bit to think that when he was going down and realized there was no way to avoid the clutches of the enemy, he did what they all had joked about: he landed safely on the Japanese base and headed right for the commander's tent to turn himself in.

Another story, as related later in a report filed with the Marine Corps Casualty Office in Washington, told a different version of events. It stated that Ryan was "shot down by enemy [anti-aircraft] fire on a bombing mission over Rabaul, New Britain and went down at sea. No record of POW."

Whatever had happened to Ryan and his fellow pilots—the fates of Brindos and Marshall also remained a mystery—it had been a bloody day in an exceedingly bloody month for pilots heading to Rabaul. In January 1944 alone, the Americans lost more than a hundred aircraft, including thirty-seven Corsairs.

"We live for each other a great deal out here, much more than they do at home, I fear—and sometimes we also die for each other," Overend wrote in the solitude of his tent about the worst day for his squadron. "There is no gain without a sacrifice."

———

The telegram, dated February 7, 1944, arrived at 1023 Ashley Avenue addressed to Mrs. Grace A. McCown. It was one of thousands delivered in cities and towns across America. The few simple words struck a fierce emotional blow:

DEEPLY REGRET TO INFORM YOU THAT YOUR SON MARION
RYAN MCCOWN JR USMCR IS MISSING IN ACTION IN THE
PERFORMANCE OF HIS DUTIES AND SERVICE TO HIS
COUNTRY. I REALIZE YOUR GREAT ANXIETY BUT DETAILS
ARE NOT NOW AVAILABLE AND DELAY IN RECEIPT
THEREOF MUST BE EXPECTED. TO PREVENT POSSIBLE AID

TO OUR ENEMIES DO NOT DIVULGE THE NAME OF HIS
SHIP OR STATION.
A. A. VANDERGRIFT
LIEUT GENERAL
THE COMMANDANT US MARINE CORPS

An accompanying letter informed Grace that Ryan "failed to return from a flight mission against the enemy while serving in the Southwest Pacific area" and that attempts were under way to find out what had happened to him.

"You may be sure that all officers and men in the active theater of operations exert their utmost efforts to learn the fate of their missing comrades," the letter stated. "Everything humanly possible is being done to learn the fate and whereabouts of your son. Please be assured that when additional information is received concerning him it will be sent to you promptly."

The news spread quickly. A Western Union telegram was soon dispatched to Claudia's husband, Captain Leonard Almeida, in Jacksonville, North Carolina:

WE HAVE JUST HAD A MESSAGE THAT RYAN IS MISSING
TELL CLAUDIE AND TELL HER MAMA IS ALL RIGHT—
URANIE.

But Grace wasn't all right. Her heartache at the news was so overwhelming that it was blamed a few days later when she crashed her car. Still, there was hope. Ryan might still make it home. "I'll wait and you hope," he had told her in his last letter, after being fished out of the Solomon Sea. Now Grace did both.

Her anguish was only compounded when a letter arrived from the Marine Corps a week and a half later, on February 18, 1944. There was no record at Marine Corps headquarters that indicated why she was receiving a hundred dollars a month from Ryan's pay. The last sentence almost surely fueled her worry for her son's fate with fears for her own future: "Payment of the above mentioned allotment has been suspended and no further payment will be made until it has been determined that payment thereof is in accordance with existing law."

She and Uranie needed the money to live. Three days later, in a rush of words expressing her worry, Grace replied to the letter, telling the Marine Corps paymaster that the notice about Ryan's pay "has come as a great shock."

> Please be advised that my son Marion R. McCown, Jr. made this allotment out of his salary for the support of the home, my medical treatment and care, and his insurance policies which have to be paid monthly also for the support of his sister whose education as a doctor was his first consideration. After he left Cherry Point, N.C. and just before going to the Pacific area he made this allotment, up to this time he had sent it to us by P.O. money order every month, he preferred to handle it this way, it seemed a little more personal. He has always felt keenly his responsibility to his home and his sisters as he was the only male member of our family. Needless to add that were this allotment discontinued, it would be a great hardship to his loved ones.

Grace also enclosed a sworn affidavit, signed in the same graceful cursive script as Ryan's, stating that her son's pay made up more than half of her monthly income. Now that she wasn't working, all she had was a small annuity she had set aside while she was employed, she reported. She had no spouse, and recounted that she filed for divorce in 1922 "on the ground of desertion [and] no provision was provided for myself or children. I worked and supported them." Ryan had been helping to support all of them from the time he was seventeen, when he worked as a shop clerk for the local U.S. Civil Service Department, earning $120 a month. Grace also included a letter from her physician stating that she had been admitted to the St. Francis Infirmary in August 1942, when Ryan was stationed at Quantico, after she suffered a "cerebral accident" that forced her to retire from her work.

When she hadn't heard anything from the Marine Corps by March, she followed up with another letter asking if Ryan's payments would be reinstated.

"If not we will have to make other arrangements here," she wrote. She was also worried that Ryan might lose his ten-thousand-dollar life insurance policy. Since he had left for the war, she was paying his monthly premium of $8.61 from the money he was sending home.

———

Grace sat and waited for more news of Ryan, often scanning up and down Ashley Avenue as if she were expecting him to pull up in a taxi. She held out hope that Ryan might have survived in the jungle or was being held prisoner by the Japanese. The next update she received on his case, in a letter from the Marine Corps dated May 10, only dampened her hopes. No additional information had been received regarding his fate, she was informed. He would remain "missing in action." She got much of the same in a letter four months later.

In July, a package arrived that was the most difficult to open of all: her son's personal effects. The large box of Ryan's belongings was filled with the items he had worn, from his uniforms and caps down to his leather gloves, aviator scarves, undershirts, drawers, and shoes. In the metal box where he had stored them at Torokina were his photographs of home, his captain's bars, his wallet, and a riding crop he had taken with him from Charleston. There was also his leather-bound diary, a Christmas present in 1939, with some of the letters he had received from Grace clipped inside its pages.

Then came a glimmer of hope—in the form of a notice from a Marine Corps colonel in Washington. President Roosevelt, he informed her, had authorized the Air Medal to be awarded to Ryan for his exploits after he went down at sea and his determination to get back in the air without delay despite the harrowing experience without a lifeboat. But it was the final sentence that grabbed Grace's attention and yanked at her emotions.

"The decoration and citation will be held in this office for Captain McCown in case he should be available for presentation at some time in the future," it read. The Marine Corps, too, it seemed, was not giving up hope that Ryan had survived the mission and might still be alive.

Grace also heard rumors from his fellow pilots that he might have survived. She received word from Ryan's squadron about their suspicion that he might have landed his damaged plane on the Japanese airstrip near Rabaul and been taken prisoner. The next day, the version went, some of the men picked up a garbled broadcast by Tokyo Rose, the English-speaking Japanese propaganda broadcaster, reporting the name McCown. Some Navy pilots on a nearby island had apparently relayed that they also heard a radio broadcast stating that a Captain McCown was a POW.

She clung to the rumors for strength of spirit and asked the Marine Corps about them. "Some of Captain McCown's friends believe that he may be alive, a prisoner of war in a rear area," Grace wrote, more than a year after he was lost, on January 25, 1945.

In June 1945, a month after Germany surrendered to the Allies and Japan had become the sole focus of the war, Grace waited for the veil of mystery to be lifted. But when she opened her mail, she found only another delivery from the Marine Corps with some of Ryan's remaining personal effects. There were two pairs of Navy wings, two keys, his Social Security card, and a check for $111.

The war ended with the dropping of two atomic bombs on Japan that August, bringing access to Japanese prison camps and the officers who ran them. But there was no word at all from the Marine Corps— not for another half a year. Then, as Ryan's birthday approached for the second time since he was reported missing, Grace's faith, like so many others', was dashed with the stroke of a pen in Washington. On January 16, 1946, the secretary of the Navy, following the legal procedure for such cases, declared Marion Ryan McCown Jr. dead.

"Inasmuch as five months have now elapsed since the termination of hostilities with Japan," James Forrestal wrote, "and neither an extensive search of all Japanese prison camps and records nor questioning of returned prisoners of war has revealed any additional information, it is only reasonable to conclude that [he was] killed in action in the line of duty."

A week later a newly grief-stricken Grace received yet more confirmation that hope was lost.

"In view of the circumstances surrounding your son's disappearance and the length of time which has elapsed without word of his whereabouts, the conclusion is inescapable that he lost his life at Rabaul, New Britain," the Marine Corps wrote.

Once again Grace turned to her beloved Unitarian Church on Archdale Street. She organized a drive to collect donations for the Unitarian Universalist Service Committee in New York, which was sending shipments of supplies for war refugees in Europe. Her notice in the church newsletter, the *Liberal Messenger*, appealed to fellow congregants to aid the needy. "Clothes are desperately needed. Your help will count." She called on her fellow Unitarians to phone her— "dial 8896"—to find out where to leave their contributions or let her know where they would like her to pick them up. Meanwhile, in her brother's memory, Uranie, now a medical doctor, donated to the church an altar set, consisting of matching brass candelabra and candlesticks.

The official reminders of what they had lost painfully continued. A month after Ryan was declared dead came a telegram informing Grace that she would soon be receiving his Purple Heart, as well as two medals for his service in the war and in the Pacific theater. Subsequent letters apologized that the medals were not ready to be issued as planned. Each time another envelope arrived from the War Department, Grace's hands trembled as she opened it in nervous anticipation of what she might learn about her son's fate—about how or where he died. Some were condolence letters from the top brass.

In May 1947, she received a notice that Ryan was being posthumously promoted to major, with the commission certificate attached "as a token of the meritorious service of one of our most gallant and faithful Marines." Another set of service medals and ribbons didn't come until the summer of 1948, another not until the spring of 1949, more than five years after he was reported missing.

By May 1949, distraught and growing more ill, Grace had had enough. The Marine Corps informed her it would like to send an officer to her home to finally present to her, in person, the medal for Ryan's heroic actions on January 15, 1944, when he was shot down over Buka Passage—the medal she was told back in 1944 that the Marine Corps was holding on to in case it could bestow it on him in person.

The Marine barracks at the Charleston Naval Base, which had been given the task to deliver the medal, reported to Washington that "presentation of this award was difficult due to the reluctance of the recipient to receive the award." The thought of a military officer in uniform bounding up the steps to her front door on Ashley Avenue was apparently too much to bear. Grace's brother Lucas served as her intermediary, and the medal was sent by registered mail to his home down on Trumbo Street, where Ryan had so many happy memories from his childhood.

Part of Grace was now lost, too. Uranie's goddaughter, young Meri Roberts, who lived down the street, kept asking why Grace always sat silently on her front porch. Her mother's explanation was always the same. "Mrs. McCown's son was reported missing during the war, but she never accepted the fact that he had died. She believed that if she waited and watched, he'd eventually come home."

Grace's grandson, Claudia's little boy, John Almeida, had few memories of his grandmother Gracie—only that she treated him to Reese's peanut butter cups and that the few times he stayed with her, she awoke startled in the middle of the night. As illogical as she knew it was, Grace couldn't help but think it might be her "inquisitive little blue-eyed boy." But of course Ryan never came.

In 1950 the Marine Corps finally returned Ryan's tattered aviator's flight log. The small brown canvas and cardboard cover revealed, in his neat script, every one of his flights, beginning as a cadet. The only exception was the last entry, for January 20, 1944, which was filled in by a fellow pilot back at the Torokina base in the Solomons— "missing in action, Rabaul area."

More tragedy befell Grace in December 1952, when she received word from Texas that Uranie, who had married a police officer and was known as "the beloved little doctor of the hill's country," was killed in a shooting ruled accidental, though some in the family suspected something more sinister. By the following year, Grace was gone, too. Whether it was from heart disease or heartache, no one could really say. Probably both. She was sixty years old.

Claudia buried her mother in the cemetery of her beloved Unitarian Church on Archdale Street. The inscription etched on Grace's tombstone was a mother's final testament to her lost children, from the poem by Elizabeth Barrett Browning: "And if God choose I shall but love thee better after death."

PART FOUR

*Should you get blown off course, look for the
stars, take a reading, and get back on course.*

Brigadier General George S. Eyster, 1945

★

CHAPTER NINE

REDISCOVERY

By the summer of 2007, George had been leading recovery teams in Southeast Asia for nearly a year and a half. He was now considered one of the more experienced officers at JPAC. He was also slated for promotion from captain to major, and it was time for him to take on more responsibility. Like others before him, he anticipated being transferred from Detachment 4 down to JPAC headquarters to work in the operations directorate planning new missions to Southeast Asia. Instead, George was unexpectedly tapped for another job.

While the search for the missing had been fueled by the Vietnam War, only a fraction of the eighty thousand MIAs recorded by the U.S. military fell on the battlefields of Southeast Asia. More than eight thousand were listed as missing in action from the Korean War, between 1950 and 1953, while the vast majority had been lost in World War II, the first truly global conflict waged on land, on sea, and in the air on virtually every continent—all told, more than seventy-four thousand. At the end of the war in 1945, Graves Registration teams traveled to far-flung battlefields in Europe and Asia to try to recover remains and locate crash sites. They also gathered clues about the possible whereabouts of men who might have been captured alive and held in prisoner-of-war camps. Nearly half of the World War II missing disappeared at sea in the great naval battles of the war, making their recovery next to impossible, yet tens of thousands were buried where they fell. But the U.S. military's ability to account for them was bound by the limits of technology, the vast distances in between, and notoriously incomplete or inaccurate records and battle reports about their last reported positions.

By the time George arrived at JPAC, however, that was no longer the case for thousands of them. Even a lifetime later, the search for the missing from World War II was becoming more practical with advances in forensic science, field excavation methods, and communications. It was an especially exciting time at JPAC as opportunities to recover MIAs were opening on battlefields that had seemingly been closed off forever.

Working out of a cubicle in one of the trailers across the parking lot from Building 45, George was now a "worldwide planner," which meant he was responsible for planning recovery missions all across the globe, from India to Indonesia. His new boss was a burly former Army sergeant with a sizable paunch and thinning, close-cropped gray hair. At first glance Rick Huston looked like a typical bureaucrat perched behind his desk in a corner office in one of the JPAC trailers. But the native Montanan and Vietnam veteran was a legend in the MIA community. Now approaching sixty, he personally carried hundreds of dead comrades off the battlefield in the Vietnam War before joining the Central Identification Laboratory when it was established in Hawaii in 1976. Huston had spent more than thirty years trekking through Southeast Asia, up and down the Korean Peninsula, across the plains of Europe, and hopping between the islands of the South Pacific searching for more missing comrades. No one would have begrudged him if long ago he had taken his Army pension to carve out a more relaxed existence. But he considered the work a sacred calling.

"These men went to war for our country; they gave up their life for our country. We owe it to them to bring them back to American soil," he explained when asked why he stayed at it so long. "This mission gets in your blood."

For Huston, as for so many others at JPAC, the search was about more than keeping a pledge to lost comrades and their families. It was also about sending a message to the young men and women currently risking their lives on behalf of the nation in Iraq, Afghanistan, and a host of other places where the U.S. military had been sent by the American people.

"It tells these guys that if we're gonna send you in harm's way, and should something happen, we're gonna come get you," Huston said. "We're not gonna leave you."

By the time George reported to Huston in the summer of 2007, the decades he had spent in wearying conditions in remote corners of the globe were beginning to show on his pockmarked face. But behind his wire-rimmed glasses the twinkle in his eyes for their mission still glowed as brightly as it had when he first earned his reputation as a fiercely committed young soldier who could swill more beer than anyone. One place on JPAC's list made him especially animated: Papua New Guinea, or, as it was referred to around headquarters, PNG.

Little appreciated outside JPAC and often overlooked in the histories of the war in the Pacific was a figure that nearly obsessed Huston: twenty-two hundred. That was how many Americans were missing in the forbidding jungles and treacherous mountains of New Guinea or had disappeared over the remote islands in the neighboring Solomon and Bismarck Seas. Indeed, there were more Americans missing in New Guinea than almost anywhere else.

The initial focus of the MIA command in the 1970s was almost exclusively Southeast Asia. But when the Communist governments were stonewalling American efforts to account for the missing from the Vietnam War, the command began looking elsewhere. Beginning in the late 1970s, then-Sergeant Huston participated in a handful of recoveries on New Guinea, where there were stories of cannibals and even American and Japanese survivors still alive in the jungles. With Southeast Asia temporarily closed off, New Guinea in some ways saved the MIA effort, which at the time consisted of only a dozen or so permanent personnel. What they discovered on the mysterious island back then was staggering. Many of the crash sites remained completely undisturbed. In New Guinea's superstitious culture, the heaps of bones and metal with American or Japanese markings were treated as shrines to be worshipped or, alternatively, as bad luck and to be avoided altogether. At the time the country was still largely unexplored and still so primitive that the first wheel some inhabitants ever saw was the landing gear of a fiery warplane crashing near their village.

After those early missions to New Guinea, attention soon returned almost exclusively to the search for MIAs in Southeast Asia. The men lost in New Guinea were once again mostly forgotten. Not until two decades later did the equation change. In the 1990s the mad rush began to tap New Guinea's natural resources. The rate of environmental destruction was staggering; logging in Papua New Guinea was estimated to be three times faster than the forests' ability to yield new growth. Therein lay a stark irony. The steady destruction of the rain forest meant that new information on missing aircraft was flooding in as never before. But the pace of development also meant that the crash sites were at greater risk of being disturbed. Tampering with them could foreclose on JPAC's one final chance to find the remains of the men who were lost. Mining or timber crews could damage or destroy evidence, making it far more difficult, if not impossible, to conduct a forensic investigation. If the sites remained undisturbed, the chances were far higher that JPAC could find signs near the wreckage that the crew had come down with the plane instead of bailed out—such as a parachute strap, a boot, a belt buckle, or a dog tag. If the aircraft was moved down a hillside or dragged to a dump in a nearby village, JPAC teams would have to rely on often conflicting memories of locals to surmise where to dig.

On top of the daunting forces of nature and fellow man that stood in JPAC's way was another group of searchers: the so-called wreck hunters, the well-financed bushwhackers hired by vintage World War II aircraft collectors to locate rare planes and parts. Some of the missing planes, if they could be restored, fetched millions on the open market. JPAC soon learned that those hunting for "warbirds" in New Guinea had little interest in finding out who had been flying the planes. On nearly every visit to New Guinea, JPAC was finding at least one crash site that had been disturbed this way. Some planes, with their original tail numbers, were showing up in the United States registered to aircraft brokers or wealthy collectors like the P-38 Lightning crash-landed on January 18, 1944, by Lieutenant John R. Weldon, who was still listed as MIA. JPAC had recently all but written off the case of another Army Air Corps pilot, Lieutenant Marion Lutes, whose P-47 Thunderbolt disappeared over New Guinea on April 29, 1944. In April 2003, the command learned, the mostly intact wreckage was hoisted off a mountainside and now sat in an aircraft hangar in Australia.

For men like Huston the pull of the remote island in a far corner of the world was irresistible. The flurry of new aircraft sightings and field investigations were reviving MIA cases that had been dormant for decades. But the command was facing a herculean task to tackle them before the evidence was lost forever.

"If we don't get off our keister," he often exclaimed, "we are going to lose our chance."

To illustrate what was at stake, Huston would often recount what happened on "Black Sunday," April 16, 1944. More than three hundred Allied planes returning from a bombing mission against Japanese bases on the western part of New Guinea ran into a fierce tropical storm over the Finisterre Range in the Owen Stanley Mountains. Large swaths of the area had never been charted, and many maps that did exist contained inaccurate elevations or simply designated large stretches of the geography with the words "No Data Available," as one survey map depicted at the time. Thirty-seven planes never returned from the bombing mission, making it the largest noncombat loss in the history of the U.S. Air Force.

"They are all in the Owen Stanleys near Lae!" Huston would insist to anyone willing to listen. If JPAC simply canvassed all the villages in the area, he was convinced, they would find some of the crash sites—maybe even all of them. "Every site is known by at least one village!"

By the time George came to work for Huston, JPAC was tracking more than three hundred crash sites in New Guinea for nearly one thousand missing Americans—almost half of all the missing in and around the island. Already, nearly half of all the World War II missing recovered since 1976, when the lab was first set up, had been found on New Guinea.

But for JPAC planners, a harsh reality remained. New Guinea was still one of the most difficult and dangerous places to operate—and not simply because it was so remote and its climate and terrain so inhospitable. When George arrived to work for Huston, JPAC operations had been suspended on the island for nearly a year because a local radio station in one of the provinces falsely reported that American soldiers had arrived not for missing airmen but for the island's gold. In a country with so little infrastructure or modern communication, it was breathtaking how far and wide the rumor spread, greatly undermining the command's ability to guarantee the safety of recovery teams.

JPAC had been working closely with the American embassy to try to undo the damage and convince provincial and tribal leaders that the only treasure they were seeking was their fallen comrades. As George reported for his new assignment, the command was eager to return.

———

Huston quickly identified George as an officer who had taken the MIA mission to heart and could be given greater independence than most officers. From his cubicle a few steps away from Huston's office, George dived into the work.

The role of the operations directorate was to make the best use of JPAC's limited resources in the field. With input from the lab staff and the historians, mission planners ranked MIA cases in order of the most likely to be solved with a full excavation at a suspected burial site or crash scene. These were cases where material evidence, such as dog tags, personal gear, or actual human remains, had already been found by JPAC investigators or discovered by locals. When George began his new assignment, the operations directorate was planning missions in countries as diverse as Germany and India.

Within days he was managing plans to mount the search for soldiers missing in Germany from World War II. He was responsible for virtually every aspect of the planning process, including coordinating with the host government, assessing the research and recommendations of other JPAC sections, and identifying the private contractors whose help in the field would be crucial. George also soon learned this would be more than a desk job. He would have to lead an advance team to Germany and, when the recovery teams arrived, run the command and control cell overseeing the entire effort.

By the late summer of 2007, George was humping through the Hürtgen Forest near the German-Belgian border. He had come to the scene of the longest battle in the history of the U.S. Army, where JPAC was hoping to locate some of the estimated 150 American GIs who were never recovered from the fierce fighting in the fall and winter of 1944–45. George's guide was a retired German Army sergeant major and amateur historian named Bernd Henkelmann, who in the 1980s had served as the German Army's liaison at Fort Knox, Kentucky. Henkelmann operated a small museum in the town of Vossenack, near where the battle took place. The fifty-seven-year-old

Henkelmann knew where local farmers, backpackers, and war enthusiasts had come across artifacts from the battle, and in some cases human remains. He soon had his American friend spellbound as they retraced some of the battle lines of the five-month struggle that took place in an area of just fifty square miles. With copies of some of the original field reports in hand, thanks to JPAC's history section, once again George was energized by the deep sense of purpose he felt and the fresh connection he was making to his own lineage. It was during the Battle of Hürtgen Forest, which proved to be the last gasp of the German Army in World War II, that his great-grandfather George S. Eyster Jr. was serving as the chief of the operations branch in General Dwight Eisenhower's European headquarters.

Also while he was in Germany, George struck up a friendship with Sandra Patricia. He was introduced over e-mail to the soft-spoken and doe-eyed Colombian girl, who was living and working in her native Bogotá. George had mentioned to a mutual friend from Florida State that he had wanted to improve his Spanish. It turned out that Sandra Pa, as her friends and family called her, was eager to improve her English. They were both single, and before long the two of them—the shy and intellectual U.S. Army officer and the petite and demure South American professional—hit it off and were sharing photographs of each other. After a few weeks, George mentioned that when he got back to Hawaii, he wanted to take a fishing trip to South America. Sandra Pa was planning to visit a friend in Panama. They decided to meet in person.

———

On Monday, January 21, 2008, a creaky turboprop touched down in the capital of Papua New Guinea, and George, Rick Huston, and two others from JPAC's operations directorate emerged into a blast of sticky equatorial heat. Wearing polo shirts emblazoned with the POW/MIA logo, they lugged their backpacks and laptop cases across the tarmac into Jacksons International Airport, the austere two-story terminal serving Port Moresby. After waiting in line to get their visas stamped by an immigration official, they hustled past throngs of passengers—some donning flowery native headdresses and bright multicolored garments, others in western T-shirts and jeans—who were waiting to board flights to outlying provinces, places with names like Wewak, Madang, Lae, and Rabaul. As George and the others headed to meet a waiting van dispatched by the U.S. embassy, he paused in front of a sign with a big red arrow: "Traveling Passengers All Weapons and Ammunition This Way."

"Is it any wonder they've got problems?" he thought.

George had been assigned as the chief planning officer for JPAC's upcoming recoveries in New Guinea. It was a testament to the command's growing trust in him. They would mark the first excavations since the false rumors spread about American soldiers searching for gold forced JPAC to halt recovery efforts back in 2006. In fact, that last recovery effort in New Guinea was considered a near disaster. The trouble began when some of the local workers JPAC hired demanded more money and the team leader refused, not wanting to set a dangerous precedent. The villagers grew angry and, JPAC concluded, spread the story that U.S. troops had invaded the area to mine for gold. It made it more difficult to work in PNG. The upcoming missions, George knew, would have to be carefully orchestrated. They would require him to rely on all the diplomatic and negotiating skills he could muster—and make up his own rules along the way.

George had spent much of the previous fall back at headquarters overseeing all the arrangements of what would be an immense undertaking, even by JPAC standards. He reviewed dozens of cases on the main island of New Guinea as well as a series of large and small islands to the north and east that had also been the scenes of fighting during the war. He arranged the cases by province, each designated as either a primary or a secondary site, based on multiple sources of information and JPAC's assessment of the evidence. He rated their priority levels by the likelihood that remains could be found, and he grouped together cases by location in an effort to maximize the work of multiple recovery teams. For example, if one site was completed early, was another nearby where a recovery team could get to work on another excavation? Cases that would require the least amount of resupply by helicopter also floated to the top. These missions could get very costly very quickly, due to the demand for private helicopters from timber and mining companies. Some cases he simply recommended for further study by future JPAC investigation teams after concluding there wasn't enough information to justify sending one of their limited number of recovery teams. Ultimately, George identified four crash sites and one location where they had reason to suspect a missing American pilot was buried. But first he had to go to New Guinea to mount a "pre-deployment site survey."

In addition to Huston, the survey team that arrived in Port Moresby included Alvin Teel, a civilian who joined JPAC in 1999 after a twenty-six-year career in the Air Force, and a twenty-eight-year-old Army staff sergeant and logistics specialist named Tremaine Jackson. The four of them planned to crisscross the country to lay the groundwork for multiple MIA recovery teams that would deploy from Hawaii for six weeks in April, when New Guinea's version of a dry season would begin. They would visit the most promising MIA sites, enlist the help of provincial and tribal officials in the area, scope out the available local labor, and make a host of preparations to ensure the recovery teams could be adequately supplied—and secured—in the field. As the senior military officer in the group, George was in charge of its safety.

It would prove to be a full-time job. Despite its stunning beauty—including fifteen-inch-wide butterflies and countless varieties of orchids—for the uninitiated Papua New Guinea was harsh and unrelenting. The mountainous jungles literally reached into the clouds, some as high as thirteen thousand feet; one nineteenth-century explorer remarked it was easier to climb a Swiss Alp than an ordinary hill in New Guinea. If you stepped just a few feet off the jungle path, you might lose all sense of direction, the rain forest so thick in places one could pass within feet of another person and never know he was there. "Just be sure you take a compass and leave a Hansel and Gretel trail behind you," one experienced visitor warned, adding with only a bit of exaggeration: "If you don't, you will die."

Other hazards George had only read about in fairy tales or adventure stories, like herbaceous swamps—quicksand—bloodsucking leeches, insects the size of your hand, and wild animals ranging from scorpions, bats, and baboons to anteaters, boars, and crocodiles. The threat from malaria, dengue fever, scrub typhus, and many other tropical diseases, meanwhile, would keep his medic plenty busy when the full JPAC team arrived.

Then there was the heat, which was nearly unbearable. Temperatures rarely dipped below the mid-nineties in a climate so humid it was one of the few places on earth where water evaporated more quickly on land than over water. The almost daily torrential rains simply turned to steam. One American soldier who had come before him memorably remarked, "If I owned New Guinea and I owned hell, I would live in hell and rent out New Guinea." Another who was brave enough to navigate through the interior put it in biblical terms, saying at first blush New Guinea appeared to be Eden and then "Eden run amok."

Yet even more labyrinthine than the terrain were the seven hundred documented native tribes of Polynesians and Melanesians, each with a distinct language, dialect, and superstitions virtually unchanged from when European explorers first landed in the sixteenth century. Many, their faces painted with lime or donning ornate shell necklaces, flowery headdresses, and colorful garments, were still subsistence farmers on the land of their primitive ancestors.

Some natives were friendly to outsiders, welcoming them in their bastardized form of English known as pidgin, where "my country" comes out as *"kantri-belong-mi"* and where the Lord's Prayer begins, *"Papa bilong yumi Istap Antap."*

Other tribes, however, were deeply suspicious of outsiders. Property was considered sacred and even treading on someone's land without permission a terrible taboo. Villagers were especially wary of the recent flood of fortune hunters and international conglomerates that had come to stake a claim to the untapped riches deep in the rain forest, from gold and copper to timber and natural gas. Like George, many of them were white men, too. There were still rumors of cannibals if you ventured far enough into the interior. Even the harmless could be jolting, like the sight of the natives chewing betel nuts, the local narcotic that turns the teeth bright red and makes a person's gums appear as if they are hemorrhaging.

George knew New Guinea was more unpredictable and potentially dangerous than anywhere the command operated—with the possible exception of North Korea. In the search for missing American aircraft and their crews, it was quite possible for JPAC to inadvertently walk into the middle of a tribal war, as Rick Huston did on a previous mission when one of the villagers where his team was working was murdered, setting off a round of bloody recriminations with a neighboring clan. A few years earlier, a fight over territory between the Ujimap and the Wagia tribes northwest of Port Moresby left hundreds dead.

Subsequent clashes in the capital and nearly half a dozen other provinces claimed scores more. Since JPAC's last mission in 2006, a state of emergency had been declared in one southern province due to the lawlessness. JPAC didn't want to be caught in the middle of a tribal clash. Though most of the tribes were still wielding primitive weapons such as machetes and bows and arrows, one advisory warned that "the advent of modern weapons . . . has greatly magnified the impact of this lawlessness." Huston, who had more experience in PNG than most of the embassy staff, knew firsthand that the only real law here was "an eye for an eye."

If George and his survey team weren't careful in their dealings with the natives, especially when it came to land rights, they could spark a conflict themselves. The arrival of so many foreigners to exploit sacred tribal land for mineral riches had only made a bad situation worse. Mysterious deaths were reported of villagers who were panning for gold near Chinese- and Australian-run mines, while other deadly skirmishes had broken out between miners and local villagers. Thousands were being displaced by the violence.

The central government's ability to maintain order was almost nonexistent. Officially at least, officials in Port Moresby had authority over the complex maze of ancient tribes on the main island and the neighboring archipelago to the northeast. But their allegiance, as demonstrated by the fractious 109-member parliament, was to tribe or clan, not national unity. The entire PNG Defense Force consisted of little more than three thousand soldiers, while local police were often outgunned by warring tribes. Indeed, a majority of the firearms in circulation were believed to be pilfered from the defense forces and the police, a by-product of rampant government corruption, which was further fueled by the influx of foreign investment. The few laws to protect the environment and the rights of local landowners were seldom enforced, and illegal logging added to the chaotic situation.

When George arrived, Port Moresby, a city of 250,000 perched on a spit of low-lying hills on the Coral Sea across from Australia, appeared to live up to its dual reputation as both impoverished and uncontrollably violent. On the ride from the airport George's driver weaved around a seemingly endless trail of potholes while trying to avoid the mess of zigzagging early-model automobiles in the series of traffic circles that made even the bravest among them a little jittery.

They passed makeshift "settlements" of shanties with names like Kila Kila and Sabama that had sprouted up on the outskirts of Town, as the center of the city was called. Port Moresby itself was mostly a hodgepodge of rickety markets and cheap wooden and cement-poured dwellings, dotted with a handful of modern buildings that ringed the port.

The gritty capital was commonly listed among the top five murder capitals in the world. Crime was so rampant that Australia, which relinquished control of its former colony in 1975, had recently returned to police its streets. Bandits—known as *raskols* in pidgin English—roamed freely in search of prey. Sightseeing advice for visitors was simple and direct: "After dark, don't walk anywhere." The *Wall Street Journal* rated Papua New Guinea one of the world's least livable places. Indeed, just as George arrived, local newspapers were reporting a spike in murders linked to black magic. As many as half of all murders were blamed on sorcery.

When George and his companions reached the corner of Douglas and Hunter Streets, the driver pulled the van through a towering security gate into the Crowne Plaza, the city's only decent hotel. After settling into their rooms and sharing a meal in the hotel restaurant, the foursome reviewed their schedule for the next ten days, went over some of their planning files, and sipped a few South Pacific beers in the lounge on the top floor of the hotel, with its view of the harbor and wharves.

PNG had an otherworldly feel about it, George thought, almost like the bar scene in *Star Wars*. The hotel guests were an eclectic collection of Chinese, South African, and other international businessmen and prospectors, mixed with some backpackers from Australia who had come to fulfill a rite of passage Down Under: hiking the Kokoda Track. The trail began north of Port Moresby and wound over the spine of the Owen Stanley Mountains to the northern side of the island—a landscape in which countless Australian and American soldiers were lost amid miserable conditions in 1942. There were also a few more mysterious characters hanging around the Crowne Plaza—rugged-looking men with mostly Australian and New Zealand accents, and a hodgepodge of mercenary types who kept mostly to themselves. Or perhaps they were the wreck hunters come to recover World War II airplanes for wealthy benefactors.

Early the following morning, George and his compatriots were shuttled a few blocks west on Douglas Street toward the harbor, passing low-slung shops and market stalls that appeared to be filled with as many beggars as shoppers. Where the street came to a T, across from a hillside bungalow that once served as General Douglas MacArthur's wartime headquarters, they pulled up to a barricaded structure of concrete blocks and iron bars. This was the American embassy, serving Papua New Guinea and the Solomon Islands.

They were quickly ushered through security and into an upstairs conference room decorated with native art and intricately carved masks representative of some of New Guinea's myriad tribes. For the next few hours they huddled with Leslie Rowe, the American ambassador to Papua New Guinea, the Solomon Islands, and Vanuatu, and her staff. After hashing out the team's plans, the embassy personnel relayed a few warnings. The provincial governor of Morobe and Madang Provinces, which included the town of Lae on the island's eastern coast, remained deeply suspicious about JPAC's intentions and was being decidedly unsupportive. They might want to reconsider going there. Another potential complication was recent volcanic activity close to several MIA sites on New Britain Island. Thick plumes of volcanic ash were disrupting air travel.

George and his team requested that the embassy staff contact the local officials near Lae to inform them that they were planning to survey the area. They also requested that the embassy contact officials on New Britain Island to let them know they were going to try to get there later in the week. George was quickly learning that there was no such thing as too much advance work in PNG. A seeming lack of coordination with the embassy and the disorganized structure of local governing authorities already posed "significant operational challenges," he recorded in his notebook. It appeared that he was now planning to operate in at least two regions of the country where local officials had no idea that they were coming.

Their next meeting was with a major in the PNG Defense Force and a technical adviser from the National Museum, which had jurisdiction over war relics and materials and would be advising them in the field. George requested that the country's armed forces and Royal

Papua New Guinea Constabulary be enlisted to provide security for the unarmed JPAC recovery teams scheduled to arrive later in the year.

Their final meeting of the day was with the governor of East Sepik Province, located in the north of the island, and a member of parliament representing its provincial capital of Wewak, where the four of them planned to begin their survey operations. They were relieved to hear the officials pledge their full support for JPAC's efforts and offer to assist in any way possible.

That left one additional task before embarking on their survey trip: lining up helicopter transport. The next morning, George and Huston found themselves in a dusty office near the airport haggling with an Australian pilot from Pacific Helicopters, an outfit that operated out of Port Moresby and Lae on the eastern coast. It didn't go well. They couldn't agree on a reasonable price or secure sufficient guarantees that the company's services would be available in an emergency. The company's fleet was in high demand from mining and timber companies, as well as a fair amount of adventure seekers. The meeting was swiftly growing confrontational when in an instant the pilot's gruff demeanor melted away. He noticed the ring on Rick Huston's finger bearing the symbol of a square and a set of compasses—the universal symbol of Freemasonry.

"Are you a traveling man?" the pilot inquired of George's boss.

It was a traditional way of determining whether a stranger was a fellow Mason.

Huston nodded that he was. In a flash this common bond washed away the distrust.

Suddenly it was as if they were old friends, and a deal was struck.

Freemasonry was yet another enigmatic piece of his heritage that George thought he might like to learn more about. He knew that some of his soldier forebears had helped to found Masonic lodges in Pennsylvania and Maryland. On several occasions in recent years he removed from its scabbard the saber of a 32nd-degree Freemason he had inherited, running his fingers over the polished metal trying to imagine the men who had owned it and its purpose.

George made a mental note to get his boss and friend, Rick Huston, to tell him more about Freemasonry.

George studied the tattered map of New Guinea, with the place-names written in German, hanging above the bar. He was sitting in the Kaiser Wilhelm, a run-down watering hole in the provincial capital of Wewak festooned with swords, pistols, and other memorabilia from the late nineteenth and early twentieth centuries, when the northeastern part of New Guinea had been a German protectorate. He had come to the area once known as Kaiser-Wilhelmsland, in honor of the German monarch. He was struck by how the competition for New Guinea's spoils was intertwined with New Guinea's modern history.

Different parts of the island were discovered by various explorers between the sixteenth and the nineteenth centuries. The Portuguese explored the region in 1512, naming it Ilhas dos Papuas, meaning "Land of the Frizzy-Haired People." Soon there followed Spaniards, Englishmen, Dutchmen, and Germans, each European empire annexing different parts of the territory to extract coconuts, rubber, coffee, and—with only modest success—gold and copper. It was the Spanish explorer Yñigo Ortiz de Retez who, in 1545, called the island Nuevo Guinea, possibly due to the resemblance of its inhabitants to those in Guinea in West Africa. But not until the 1870s was the coast of the island accurately charted. Even now, much of the interior remained unexplored by outsiders.

The town of Wewak was a small commercial center on the shores of the Bismarck Sea, at the foot of the Prince Alexander Mountains. One person JPAC recently consulted about it bluntly advised that accommodations were "generally disgusting and the town continues to fall apart." But the area was high on George's list. It had been the scene of fierce fighting in World War II, beginning in 1942, when the Japanese established an air and naval base. Driving through the town earlier in the day in a rented pickup, George saw the remnants of the bunkers and tunnels that the Japanese had constructed to withstand American and Australian bombing attacks. But it was what took place on the small barrier island of Kairiru, which after some difficulty he finally located on the old German map, that brought him here—and the enduring mystery of what happened to a twenty-one-year-old

Army Air Corps pilot from Rhode Island with a slender face, kindly eyes, and a toothy grin.

George had studied the case, designated Missing Air Crew Report 5754, intently. Lieutenant Robert Thorpe was reported missing on May 27, 1944, after taking off in a P-47 Thunderbolt from an airfield near Lae to strafe the Japanese airfield west of Wewak. Efforts to locate him by Army Graves Registration teams after the war proved unsuccessful. The subsequent search by authorities from the United States and Australia was also futile. As was the case for so many families of the missing, the letters to his distraught parents from the War Department contained those painfully unsatisfying words that "your son second Lieutenant Robert E Thorpe has been missing in action since twenty seven May over New Guinea." Yet there emerged glimmers of hope over the years that answers might someday be found.

A few months after the Japanese surrender, an Australian team interviewed a Japanese prisoner who told them an American pilot fitting Thorpe's description had floated ashore on Kairiru on a log, was captured by natives, and was handed over to the small Japanese garrison. The story went that he had died of malaria while in captivity. But when Australian mortuary specialists later exhumed a grave on Kairiru that they were told was Thorpe's, the remains turned out to be those of several Japanese. Not until a half century later, when JPAC began to scrutinize anew the records relating to hundreds of aircraft losses in New Guinea, did a fuller picture begin to emerge. Later testimony of Japanese officers assigned to the Twenty-Seventh Special Naval Base Force headquarters on Kairiru told another version of what happened. Records previously overlooked showed that under questioning by Americans in Tokyo in 1947, a Japanese Navy officer named Keoru Okuma who was stationed on Kairiru at the time offered startling details of an American pilot he encountered on the island:

> He was about 20 years old, 5'5" tall, slender build, medium brown long hair, brown eyes, unshaven, body and face sunburned. He wore light blue short pants—torn above the knees—probably Japanese Navy pants given to him by his captors. No hat, barefooted, naked from the waist up, no hair

on chest; not blindfolded, hands tied behind, feet not tied, no scratches or wounds that I remember.

He said he was born and lived near Boston. He said he was a first lieutenant Army Thunderbolt pilot, shot down east of Kairiru, and swam to Kairiru with a floating log. . . . The POW was first beaten after I completed my interrogation by about three noncommissioned officers with their hands and sticks about his face and buttocks. His back was bleeding somewhat. The POW just bowed forward.

Later that same afternoon, the officer recounted, the order was given for the American prisoner to be executed. He described the gruesome final moments, which he said took place in front of about thirty Japanese troops next to a coconut tree near a native cemetery where a fresh grave had already been dug:

They held him up so he could walk. The crowd was yelling but the POW was quiet. When we reached the execution spot, the POW stood beside the hole, blindfolded, hands tied behind him. [One of the other Japanese officers] said in English to the POW, "I will kill you with my pistol." Then he stood beside me and shot at the POW's left ankle, but missed both times, and said, "I'm not so good." The crowd laughed. [The Japanese officer] stepped up and then pushed the POW into a kneeling position before the hole with the head bowed and forward. The POW's lips were moving, but I heard no sound. Then he poured water from the bottle on the POW's neck and washed it, and also poured water on his heirloom samurai sword. He then beheaded the POW. When I next looked I saw the POW's body in the hole with only a part of one leg sticking out of the hole. I think I saw blood on the ground. Later I learned [another officer] had cut open the POW's corpse.

Several other Japanese officers corroborated key details of the incident. One recalled the pilot said his name was Robert. Another identified him from a photograph as the prisoner in question. A third,

JPAC historians learned from long-forgotten records, even sketched a map of where the execution took place. It pinpointed an area on the west side of a small stream running behind a Catholic mission on Kairiru that had served as the Japanese headquarters.

George now had a copy of the map, which was little more than a few pencil lines and arrows to depict a jungle path, nearby fields, and a circled X marking where the Japanese officer recounted Thorpe was executed and his body buried.

George also knew something else. Still awaiting answers back in Rhode Island was Robert Thorpe's seventy-seven-year-old brother. Gil Thorpe, whose angular face and bushy eyebrows bore a striking resemblance to those of his older brother, was thirteen when he answered the door on a late Tuesday afternoon in early June 1944 and was handed the War Department telegram reporting simply that Bobby was "missing in action" over New Guinea. Picking up where his father left off, Gil, now a retired dentist, never gave up hope that his brother might someday be buried in the family plot. He penned letters to his U.S. senator, attended family updates that JPAC held periodically in nearby Connecticut, and even teamed up with a historian friend to try to glean more information about his brother's fate from Japanese war records. His older sister, Nancy, who had recently been moved to an assisted-living facility, continued to ask Gil whether there was anything new to report about their missing brother.

No one from JPAC had ever been to Kairiru. Now George and Sergeant Jackson would make their way out in the morning. As George gazed up at the mysterious island on the map above the bar, which he located just north of a smaller one called Muschu, he tingled at the prospect that Bobby Thorpe might still get his long-overdue homecoming. He also knew it might be too late.

When JPAC first concluded that Thorpe's remains might still be buried near the Catholic mission on the island, commanders were concerned that if word leaked out the Americans were coming the grave could be disturbed. JPAC knew from firsthand reports that the inhabitants of Kairiru were particularly superstitious and the knowledge that a white man might be buried in their midst would be considered bad luck. One of the documents in the JPAC file reported "recent activity regarding the removal of body parts from graves used in sorcery practices." JPAC was told there were "lots of stories about ghosts, mass graves," tales that like virtually everywhere else in New Guinea "get expanded by each person you talk to." Any local inhabitants who helped the Americans, JPAC was also warned, might be at "real risk" of retaliation by their fellow islanders.

———

If George was looking for the archetype of New Guinea's ancient customs and cultural rites, he couldn't have come to a better place. Even by the standards of Papua New Guinea, Kairiru was shrouded in myth and legend. Black magic and evil spirits were part of everyday existence. The most common tales, passed from generation to generation in the glow of torches of dried coconut and sago leaves, spoke of devils with supernatural power that took human form and wandered in the darkness with an insatiable desire for human flesh, especially children's. In their rituals, the inhabitants of Kairiru prayed to devils known as *tambaran*, who were said to live in rocks, caves, and mountains. They prayed to *tambaran* for help fishing the surrounding waters and harvesting taros, yams, and other staples, and in times of *birua*, or war, they invoked these spirits to bestow magical powers on their spears of soft *limbum* wood.

But many devils brought only bad luck, which in the ancient culture of the people of Kairiru was synonymous with death. Like the *masalai*, who lived in rivers and seas and could change a man's mind or make him do evil things. These devils could bring destruction by rain and earthquake. They could also be more easily spotted: they were often white-skinned or had light-colored eyes.

George's only means of reaching the island was crouched in a rickety sixteen-foot banana boat with an outboard engine he had rented the day before on the Wewak waterfront—for a whopping four hundred dollars. It was far more than he had planned to spend, but the craft was the only available mode of transport.

As the officer in charge of safety, George ordered Huston and Teel, much to their consternation, to remain in Wewak while he and Sergeant Jackson went on to Kairiru. There were only two life vests, and visions of having to pull the two middle-aged men out of the waves didn't exactly appeal to him.

Now, with the early morning gleam of sunshine reflecting off the aquamarine waters of the Bismarck Sea, George, Jackson, and a local,

Anton Sakarai, the minister of culture and tourism for East Sepik Province, soon pulled around the headlands off Wewak, passing a tuna-processing plant. Spying the massive tunas jumping near the boat, George wished he had some fishing tackle. But his decision to leave Huston and Teel behind was quickly reinforced. The banana boat entered the open water and began to rock violently in five-foot seas as it chugged around the southern rim of Muschu, Kairiru's neighbor, with its idyllic black sandy beaches and thatched-roof huts framed by swaying palmettos.

Then they headed northwest in the Muschu Passage and cut through a breakwater. There the seas grew even choppier, the waves now topping eight feet.

Finally, about an hour after leaving Wewak, George sighted Kairiru in the distance. About twenty-five miles around, the tropical island resembled a brilliant green dome, with its mountainous spine running east to west and centered on the three-thousand-foot Mount Malangis. As the boat approached the southwestern shore, George eyed the four or five clapboard buildings of the St. John's Mission and the adjacent St. Xavier School cut out of the bush. On the eastern side of the grounds he could also see what remained of the Japanese airstrip. For the first time, the war had an immediacy for George. Until now he had only really experienced Port Moresby, which he knew had changed significantly in the decades since General MacArthur paced the balcony of his headquarters. But Kairiru, he thought, must have looked much the same back in 1944, when planes lifted off and landed at Ulbau Beach and Imperial Japanese Navy warships anchored up the coast in Victoria Bay, where the hulks of two Japanese ships sunk by Allied bombings still rested beneath the deep. He imagined what it must have been like to be held prisoner in this idyllic setting, knowing—as all American fliers did back then—that capture was a fate worse than a fiery death in aerial combat. George recalled a photograph in a Time-Life picture book he had seen as a kid of an American POW being beheaded by a Japanese soldier, an enduring image that encapsulated for him the barbarity of the American enemy in the Pacific theater. He would now forever associate the photograph with Robert Thorpe.

As the boat approached the shores of Kairiru, George's momentary reverie was interrupted when he spied Brother Graeme waiting for him onshore. Graeme Lynch was a Catholic missionary from Australia who had been running the St. John's Mission for more than twenty-five years. George first approached him on the beach in Wewak the day before after learning he made regular trips from Kairiru to sell chickens and eggs to raise money for the mission. Brother Graeme greeted George warmly as the boat came ashore. The mission and the nearby St. Xavier School consisted of the remnants of the Japanese naval base. The former headquarters building was now the main school building and the dilapidated barracks the student dormitories. Even the grass airstrip was now a ball field. George could quickly see that Kairiru had virtually no infrastructure, not even electricity. He asked about the island's water source and was told it came from a volcanic lake in the mountains. The living would be sparse, but George concluded that a well-supplied recovery team using generators could probably make do on the island during an extended excavation, particularly if it could house in some of the school's buildings. However, the mission would be risky without reliable air transport. If the team needed to evacuate an injured team member, it would simply take too long to get back to the mainland by boat and then arrange for air transport to a modern hospital. As he jotted details in a notebook, George noted that the remote island presented a "difficult scenario in absence of helicopter availability."

Most of all, he still needed to survey the possible grave site of the lost American airman, which he was told was a short walk across the grounds of the adjacent St. Xavier School.

"It's over there behind the bunkhouse," the headmaster told him.

———

George could picture Robert Thorpe standing over his own grave, his lips moving silently. He could almost hear the Japanese officers taunting him as dozens of Japanese sailors standing in a circle shouted and jeered at the bloodied American. As George scanned the ground around his feet, he imagined Thorpe's captors firing their pistols into the dirt around him, the crackle of gunfire feeding the frenzied atmosphere.

The St. Xavier schoolmaster and Brother Graeme had led George down a slope from the main school buildings, past the remnants of a prewar Catholic church and a well-preserved Japanese Shinto shrine. At the end of an old track road they crossed a small bridge over a stream and continued up the streambed about 130 feet. They then walked a few paces up the stream bank to a shallow, unmarked depression about six feet long. It was covered by low-cut grass and located just east of a lavatory used by the school's students. It was also a short distance from the native cemetery, located farther up the slope, where similar-looking depressions were marked with brown, green, and clear glass bottles and a mixture of colorful shells and rocks. The depression before him appeared to roughly coincide with where the records indicated Thorpe was executed and buried. Some of the locals told him that the coconut grove that had been in the vicinity during the war had been removed and a dormitory built, but otherwise the area had not been developed. The site looked very promising, George thought.

As he surveyed the terrain and took notes, he was again seized by the image of Robert Thorpe in those final moments more than six decades earlier. Stripped down to his shorts, Thorpe was kneeling now before the hole in the earth, praying silently for salvation. George was confounded by how his fellow pilot, just a kid at twenty-one years old, was so steady in the face of death, how he had so stoically met his horrific fate. Under intense questioning earlier that day, George knew, Thorpe had reportedly given his name and rank and hometown, and nothing else, as he was trained. He volunteered nothing that might help the enemy. Under similar circumstances, George felt sure many men would have broken down and begged for mercy.

"What would I have done in that situation?" he wondered to himself.

He didn't know. But he realized in that instant that no matter how many challenges he had confronted while wearing a military uniform, and despite the horrors he witnessed and the dangers he confronted in battle, it all paled in comparison to what so many others before him had faced. As the final moments of Robert Thorpe's life played across his consciousness like an old grainy film, George felt embarrassed. He hadn't had it that rough at all.

What he heard next, though, was like a punch to the stomach.

"There is a lot of black magic here," the headmaster told him. "The schoolboys removed the bones."

———

Back on the mainland, the wreckage of the U.S. Navy dive-bomber, resting in two heaps on the edge of a steep slope partially covered in thick foliage, had been nearly impossible to locate. George and Sergeant Jackson, along with a local landowner, had set out to find it hours earlier from the remote village of Saunam.

The crash site had been reported to JPAC the previous year after an elderly local man cutting down a tree found a piece of iron sticking out of the ground. Amid the wreckage were found a dog tag, a shoe, canteens, and some human remains. A review of the war records strongly suggested it was the SBD Dauntless flown by Navy Lieutenant Francis McIntyre of Mitchell, South Dakota, and his gunner, the aviation radioman second class William L. Russell, of Cherokee, Oklahoma. They were reported missing on November 10, 1943, after a strafing mission of a nearby Japanese airfield.

The villagers in Saunam were Seventh-Day Adventists, led by a former officer in the PNG Defense Force. They insisted it was only a short hike to the crash site. But as George knew all too well by now, the time it might take a local to hump the distance was usually a fraction of what it required for an outsider unfamiliar with the terrain. He had to ford a winding river seven times, wading for several long stretches in waist-deep water because the ravine walls on either side were so steep. The wreckage itself was more than three hundred feet up a sharp incline.

"The difficulty of the terrain will require that the team fix rope guides to assist in traversing the area," George recorded after assessing the area for a possible recovery operation. "The steepness of the terrain will challenge the team and could make excavation operations precarious during inclement weather."

It was also clear to George that a recovery team would need a helicopter to operate at the site, something that was exceedingly difficult to guarantee for a reasonable price. Otherwise, they would have to carry anyone injured back to the village of Saunam on a litter and then drive the person by 4x4 to Wewak, a process that could take up to three hours.

When George got back to the village later in the day, something else gave him serious pause about recommending the site for the upcoming recovery efforts. The young men of the village were gathered together, spears in hand. When he asked what was going on, he was informed they were preparing to march off to a neighboring village to settle some scores.

———

George and the others huddled together back at the Crowne Plaza in Port Moresby to review the bidding. Their plans to launch multiple recoveries out of the Wewak area were quickly falling apart. They had run into a series of obstacles. First, as George was learning with each passing hour, all the planning back at JPAC for an undertaking such as this only went so far. At the hotels and guesthouses he visited in and around Wewak—if you could even call them that—George was offered lodging for the JPAC teams at outrageous prices. As soon as the proprietors knew who he was, they sought to fleece the Americans for all they could get. One asking price was actually three million dollars. The outlook temporarily brightened when George secured permission to set up a base of operations for multiple teams at a PNG Defense Force outpost on Cape Moem east of Wewak. But bigger issues arose. The two sites they had surveyed so far were both problematic for full recovery operations. On Kairiru there was now more conflicting information on where Thorpe's remains might be. Claims by some of the natives that the grave had been exhumed and the bones reburied in the native cemetery would require a more intensive search on the island. This made the case, much to George's disappointment, less promising than it had seemed to be. Meanwhile, the crash site believed to be where McIntyre and Russell were lost posed its own logistical problems. It would require helicopter support and setting up a base camp at the crash site for the duration of the recovery. On top of that, they weren't developing enough other promising MIA leads around Wewak to justify bringing full teams to the region. For an organization operating on a shoestring budget like JPAC, the more locations that could be excavated during a deployment, the better. George needed to convince his superiors back in Building 45 that every dollar spent trying to bring home MIAs—and every soldier enlisted in the effort—was being maximized to the fullest extent possible. He just wasn't there yet.

The numerous crash sites on his list that were farther south in the highlands also proved elusive. Passing through Lae, where the local officials had still not responded to their advance requests for assistance, what they were hearing from the embassy was only more discouraging. There was too much lawlessness and political strife, too many recent reports of roving bands, to bring in a large number of American troops for an extended period of time—especially with provincial leaders so unwilling to provide security. At minimum, he reported back to JPAC, a small investigation team could operate in Lae and in Madang in the highlands developing the leads for future recoveries. But George was running out of time to lay the groundwork for the large recovery teams that were set to deploy in a few short months.

Their best bet, they all agreed, was now New Britain Island, where they had relatively solid information on nearly a dozen possible crash locations, several of them in relative proximity to each other in the thick jungle blanketing the northern tip of the island.

But the still-active volcano they had been warned about when they arrived in Port Moresby was in a decidedly sour mood, choking the skies with thick clouds of ash and shutting down air traffic. On January 26, after a tedious delay, George and the survey team finally got a flight to New Britain. The two-hour journey, in an aging jet operated for New Guinea's national airline, took them out over the Coral Sea, the scene of an early naval battle between the U.S. and Japanese Navies and where the USS *Lexington* had been scuttled after sustaining heavy bombardment in May 1942. The aircraft turned northeast and traversed the majestic Owen Stanley Mountains, where many American GIs, mostly from the Michigan and Wisconsin National Guard, had met their doom later that same year and countless airmen had disappeared. Once they were over the Solomon Sea, the aircraft soon began descending toward the rugged, crescent-shaped jungle island of New Britain.

New Britain, known by the Germans who once controlled it as New Pommern, or New Pomerania, was the largest island in the group known as the Bismarck Archipelago, which stretched eastward from the Bismarck Sea on the northeast coast of New Guinea about five hundred miles to the island of Bougainville in the Solomon Islands. Covered in rain forest and dotted with volcanic peaks reaching as high as 6,000 feet, the island is 370 miles east to west and at its widest point about 60 miles across. It is blanketed with trees up to 150 feet high that form a canopy over a second layer up to 30 feet high, and tangled clumps of bamboo and palms sprouting from thick undergrowth. There are numerous rivers and streams running out of the mountains, and where the island isn't covered in forested swamps, the earth is made up of a thick reddish-brown soil that turns to mud in the frequent torrential rains. Cross-country movement is extremely difficult. Meanwhile, the native population, mostly a mix of Melanesian and Polynesian blood, are still largely governed by tribal allegiance, not central authority. Even though the modern world has reached most areas, there are lingering reports of isolated cannibalism and head-hunting in the island's interior.

JPAC's interest lay mostly on the northeast end of the island, where scores of fighter pilots and bomber crewmen had been lost in the siege of Rabaul from 1942 to 1945. That was where George's hopes of bringing home some of his lost comrades were now pinned. Their immediate destination was Tokua Airfield near the town of Kokopo, which had replaced Rabaul as the region's commercial center after the volcano erupted in 1994. Flying in from the east over St. George's Channel, making landfall just south of Cape Gazelle, the aircraft approached a small airstrip cut out of the jungle near the shores of Blanche Bay. As it descended over the bright green carpet of the coastal plain below, up ahead, just visible from the right side of the aircraft, was a striking view of the hook-shaped caldera enclosing Simpson Harbor—and at its tip the belching Mount Tavurvur.

———

George spit out the pinch of chewing tobacco. He pulled his lucky camouflage cap, the tattered one with the Florida State University logo, low over his forehead. He climbed up the steep slope, peering through the dust. The landscape was a pallid charcoal gray, utterly barren save for the tops of a few palm trees poking through the surface. He halted on top of one of the mounds of ash and looked out at the geography around him.

The bleakness of his immediate surroundings contrasted sharply with the vista beyond. The blue waters of Simpson Harbor sparkled in the distance, enclosed on three sides by a fishhook-shaped caldera of jagged mountains and triple-canopy jungle, which blinked brilliantly green in the equatorial sun. George, who was perched near the tip of the fishhook, glanced south to the opposite shore and a trio of mountains that formed the spine of the Gazelle Peninsula, a vista covered in bamboo forests and large-leaved mango trees. The scene was at once more beautiful and more forbidding than any he had ever seen—and he had seen his fair share these last few years.

It was an unusual duty post for a thirty-four-year-old U.S. Army officer. Nor did George look the part. Instead of a uniform, he wore a pair of well-worn jungle khakis and a light cloth shirt unbuttoned at the collar. Rather than the sands of the Middle East, his hiking boots were caked in dried reddish-brown mud from trekking through the rain forest. He had a couple of days' worth of stubble on his ruddy square-set jaw and a few extra pounds on his stout five-foot-seven-inch frame. His standard military crew cut had been replaced by the strands of dirty-blond hair poking out from under his cap, and he was unarmed, save for his machete, the gift from the village chief in Laos.

Now, as he gazed out over Simpson Harbor, for the first time he fully grasped what had taken place here. On the shoreline below, partially obscured by the billowing peaks and valleys of volcanic ash, were the outlines of a vast concrete bunker, where a rusted anti-aircraft gun was still perched outside the entrance. Inside the warren of damp, subterranean rooms had been the headquarters of Admiral Isoroku Yamamoto, which George had toured after paying a few kina to the locals. The skies above him had been the scene of one of the most bitterly fought air campaigns of the war. Though the guns had been silent now for more than sixty years, George could still see the evidence of the colossal clash that took place here. Rusted Japanese vessels still sat in their cave berths around the harbor. Crumpled fighter planes lay amid the coral just off the beach. Even the remains of Japanese soldiers were left undisturbed in the twelve miles of caves that snaked deep into some of the surrounding ridges. On the very ground where he now stood had been the Lakunai Airdrome, one of the Japanese's largest fighter bases. This was Rabaul, the place that had "terrified a million Allied fighting men."

It had been all but forgotten by the outside world, eclipsed by more famous battles with names like Iwo Jima and Guadalcanal or the Battle of the Bulge and Stalingrad. But not by the small military unit that George was a part of. Hidden in the swamps and bogs or covered in thick scrub growth were clues to what happened to hundreds of pilots and crewmen. Their crash sites, buried beneath the vines, creepers, brush, and razor-sharp kunai grass, beckoned for someone to unlock the mysteries of their ultimate fates—and at long last try to bring them home.

George's main focus would be several crash sites relatively close to each other. One case, designated simply "Bureau Number 02402," was particularly intriguing. It contained the GPS coordinates of a remote village called Vunakaur about twenty miles south down the peninsula along the Tomukavar River. That was where the wreckage of a Marine Corps fighter plane had been located, its charred fuselage rusted and weather-beaten, with its serial number only partially visible. Bones and other evidence had been recovered in the vicinity, but whom they belonged to remained a puzzle. George and his team had one last chance to try to complete it.

———

Like so many cases George had studied, Bureau Number 02402 was a stubborn one. But he also knew that just as obstinate were the men and women—generations of them, really—who never gave up on solving it.

Four years after the war, the search for the pilot who JPAC suggested had been lost in the crash had effectively been deemed a wild-goose chase.

"The remains of the subject named decedent have been declared non-recoverable by Special Boards convened in the field and in the Office of The Quartermaster General," the Department of the Army, which ran the Graves Registration Service, concluded in November 1949.

It might have been forgotten altogether if it had not been for a timber salesman and World War II aficionado from New Zealand named Brian Bennett, who was working in Rabaul in the fall of 1981. Bennett, a slight man who by the time George arrived on New Guinea had a shock of gray hair, had identified dozens of lost U.S. warplanes in New Guinea during his travels across the islands and painstakingly recorded all the details of the wreckages and passed them on to the Central Identification Laboratory. For a time he was a paid consultant for JPAC.

Bennett wrote a letter to the U.S. Navy at the time reporting the wreckage of a Corsair on New Britain near a village that was then known as Viveren, where he recovered a small piece of aircraft stamped with the partial serial number 2402. In response the Navy told him that a review of war records indicated that the aircraft was last assigned to the Marine Corps captain Nathaniel Ruggles Landon Jr. of New York City, a member of Marine Fighter Squadron 211, who was reported missing over Rabaul on January 20, 1944.

Seven years later, in March 1988, a small team from the Central Identification Laboratory visited the crash site for the first time. They found no additional identifying materials and only a partial data plate from the rusted and fire-damaged Pratt & Whitney engine. Interviews with locals at the time also suggested that the body of the pilot might have been removed years before.

"No evidence of remains could be found," the U.S. team that visited the crash site in 1988 concluded.

The U.S. military still hadn't given up hope. Three years later, over a few days in May and June 1991, another U.S. team searching for lost planes on New Britain Island visited the wreckage again, finding that it had been "thoroughly picked over" and reporting that the cockpit area had been "consumed by fire." It also appeared that parts of the wreckage had been moved to make way for local crops.

Then they found a new glimmer of hope. A single bone was pulled from the crash site that was later identified by the Central Identification Laboratory as part of a left humerus, or upper arm, but it could not be matched to an ID. What they found next, after digging underneath a part of the remaining fuselage, forced authorities back in Hawaii to reevaluate their earlier conclusions about who had been piloting it. It was a dog tag. But it was not stamped with "Nathaniel Ruggles Landon," who the records indicated was assigned the plane. There was another name etched into the metal ID plate: "Marion Ryan McCown Jr."

But when JPAC checked the records for a crash report involving anyone by the name of McCown, it only found a one-page typewritten form dated January 15, 1944, that stated: "Pilot made water landing 47 mi. from Torokina" in the Solomon Islands. "Was later picked up by PT boat." On the line on the form next to "injuries" was typed one word: "Safe." For all they knew, McCown could be retired and living in his native South Carolina. It was not uncommon to discover identification tags left behind in the cockpit by previous occupants. Other records, meanwhile, indicated McCown was assigned a Corsair with a different tail number, 17448, while secondary sources suggested McCown might have been held prisoner and executed by the Japanese.

Nonetheless, the likelihood of finding more remains at the crash site was deemed remote. "Plane # not definite, but no further work needed at site," the archaeologist who was part of the 1991 team recommended. He concluded that with the command's limited resources there were simply too many other cases that had better prospects. "If any human remains had been close to the surface or associated with the removed metal, then those remains probably would have been moved. Dogs and pigs would have also disturbed the human remains. The possibility of there being additional recoverable remains at the site is remote. No further work is recommended for this site now or in the future."

———

Then a new break came in 2003, when JPAC's chief historian, Christopher McDermott, was forwarded an e-mail from an Australian helicopter pilot reporting that he had found a fire-damaged dog tag next to a Corsair near Rabaul stamped with the name "Marion Ryan McConn Jr."

McDermott, a slight, soft-spoken man with short brown hair and spectacles, was a World War II historian by training, and so was his wife, who also worked for JPAC. With his near-photographic memory, McDermott spent countless hours poring over piles of old records typed on onionskin to find new leads and uncover additional information that might revive some of JPAC's cold cases.

A few days after receiving the e-mail about the recovered dog tag, McDermott wrote back to the Australian pilot saying there was no record of a World War II pilot with that spelling but asked for more details about the location of the wreckage. A week later, the Australian helicopter pilot responded that he had been mistaken. After cleaning the damaged dog tag, he discovered the correct surname. It was McCown. Not McConn.

Still, the name meant nothing to McDermott. He did a cursory search and reported back two days later that data "suggests that he may have been a POW in Rabaul, but not returned following the war." In the meantime, McDermott contacted the National Archives in College Park, Maryland, to request a copy of McCown's Individual Deceased Personnel File, or IDPF. For JPAC's history section, the IDPF had come to be "the best primary source document for casualties." While all members of the military had a personnel file, those killed in combat or declared dead after being missing for years generated an IDPF, which could include reports associated with their loss; information on what steps had been taken at the time to search for them; whether they had been taken prisoner; any correspondence between the government and their next of kin; or anything else the bureaucracy generated over the years related to their case.

The National Archives responded to McDermott's request for a copy of the file by reporting that it couldn't find it. JPAC would ultimately request a copy three times, only to be told the same answer. The case was put aside again.

―――

"How do we get momentum in this case?"

It was a question that McDermott was asking often in the summer of 2005 as he reviewed a number of stalled MIA cases in New Guinea that once seemed promising. He knew that DNA analysis was now far more advanced than it had been in the 1990s when the bone found at the crash site was first tested—without results—for genetic code. He also knew that JPAC's field methods were much more rigorous and precise than they had been back in 1991, when the archaeologist concluded nothing else could be found.

He decided it was time to resample the piece of the left humerus stored in the lab since the visit to the crash site fourteen years earlier. But once again, the report came back "inconclusive." What the case needed, McDermott concluded, was new information that helped confirm who actually died in the crash. Then they might have justification to go back and look for more remains that might have a better chance of being identified.

McDermott and his staff began looking for any additional records that might shed more light on the case. "We may, if we did some historical type research, try to figure this puzzle out," he wrote in July

2005 to one of the other historians, "but it is a big problem with at least 73 F4U-1s recorded as lost over Rabaul."

He set aside for the moment the indications that McCown was flying another plane—the one that crashed on January 15, 1944, when he was rescued at sea. He studied records from his unit, VMF-321. On a trip to the National Archives facility in College Park, JPAC staff pulled all the combat reports from the Hell's Angels. They learned that McCown was reported missing on January 20, along with two other Corsair pilots in the squadron. The records also reported that one of them, Roger Brindos, was killed in the POW camp at Rabaul and his remains were buried after the war in the U.S. military cemetery in the Philippines. The other pilot, Robert Marshall, was still MIA.

McDermott was finally beginning to see how this case might still get another chance. The fact that McCown and the pilot they originally thought was flying the plane—Lieutenant Landon of New York City—were lost the same day might have started the confusion years ago. He also learned that the bone and the McCown dog tag recovered in 1991 were stored in different places, possibly explaining why more research wasn't done earlier. Based on what they had learned, it also seemed likely that both dog tags—the one recovered in 1991 and the one found by the Australian helicopter pilot in 2003—came from the same crash site on New Britain Island. Two dog tags would be more than mere coincidence. McDermott was now almost sure Marion Ryan McCown Jr. was lost in that crash and part of his humerus was sitting in the lab. The only way they could be certain would be to go back to the crash site in the hopes of finding more remains.

————

George gripped the steering wheel, and his eyes darted at the daunting scenery around him. He was heading south along a rough mixture of asphalt and thick mud, with Sergeant Jackson and their escort from the National Museum in tow, a Mr. Polum. The white Toyota 4x4 steadily climbed into the mountains. The thick rain clouds hanging low in the sky grew closer as the vehicle wound hundreds of feet up into the jungle. George noticed that on both sides of the narrow trail the terrain dropped into the jungle abyss below. He made a mental note to fully brief his team leaders on the safety concerns. The slippery surface had no guardrails, making the journey painstakingly slow and nerve-racking. The route became particularly treacherous as it passed a small village perched on top of a mountain. There was little room to maneuver safely past without driving off the road and plunging into the rain forest below.

After about half an hour the trail began descending steeply again. To pinpoint their location, George consulted his Global Positioning System, a Garmin 60CS receiving signals from six satellites. The spot they were searching for on the Military Grid Reference System, the geo-coordinate standard used by the United States and its NATO allies, was supposed to be in the village of Vunakaur, in the Gazelle district of East New Britain Province. Like any good Army Ranger, George also studied his map of New Britain, a 1976 edition plotted by the Royal Australian Survey Corps, the most recent that JPAC could find.

He felt that they were getting close just as he looked up and spotted a group of barefoot children carrying machetes darting in and out of the thick banana trees beside the road. It seemed everyone in this country carried a machete, he thought—even just to go for a short walk through the bush. But George was growing a bit nervous for another reason. They were now in a pretty remote area, and he was concerned about just walking onto someone's land unannounced. He knew that trespassing could be a severe violation of tribal rights. If he wasn't careful, he might make enemies of the very locals whose help would be critical to a successful recovery operation.

Off to his left he made out the outlines of a few structures set back in the forest. George pulled the white Toyota into a small clearing beside the washed-out track and slowly came to a stop. He checked the GPS again. This had to be it. They were just a few hundred feet off from the coordinates of the crash site, last recorded by a JPAC investigation team in 2006: 56M MA 05313 09248.

The village of Vunakaur could barely even be classified as such. Situated about three hundred feet above sea level in a thicket of pungent banana and papaya trees, it was a collection of about half a dozen thatched-roof huts built on stilts around mud-packed courtyards and surrounded by small, neatly manicured hedges and vegetable gardens and strung with clotheslines. It looked more primitive than impoverished. The village, also referred to as Viveren in some JPAC records, was actually the homestead of the Wartovo clan. At the entrance was a small outdoor Christian shrine fashioned out of old World War II bomb casings etched with Japanese characters. The missionaries had apparently reached here too, George thought.

Moments after the three men stepped out and walked toward the village, a middle-aged woman in a bright-colored native dress appeared, eyeing them warily. In pidgin English sprinkled with a few phrases in the local dialect, Mr. Polum greeted her and said that his two companions—George and Sergeant Jackson—were members of the same American organization that had visited the village some years earlier to search for a plane that had crashed during the war. They were hoping to speak to Mr. Enis Wartovo, he told her.

"*Poppa me*," the woman responded with a look of recognition. He was her father.

She led them a short distance into the heart of the village, where chickens roamed between the thatched native dwellings, and fetched the old man while they waited.

Enis Wartovo soon emerged from one of the huts clutching a walking stick. Scrawny and hunched over, he appeared to be well into his eighties—no one, including himself, knew his exact age. His sparse teeth and lips were covered in the bright red of the betel nut, the locally grown narcotic chewed by man and child alike. He had rough, leathery skin, a tuft of gray hair, and wide expressive eyes. One of his seven sons was now the landowner, they learned, but Enis was still the patriarch of the Wartovo clan, and his permission would be needed for JPAC to dig in their village.

Wartovo greeted them warmly and told them he remembered when the Americans visited the village in the years before. George instructed Mr. Polum to ask him if he could bring a large team of Americans to the village from April 1 to May 15 to dig around the plane. George assured him they would be compensated for any damage. He also inquired of the man how much local labor might be available to help the recovery team.

The old man told George that the clan would help them in any way they could and would provide up to several dozen laborers, men and women, to work for them. Wartovo had only one request: that the Americans erect some type of marker to inform future visitors about what happened here during the war. Apparently, over the years a fair share of wreck hunters and World War II aficionados had come looking for war relics, and the attraction of a crumpled American warplane had been a minor source of income for the village as a tourist site of sorts.

George could see that the patriarch, whose elderly wife, Siel, soon joined them, understood why the Americans kept coming back here—and why George and the others were here now.

"It is like what we do," Wartovo said in a low whisper. "We do our best to bring them home and bury them in our cemetery."

Wartovo knew firsthand the scale of the losses that the Americans had suffered during the war. As a young man, he had been a forced laborer for the Japanese troops after they invaded the island, helping them scavenge for food to feed the soldiers and sailors who were living in the caves near Rabaul. He recalled one incident where an American plane had crashed and he and his friends removed the dead bodies and buried them. George made a note to ask more about that incident later.

When the Japanese invaders were finally defeated, Wartovo recounted, he first thought that the Americans who soon arrived on New Britain were Germans, the white people the natives had the most interaction with in the early twentieth century. Many of the Americans then were searching for lost pilots, he said. George knew he must have been referring to the teams from the Graves Registration Service who scoured the region in the immediate aftermath of the fighting.

Then Wartovo's daughter took them to the plane. Hacking his way through the thick jungle foliage and vines, George finally came to the edge of a steep slope overlooking a small floodplain and a muddy stream, where stands of giant bamboo lined the water's edge. Off to his left, nestled near where the locals cultivated banana, cocoa, papaya, pumpkin, and taro plants, lay the tail section and several other large pieces of wreckage, rusted and faded but still the telltale blue of a Corsair. George swiftly made his way to where the large pieces of wreckage lay. He glanced around, trying to imagine what might have happened in the final moments before the Corsair came to rest here. The aircraft probably ripped through the tops of the broad-leafed trees, shearing off the wings, before the cockpit section shot like a comet through the layers of vines and dense vegetation and gouged into the hillside in a fireball.

———

Three months later, in April 2008, George's temporary headquarters—in JPAC lingo the "command and control cell"—was room 303 of the Kokopo Beach Resort, a collection of wooden bungalows on the shores of Blanche Bay that were usually rented to traveling merchants and the steadily rising number of adventure tourists who came to dive for sunken ships and aircraft wrecks or scour the rugged peninsula for other war relics. By New Guinea standards, the accommodations were about as good as it gets. The sleeping areas, lined with three simple beds, were clean if spare and even had their own toilets and primitive showers. The electricity was decently reliable, and some rooms even had air-conditioning in the form of battered but workable window units. There was no hot water, but the lodgings were still light-years ahead of what many assigned to JPAC had experienced on other recovery missions, where jungle camps were common.

On his survey trip in January, George worked out a deal with the middle-aged proprietor, a generous spirit who went simply by Dougie, who for a reasonable price agreed to provision George and his soldiers with staples like eggs and meat in the mornings and chicken and rice and fried potatoes following their long days in the jungle. Dougie assured George that there would also be plenty of South Pacific beer for purchase in the enclosed picnic area at the back of the main lodging building, where he could huddle each evening with his personnel. There was even dial-up Internet for them to check e-mail or surf the Web, though that proved to be almost totally unreliable. One drawback that was no fault of Dougie's was the coughing fits and constant sinus irritation suffered by virtually everyone on the mission. There was simply no avoiding the film of volcanic ash that settled each day on the ground, on their vehicles, in the eaves, and on virtually every other outdoor surface from the belching volcano standing sentry across the bay.

George spent most of his days—and often much of the evenings—crisscrossing the peninsula in the Toyota 4x4 to meet with local officials and police, secure additional supplies, and monitor the progress of the two recovery teams that would be heading out each morning to the pair of Corsair crash sites. As the officer in charge, he was also responsible for coordinating the activities of a small JPAC investigation team operating in the highlands of Madang Province on the mainland in search of new leads. For the few precious hours he could relax, George brought along an Xbox video game console and some of his favorite DVDs to watch on his laptop, including the *Band of Brothers* series and *The Big Lebowski.*

On Saturday morning, April 5, already hot and sticky before the sunlight reflected off the Solomon Sea on the eastern horizon, George led a small team from Kokopo to the Wartovo homestead in the village of Vunakaur for a "leaders' recon" of the first recovery site. When they arrived around 8:00 a.m., they followed Enis Wartovo's eldest son, Walia, through the foliage on the edge of the village to the crash site, where more than twenty local kids were scattered around eagerly awaiting their arrival.

George turned to his soldiers and the team anthropologist and signaled for them to get to work. The recovery team leader designated for Bureau Number 02402 was the thirty-year-old Marine Corps captain Bo Bergstrom, a tall and lanky combat veteran from Sheridan, Wyoming, with a wide grin. Bergstrom considered his JPAC tour a once-in-a-career assignment, almost too good to be true, and was eager to begin preparing the area for the excavation.

But George knew that the man most likely to determine if this cold case would be solved was Dr. Owen Luck O'Leary, the tall and sinewy twenty-nine-year-old anthropologist from Bozeman, Montana, with a shaggy beard, who was the team's forensic anthropologist.

Drenched in sweat, with his baseball cap permanently flipped backward, the energetic O'Leary often spoke in the vernacular of one of his other pastimes: surfing. Like when he was describing what it felt like to successfully close an MIA case as being "stoked." But when he was overseeing an excavation or working in the lab, O'Leary was singularly focused on the task at hand. He was keenly aware that the bits of bone and enamel that he had gingerly held in his gloved hands likely belonged to young men like himself—he often didn't even know their names—who gave their lives for their country. He saw it as his special duty, often as the sole civilian on the recovery team, to conduct himself in the field with the utmost professionalism. This was his fourth mission in fifteen months, including to Vietnam, Laos, and now PNG.

George and the advance team got to work recording the details of their surroundings. The remnants of the cockpit and engine and the rusted shell of the tail section rested on the upper portion of the hill, near a large pile of propellers and other aircraft wreckage. All around the area grew cocoa, taro, pumpkin, and papaya plants. Small vines covered the jungle floor, and a thick canopy of banana and mango trees shaded part of the area. Down the slope, on the floodplain leading to the small muddy river, lay part of a wing, probably strewn there by salvagers, they surmised.

They recorded the key features of the topography, as every detail would have to be considered to ensure the safety of the team. There was a steep drop just a few steps away from the main aircraft wreckage, and the sloping terrain covering much of the area would likely become very slick during what they expected to be almost daily periods of tropical downpours. To reduce the potential hazards and ensure a steady pace of work, they decided the team would have to cut some makeshift stairs into the earth and lay sandbags in key places. O'Leary also noted the presence of "poisonous spiders and centipedes."

To the northwest of the wreckage were a series of small terraces cut into the hillside leading to a flat area at least thirty feet across that the Wartovo son told them was a ceremonial space for members of the local Togogomac clan. The team carefully sectioned the area off with engineer's tape to make sure it wasn't disturbed. The entire area where they would be digging had clearly been picked over by both man and beast since the Wartovo family first arrived there in the mid-1960s. The mud-packed trail that ran from the small village down to the river cut directly through the middle of the debris field. They were also told, to their dismay, that the tail section and the large portion of one of the wings at the bottom of the hill had been moved over the years. There were other disturbances that might affect their ability to find evidence of the pilot. The logging of large trees in the area had taken place periodically, villagers said, and every few years the river flooded its banks. The good news was that a large tree was growing right through the middle of the engine, a sign that it probably hadn't been moved in decades, if ever. It was the surest indication that they should begin digging there. O'Leary decided they would fasten the engine to some nearby trees so they could safely excavate beneath it.

Dr. O'Leary, trowel in hand, knelt down to take soil samples. The earth ranged from dark brown silt-like clay, which was moist and loose, to a yellowish-brown and light olive-brown loam that he described as "structureless." He also found bits of metal and other "incident-related" materials. After a few shovel tests he concluded the sediment was suitable for dry screening. But due to the frequency of rain in the area, he told the others he was tentatively planning to use the nearby river as a water source for wet screening—the dirt was likely to turn to muck anyway. In order to avoid sediment runoff downstream to the next village, they would have to dig a settling pond to dump all the earth after they screened it for evidence.

George again played the role of diplomat, ensuring that the Wartovo clan was in agreement with their plans. The local workers would be paid fifteen kina, or about five dollars a day, he confirmed, to be doled out individually in cash once a week. At the conclusion of the excavation he would negotiate compensation for any damage to the village's crops or trees or other property. He also ordered the team's medic to set up a temporary medical clinic for the surrounding villages to ensure goodwill.

———

On April 6, with the help of some local laborers, George oversaw the off-loading of an Air Force C-130 packed with the final delivery of field equipment. He now had the shovels, hoes, picks, buckets, ropes, tarps, hoses, chain saws, lumber, bottled water, medical supplies, and various other items large and small that he had anticipated the teams would need, drawn from a warehouse that JPAC rented near the docks in Port Moresby.

"All teams are now prepared to transition to steady state operations," he reported to JPAC headquarters.

That same morning, O'Leary, an explosive-ordnance-disposal specialist, a life-support investigator, a medic, and several others arrived at the Wartovo homestead at 8:00 to begin identifying the size of the debris field around the wreck. Using metal detectors, they almost immediately located what appeared to be .50-caliber rounds of ammunition along with what O'Leary knew immediately was crucial confirmation that the pilot came down with the aircraft: projectiles from a .45-caliber pistol, just what Corsair pilots carried with them into battle.

More pieces of wreckage, large and small, and other potential evidence from the crash appeared to extend from the upper section down the slope and almost out to the lip of the river—including material lying on the ground as well as some that had apparently settled beneath the surface over the years. Because the wreckage was believed to be that of a fighter plane rather than a bomber, there was no sign of large unexploded bombs, nor did they expect any. The only ordnance they were finding were lots of .50-caliber rounds. There was also evidence of oxidized aluminum, the result of the oxygen eating away at the aircraft metal, which after so many decades appeared as a bluish-white dust. It slowed things down a bit because it caused the metal detectors to go off in areas that didn't necessarily contain actual wreckage, just remnants of the tainted soil from years of rain and flooding. Within a few hours, however, O'Leary determined the edges of the crash site using a standard of 12 feet without any metal "hits"—a total area about 140 by 125 feet.

The rest of the team designated for the recovery site arrived at 10:15 a.m. after collecting their gear from a warehouse in Kokopo where George had arranged for it to be stored—just in time for a nearly three-hour downpour that turned the entire area into a mud bog.

When the weather finally cleared, leaving in its wake a thick, steamy mist and ankle-deep mud, the team began clearing the debris field of all low-lying vegetation, leaving the banana and taro trees standing. They also cleared an area along the riverbank to construct the screening station and set out to fashion a set of stairs with sandbags running down from the village to help ensure operations wouldn't grind to a complete halt each time the heavens opened up, and to prevent injuries. They also dug a hole for a latrine that they shielded with tarps, including a long piece of bamboo sticking out of the ground where the men could urinate. They cut logs and strung together some bamboo for a covered break area with stout and thick logs placed upright as stools, as well as a makeshift rack to hang their backpacks. For the next several days, relying on the help of between twenty and twenty-five local workers, the team battled the moisture and the muck to complete the site preparations. On April 7, they had to quit at noon because "the rain had made the site very unsafe and the scientific integrity was compromised," O'Leary recorded in pencil in his field notebook. The team's engineer decided to dig artificial gullies to help deal with the runoff. Captain Bergstrom, the recovery team leader, also got the go-ahead from George to begin arriving an hour earlier each morning to get a head start before the daily downpours.

Finally, by the end of the fourth day, everything was mostly in place. Using ropes fastened to stakes in the ground, they sectioned off the debris field into forty-seven grids, each roughly twelve feet square. The area was treated like a crime scene, where every person's movements were closely tracked and recorded. With the help of some team members standing at the four corners of each grid holding a prism, O'Leary used laser survey equipment to create a digital map of the recovery scene.

They also completed the screening station, which was fed from the river by seventy-five feet of garden hose leading to smaller black rubber hoses dangling over the sifting screens. A tarp-lined trough running beneath the screens would carry the brackish water to a nearby drainage pit. A zip line running down the slope from the main wreckage was erected to efficiently deliver buckets of earth to the screening stations. The team also practiced its evacuation drill by simulating carrying a wounded person on a stretcher up the steep slope to the village to be transported off the island in an emergency.

O'Leary was happy to report that they would open the first grid on April 9—and from there "follow the evidence."

———

"A wreck a day" was how George came to describe New Guinea, where it seemed nearly every outing by JPAC personnel turned up a new potential lead. He barely had to step out of his bungalow in Kokopo for the leads to find him.

One night a local man named David Atomo showed up at the lodge with what he said were the remains of an American pilot and a basketful of rusted and mangled aircraft parts that came from an American plane that crashed during the war in the village of Makurapau. George and some of the others more familiar with World War II aircraft inspected the gear. One piece looked like the remnants of an electrical motor, stamped with "Dynamotor DM-28C - Signal Corps US Army - RCA Manufacturing Co. Inc. Camden, N.J." Another, which resembled an aircraft magneto like those used during the war, was stamped with "American Bosch Corp. Springfield, Mass." It also had the date of manufacture and a serial number. The potential human remains were placed in an evidence bag and carefully labeled.

They weren't sure what to make of all this. Mr. Atomo, dressed in western attire of pants and a T-shirt and apparently in his thirties, could simply be seeking to make a buck from the endless scraps of metal and chunks of lead—American, Japanese, and Australian—that littered the island but were not necessarily tied to an MIA case. Or his information could be a new piece of the puzzle. George peppered him with questions. Atomo stated he knew of eight crash sites in the Kokopo and Rabaul area. George jotted down some notes and logged on to his laptop. He pulled up a list of known crash sites in the area to try to cross-reference the information with previously investigated ones. No matches were apparent. George pointed to the basket of aircraft parts and asked if the man knew how many engines the plane had. Two, he was told. A quick search of his database confirmed that at least twenty two-engine planes had been reported missing in the general area during the war. George decided he would try to visit all the sites in the coming days with Atomo as his guide.

Another site reported by a local, near the village of Karu, was especially intriguing. It was said to involve a plane that crashed about 160 feet offshore in a lagoon sixty feet deep. The aircraft could supposedly be seen below the surface at low tide. The locals said they were told that most of the crew were killed in the incident and buried beneath some coconut trees just off the beach. One survived, or so the story went. But when George arrived in the village, he heard conflicting tales of the circumstances. One person said that one of the pilots swam to shore and was captured by the Japanese; another that the pilot never got out of the aircraft. All the information "was oral history passed down from parents, relatives, or community members," George wrote in his daily report on April 18. "Locals stated that they thought there was no one left alive in the area that would have firsthand knowledge of the event."

He received more promising news from the investigation team working on the New Guinea mainland. They requested that he contact the history office at JPAC headquarters and ask them to search the records for a .50-caliber machine gun with the serial number 10873805, which had been turned over by a village chief. Locals said the story passed down from elders was that it came from a burning aircraft that circled twice during the war before crashing into a tree. No parachutes had been seen, they said. The investigation team also found a section of a fuselage, believed to be that of an Army Air Corps P-47 Thunderbolt, that possibly had the last two ID numbers of either 05 or 09. They also found two wrecks that appeared to be Army P-38s. One had an engine block printed with the number 42903, along with "SER3853" and a "sideways eight stamp." The other appeared to contain the tail number 2667x9—the x for where a hole in the tail section had blown away the second-to-last digit.

———

Just after 8:00 a.m. on April 9, under sunny skies, Dr. O'Leary gave the go-ahead to open up the first grid, designated 516N 504E, adjacent to the engine with the tree growing through it. The team began swiftly but methodically digging up the earth, shoveling it into plastic buckets and then sending them down the zip line, where they were carefully set aside to be screened by pairs of American and local workers. Thirty-five local workers were on hand to complement the team of a dozen Americans, which made sure each bucket was hosed out above the screens to ensure as little soil was missed as possible before it was passed by a bucket line back up the slope to the main crash site.

O'Leary's instructions for the screeners were simple and direct: "Anything in the screen that is not naturally of the forest will be pulled out—metal, plastic, glass, bone, teeth—including a candy wrapper from yesterday or a cigarette butt."

The process was repeated like a well-oiled production line. Before long, the entire area was a hive of activity. Buckets, filled little more than halfway to avoid spillage, whooshed down the rope line. They were off-loaded and carefully passed to the screeners and dumped onto the screens. The soil, drenched by the black rubber hoses dangling above each wood-framed screen, was broken up by hand before being pushed through the wire mesh. All the American screeners wore thick canvas gloves to avoid coming into contact with the soil, which was high in tetanus. O'Leary kept track of where exactly the dirt was being pulled from in the grid—in scientific parlance its "provenience"—down to the depth where the soil was removed.

Senior team members monitored each step of the process, periodically giving orders to the more junior ones, to ensure the integrity of the excavation. Due to the sweltering heat, breaks were ordered every hour to drink water and replenish bug repellent and sunscreen. Smoking and chewing of betel nut were prohibited in the work areas.

It didn't take long. After a few hours of digging and sifting, O'Leary was called down to the screening station. He was handed a small fragment that came from the first grid less than twenty centimeters below the surface. He held it between his thumb and his forefinger and tentatively concluded it was "osseous material"—a tiny shard of bone that appeared to have been burned. After digging deeper in the grid, they found what looked like buckle fasteners and fragments from a pistol grip. They also found bits of glass and what looked like a section of piano wire—perhaps from a gearbox, someone proposed. Then they pulled from the screens a parachute locking cone and grommet, a hook that could have been used to latch a small pack, several buckles of different sizes, and a rusted and bent steel key they knew was designed to open a can of rations.

To whom the remains belonged, of course, remained a mystery. Natives had been living in the area for thousands of years. It was also a big question mark whether the identity of the remains could even be learned; like the other fragments, they appeared to have been badly burned. But O'Leary—and the rest of the team—were "stoked." So was George.

"RT 1 currently making steady progress," he reported to headquarters during the second week of the mission, referring to Recovery Team 1. "While only a small percentage of area has been excavated they have been very successful. Believe they are operating at a high tempo and will begin to make a large impact on their overall area in the next few days."

———

Things were not progressing as well at the second excavation George had organized—where they hoped to find the remains of another Marine Corsair pilot who was lost a few weeks later in 1944.

Like all of the MIAs, it was another heartbreaking case. Lieutenant Allan S. Harrison, from Houston, Texas, was an only child, whose distraught parents, Cora and Allan, desperately waited for answers that never came. A month after he was lost, they wrote to the Marine Corps that "this boy . . . is all we have in the world—we've lived the best part of our lives for him."

George made multiple trips—several hours up and back—to check on the progress and huddle with the team leaders. The site was located in Kadaulung Settlement to the northwest on the territory of a well-off landowner who was very friendly and cooperative. The journey required driving on a mixture of washed-out roads, over a rickety plank bridge, and down several primitive jungle tracks barely wide enough for the Toyota to pass. Along one of them George had previously overseen the laying of logs and sandbags to make it passable. The excursion finally ended after hiking through a thicket of banana trees and cocoa plants where some of the native women regularly emerged to hand him large and prickly melons to show their hospitality. "Thank you, Momma," George would reply in the best pidgin twang he could muster.

The team searching for signs of Harrison had to slash, cut, and clear a large swath of a thickly forested valley where comparatively few pieces of wreckage were strewn over a great distance—requiring a tremendous amount of backbreaking work even before any excavation could begin. It was clear that the site had been heavily scavenged for metal; very little of the wreckage previously documented by JPAC investigators could be located. An earlier JPAC excavation of the site had not included an anthropologist, so there were questions about the scientific validity of the information in the files. Nearby villagers reported that the pilot's skull might have been buried some years after the crash at the far end of the site, but numerous tree roots in that area slowed the work. The nearest water source was more than sixteen hundred feet away, so the less preferable dry screening was the only option. To make matters worse, the rains turned the area into a "big mud pie," making it decidedly unsafe and difficult to maintain the scientific integrity.

Another reminder that the safety of George's men and women remained job one came when one of the second team's rented vehicles slid off a muddy track into an embankment after the driver tried to negotiate a series of small gullies awash with rainwater. One side of the van was smashed in, but luckily no one was injured. The accident, George reported to his superiors, was "due to difficult conditions and not negligence."

The security of the team's equipment was also a concern at the second recovery site. One night the armed guards George had hired caught five men trying to sneak into the area, hog-tied them, and turned them over to the local police. As if he needed another reminder of the Wild West nature of New Guinea, the district police official informed him without any hint of emotion that the security guards had permission to shoot potential poachers on sight. George made it clear that he did not support such extreme measures.

The second recovery was going more slowly—and with far less success. Even when the team began excavating, they found nothing. Grid by grid they dug and sifted, but there was no sign of remains or other evidence of Lieutenant Harrison.

———

When George negotiated the terms with the Wartovos, the family patriarch, Enis, deferred the details to the eldest of his seven sons, Walia. But Walia did not live on the land. His younger brothers did. That soon spelled trouble.

At 3:00 p.m. on Friday, April 11, the steady hum of the work came to an abrupt halt with a series of shouts. One of the locals standing near the bottom of the zip line began throwing bucketfuls of dirt, hitting another in the face. Half a dozen buckets were dumped on the ground before the man stormed up the hill toward the village.

The troublemaker was one of the younger Wartovo brothers who lived on the land. He apparently had not been consulted by his older siblings and was upset about the damage being caused by the excavation. Another brother confronted the team leaders and accused them of ignoring two requests by a third brother to stop digging.

Captain Bergstrom, the recovery team leader, decided to stop all work for the day to let the brothers talk it over. The last thing the Americans needed was to spark a family feud that could end the mission just as it was getting rolling—and possibly cause bad blood that would prevent JPAC from returning in the future. George would come to the site the following morning to talk to them, the brothers were told.

All the spilled dirt was collected and screened before they packed up and headed back to Kokopo.

———

George arrived at the Wartovo homestead before 8:00 a.m. on Saturday, April 12, to try to salvage relations. He brought with him a wad of cash he withdrew from the JPAC account he'd set up at the Westpac bank in Kokopo; for security he enlisted two local policemen to go with him to make the withdrawal. He was calculating that the weekly wages might help break the impasse. The representative from the PNG National Museum in Port Moresby, who had accompanied George on his first trip to New Guinea, acted as translator. The brothers, once they learned George would pay the workers their first weekly wages, told him the excavation could continue. George was relieved. It appeared the delay in recovery efforts would be brief. But after the local workers were paid—a process that took more than an hour as the kina were doled out to each individual on a daily roster kept by the team sergeant—there was more trouble. Another Wartovo brother arrived on the scene and demanded more compensation on the spot for the damage to the land—something George had previously agreed they would work out after the team closed the site the following month.

George had to make a quick decision. If he changed the original terms he had agreed to with the eldest son, Walia, there was no telling where the demands would end. His funds were limited, and he had to do everything in his power not to set a bad precedent that could imperil future recoveries in Papua New Guinea. The island may have been primitive, but he knew from Rick Huston that word—not to mention rumors—spread far and fast through the countryside.

"No," he said and walked away, abruptly ending the discussion. Then he ordered the team to pack up and head back to the coast.

The gamble appeared to pay off. The brothers said they would come to Kokopo later in the day to continue negotiations. A few hours later one of them arrived with a letter of apology. There would be no more problems, George was assured. The brothers had settled their differences. The Americans could resume their work on Monday.

No one worked on the Sabbath in New Guinea, so the recovery teams took the day off out of respect. George had budgeted a little for what the military dubbed "morale, welfare, and recreation," or MWR. His teams deserved some fun. He rented some beat-up motorboats through Dougie at the hotel, packed up cold beer and soda, and took them out to an idyllic deserted island named Little Pigeon a few miles off the coast. In the shadow of the volcano, they went swimming and snorkeling and had a pig roast.

———

George spent more time with the first recovery team to make sure good relations were maintained with the Wartovo clan. For good measure, he offered to drive the village's barefoot children to their schoolhouse, sparing them the long trek each morning along muddy tracks in sweltering heat.

Dr. O'Leary, meanwhile, continued to follow the evidence. As the second week was drawing to a close, he concluded that the recovery scene was smaller than he first thought. A test grid opened down near the river turned up no suspected human remains. The crucial discoveries were concentrated around the engine, leading in the direction of the grids near the partial tail section a short distance away. It was time to flip it over so they could dig underneath.

"Watch the sharp edges. You don't want to get cut," the thirty-six-year-old Army staff sergeant Jimmy "Big Poppy" Bonilla from Beacon, New York, instructed as he led a group of Americans and locals in lifting the hulk that had once been the aft section of an F4U Corsair, now flaking with rust and rotted through in several places.

The team sergeant, Bonilla, a tattooed infantry soldier with a scar in the middle of his forehead, repeated the warning.

"Nice and slow, we don't want to get anybody hurt."

They rolled the tail section over, and it slid partway down the slope.

O'Leary methodically opened a new grid for excavation and, after concluding it had been sufficiently excavated and screened, moved on to the next. Over the next several days JPAC personnel found more fragments of a pistol grip and what looked like a four-holed plastic button, faded and chipped—similar to the kind commonly used on coats, suits, jackets, caps, and other apparel supplied to military personnel by the U.S. Army Quartermaster Corps during World

War II. Oddly, they also found a pecked and battered but relatively well-preserved glass marble with an orange ribbon at its core.

Most important, they found what appeared to be human remains, including parts of a clavicle and a left humerus. They tried not to think about the macabre nature of what they were doing and instead relished the thought that each shovelful might bring another one of the missing closer to his long-overdue homecoming. Some of the local workers seemed to instinctively understand the importance the Americans attached to returning their elders to their native land.

Twentysomething Gesling Mutumuy, who in his dreadlocks and T-shirt emblazoned with a marijuana leaf resembled the reggae performer Bob Marley, couldn't care less about what was buried beneath his feet. But as he leaned against a tree branch chewing betel nut and watching the Americans—in awe of the small village of their own they had erected almost overnight in the middle of the jungle—he could see they were completing their own sacred ritual. The clans of the lost American warriors needed to know where their kin had fallen.

But to determine that, and to maximize the likelihood of a positive ID, JPAC needed more evidence. While extracting DNA from bones that were exposed to the elements for a lifetime was increasingly possible with the advance of forensic science, it often couldn't be accomplished—as was the case with the small amount of remains recovered years before.

The team plowed through more grids as the local workforce swelled to nearly fifty. What George's team found next was like striking gold: human teeth. There were nineteen in total, including maxillary teeth such as incisors and canines and some molars connected to part of a left mandible. Clearly visible on some were fillings, which could be compared to dental records.

The team's photographer, the twenty-two-year-old Army sergeant Kaily Brown of Salt Lake City, Utah, snapped images of some of the material before O'Leary placed the items in labeled evidence bags and locked them in a heavy-duty black case with two combination locks.

Captain Bergstrom, the team leader, now understood why the cursory excavation that had been conducted at the crash site seventeen years before had found so little evidence. "They didn't go nearly deep enough."

They pushed ahead. Under O'Leary's watchful eye, the recovery team braved the heat and torrential downpours—now often accompanied by deafening thunder and dangerous lightning—to complete the excavation on schedule. Tarps were laid out across the completed grids and suspended from trees, while slit trenches were dug and lined with sandbags to try to keep the heavy rains at bay. The pump feeding the screening station conked out one morning and had to be replaced. A power outage in Kokopo that shuttered the local bank where George had deposited JPAC's funds also delayed the scheduled payday for local workers on April 18. The team then lost a full day of work on April 23 when they arrived to the news that two locals had died in the area overnight and the villagers were in mourning. George didn't ask any questions; he was afraid of the answers. Finally, after nearly three weeks, O'Leary determined they had done everything they could; in fact, they had recovered more biological evidence than they had hoped for. They cleaned the area, snapped more photographs of the scene, and broke down the screening station and other structures they had constructed. George arrived to conduct a final round of negotiations with the Wartovo clan to compensate them for the damage to their property.

———

At the other recovery site, where the team was still searching for signs of Lieutenant Harrison, the frustration only grew. The team had recovered small bits of what appeared to be human remains as well as some possible "life-support equipment" suggesting that the pilot had gone down with his plane on February 11, 1944. But even as they dug deeper—in some grids more than three feet—they grudgingly came to accept that the lab would probably have very little to go on to close the case. George had another idea.

JPAC records indicated there was another crash site not far away. It was believed to be the wreckage of an Army P-38 fighter that had been lost on January 20, 1944—on the same bomber escort mission as McCown. George wanted to reach the site and see if he could make arrangements to move Recovery Team 1, which was scheduled to wrap up in several weeks and return to Hawaii, to the adjacent area, and begin excavating for clues to another MIA.

This P-38 was believed to have been piloted by Lieutenant Dwight

Kelly, who had taken off with the B-25s from Stirling Island before linking up with the rest of the fighter escorts, including McCown, over Torokina. Testimony from a Japanese pilot who had been shot down the same day suggested that Kelly might have survived the crash and been subsequently killed, but no one knew for sure. The case, designated Missing Air Crew Report 1781, was still on JPAC's list of recovery sites.

The hike to the crash site near the village of Kadaulung took nearly an hour from the Harrison crash site, leading George through thick jungle and a thigh-deep river about 115 feet across. Along the way he identified two potential tracks that might serve as access roads, but upon closer inspection he concluded that only one of them, with some repairs, might work. He coordinated with some local village elders and arranged to have thirty workers available the following day to help make the necessary road repairs. But when he returned as planned, a man whose property bordered the jungle track demanded payment as well as a toll for all JPAC vehicles that would pass. The leaders of the adjacent villages of Waiware and Kolong became very angry with the man, telling George he had made similar demands of the district government, which was why the road had fallen into disrepair in the first place. They accused the recalcitrant landowner of preventing them from earning much-needed wages from JPAC and denying them an access road to deliver their crops to market. George decided it was too risky for JPAC to get in the middle of it. "My assessment of the situation was such that it was not in JPAC's best interest to become embroiled in a community issue that would likely create further problems," he reported to his superiors that night.

———

With both of the Corsair crashes on New Britain fully excavated, the mission was nearing its end, and George sought to maximize the Americans' time left in the country. The investigation team he was coordinating in the highlands on the main island of New Guinea had run into some severe weather that made travel by helicopter too dangerous, so George dispatched them to Lae, in the neighboring coastal province of Morobe, where the weather was more predictable and they would be able to investigate more crash sites on foot. But as George knew from his travels there earlier in the year, it wouldn't be easy. He reported back to Hawaii that JPAC's files covering the area were not uniform, making it difficult to determine which crash sites were already known and which were new discoveries. The investigators also found that so-called independent researchers—often the bureaucratic code for wreck hunters—had been to some of the crash sites. That made negotiating with local villages for rights to hack out landing zones much more difficult. JPAC simply couldn't pay what the better-financed privateers could. In one case, the investigation team found what looked like the scavenged wreckage of a P-40 near the village of Kaiapit. The villagers living near the crash had a letter from a California man who had been there before and might have photographs of the tail number and more information about the case. By the first week of May the investigation team had surveyed more than a dozen crash sites for possible future recovery operations in Madang and Morobe Provinces as well as on Bougainville Island in the nearby Solomons. George kept the rest of his soldiers busy the last several weeks by breaking up the two main recovery teams into smaller groups and dispatching them across the northern districts of New Britain to conduct site surveys in an effort to update JPAC's files, search for clues, and follow up new leads.

That left one last thing to do before returning to Hawaii.

———

On May 15, after washing off the mud and the grime, nearly thirty members of JPAC donned the crisp and clean military uniforms they had brought with them and stood at attention in the small chapel of Murray Barracks, headquarters of the PNG Defense Force in Port Moresby. Representing all the branches of the U.S. military, they stood silently before two flag-draped metal coffins, known as transfer cases, to conduct a repatriation ceremony for their fallen comrades.

JPAC would not know for some time whether it had accomplished its mission and recovered the remains of the missing Americans it had come for. That wasn't the point. The evidence strongly suggested that both men—McCown and Harrison—had given their last full measure in the skies over Rabaul. Even if their remains could not be positively identified for burial, they would be given this well-deserved honor.

To George's surprise, the brief ceremony in the small military chapel was attended by nearly fifty people—including representatives of the PNG Defense Force, the British and Australian embassies, the deputy chief of mission from the U.S. embassy, and some local media. The speakers reiterated the importance to the United States of the MIA mission in Papua New Guinea, which was an ally against the Japanese and now helping to continue the search for fallen Americans.

Then, in a carefully choreographed ceremony, each transfer case was slowly carried by four members of JPAC to the cargo hold of a military cargo jet waiting on the tarmac at the Port Moresby airport. As George looked on, he was struck by the thought that the young men and women under his command never knew the Marine pilots, who lived and died long before they were born. But just like the comrades they lost in Iraq and Afghanistan, they considered them their brothers. He smiled.

The identification of human remains in the United States is covered by civil rather than criminal law, meaning the burden of proof is almost always the "preponderance of evidence." U.S. military guidelines, however, dictate that when it comes to identifying war dead, that standard isn't enough. Any mistaken identification of a loved one was undoubtedly very bad, but burying the wrong soldier in a family plot, as had happened in rare cases in the past, was one of JPAC's biggest fears. The lab's burden of proof, therefore, was to be "clear and convincing." That meant maintaining a solid chain of evidence, which began with the chain-of-custody documents initiated in the field by anthropologists.

The handoff of remains to the lab—JPAC called it accession—was a carefully orchestrated process overseen by the lab's evidence manager, Ben Soria. A spectacled middle-aged Hawaiian with a master's degree in chemistry, Soria was partial to baggy floral shirts and had been a fixture at JPAC for years. On countless occasions he had greeted an arriving cargo plane on the tarmac behind the lab. This time was no different. Soria, along with a required witness, took custody of the metal coffins when they arrived at Hickam Air Force Base with the personnel returning from New Guinea.

Upon receipt, all the evidence was photographed and assigned a case number. Because the case of Bureau Number 02402 included remains recovered from a site where evidence had previously been found but not identified, the new material was incorporated into the previously assigned case number—CIL 1991-095-I-01, with 1991 referring to the year of the first excavation.

The multifaceted laboratory analysis was assigned to a team of scientists. A forensic odontologist was responsible for completing a dental profile that could be compared with the dental record of the suspected MIA. Another person would study the material evidence— the equipment and possible personal belongings found at the recovery site—and compare it with similar items carried or worn by Marine Corps pilots in the 1940s. But while they had access to all the case files, the forensic anthropologist in charge of evaluating the skeletal remains did not.

"The anthropologist is not told the circumstances of the loss nor told any details that might be known or suspected about the case until after their analytical report is written," the lab's science director stipulated at the time. "By following this policy of blind analysis, the anthropologist is insulated from any preconceived conclusions that might impart bias into his findings."

To further ensure the maximum level of scientific integrity, strict guidelines governed the investigators' ability to interact with each other on the case. Dr. O'Leary, as the field anthropologist, was prohibited from participating in the lab analysis at all, a practice meant to ensure that "the field conclusions and the lab conclusions form separate and distinct lines of evidence." All the analytical conclusions would also be peer-reviewed.

Due in part to the lab's high workload, it took several months before any tentative conclusions could be made. "Overall, the available evidence indicates CIL 1991-095-I-01 is male," the anthropologist who analyzed the pieces of bone determined in September. It was also apparent to the laboratory staff that the remains were those of a person at least eighteen years of age.

But making a successful DNA match with relatives was considered a long shot. Most of the skeletal remains were black-brown or grayish in color and appeared to have been exposed to high temperatures, some for a prolonged period of time. "The remains are in fairly poor and fragmentary condition," one early draft of the lab report stated.

The odontologist's investigation on the collection of recovered teeth went much better. A profile of the dental remains was inputted into a special computer program called the OdontoSearch Combined Database, where it was compared with 37,955 records. The results, the Army dentist assigned to the case reported, indicated that the pattern of restoration in the teeth—the cavities that were filled—and a review of those that were missing but present in the war-era dental record were "rather unique."

She closed her report with a one-paragraph opinion. They were the words that the U.S. military had been seeking for a lifetime.

"Due to numerous concordant features and no unexplainable discrepancies, it is my opinion that the dental remains of CIL 1991-095-I-01 are positively those of: *Major Marion Ryan McCown, Jr., 0-9610, U.S. Marine Corps Reserve.*"

But that wasn't the last word. JPAC sought another opinion from a member of the American Board of Forensic Odontology in Seattle, Washington. "The identification is established by the comparison of the dental record recovered from a site 15 km southeast of the Blanche Bay in Vunuakair Village, gazelle District, Eastern New Britain Province, Papua New Guinea, to the military dental records of Maj. McCown," the outside expert concluded. Supporting the conclusion was wreckage consistent with the type of aircraft that Maj. McCown was piloting and the ID tag that had been previously recovered near the wreckage. Together, the information was "definitely adequate to establish the positive identification."

On September 29, 2008, sixty-four years, eight months, and nine days after Ryan flew his final mission, JPAC's scientific director, Thomas Holland, signed a two-page memorandum making it official. Ryan McCown would finally be put to rest. But the only family member listed as next of kin in military records was his mother, Grace Aimar McCown, who had been dead for fifty-five years.

———

In a modern redbrick office building in Quantico, Virginia, Hattie Johnson was at work in her maroon cubicle one morning in the fall of 2008 when the phone rang. Johnson, an outgoing and attractive African-American woman in her forties, was a fixture at the Marine Corps Headquarters' Casualty Section, the office primarily responsible for arranging the details for the return and burial of fallen Marines from Iraq and Afghanistan. Hattie was the casualty officer in charge of handling a special category of cases: those who had been missing in action from previous wars.

It was a job that required a natural empathy, and like so many others involved with the MIA issue, she considered it a sacred trust. A clock displaying the telltale POW/MIA flag hung in her cluttered work space, while taped to her file cabinets were photographs she had received from grateful relatives across the country of Marines recently recovered in Korea and Southeast Asia. The quotation she added to the bottom of her e-mails gave voice to her abiding faith: "There are no mistakes, no coincidences, all events are blessings given to us to learn from."

When Hattie answered the phone, a man on the other end politely introduced himself. He said his name was John Almeida, and he began to tell her why he was calling. One of his relatives had seen an article published on Memorial Day in the *Boston Globe* about the search for missing pilots in Papua New Guinea. The story mentioned a name very familiar to him.

"McCown was my mother's brother. I have his flight log, and I think I have a picture," he told her, trying to contain his excitement. "My uncle has always been an inspiration for me. I joined the Marines partially because of him."

Hattie began scribbling notes and then asked him to please hold.

Almeida was a retired Navy doctor. He had been commissioned an infantry officer in the Marine Corps and fought in Vietnam before entering the Navy Medical Corps, where he eventually became a pathologist. Now sixty-three, he had been born a year after his uncle was reported missing. But he grew up hearing endless stories about Ryan from his mother, Claudia, whose wedding Ryan had so regrettably missed the week after Pearl Harbor. Ryan's beloved "Claudie" never stopped telling her boy about her big brother. For years after he was reported missing, she spoke of him in the present tense, as if he were still alive. Almeida had a picture of Ryan in his bedroom when he was growing up and had inherited his dress blue uniform. Even now, paintings of Corsairs decorated his den in Jacksonville, North Carolina. Almeida also never forgot the times he spent with his grandmother Grace. Though only eight years old when Gracie died, he understood that part of her had been lost with Uncle Ryan. John and his sister, Grace Emilie, whom Ryan had met that last Christmas before he shipped out, were the only close relatives on Grace's side of the family who were left. John's mother, Claudia, had died in 1993.

Almeida heard the sound of shuffling papers in the background before Ms. Johnson was back on the line. She did not hide her excitement.

"We've been looking for you."

———

This time it was the good news that spread fast. The details of Almeida's call reached Jane McCown McKinney, Ryan's only surviving sibling. Now sixty-five and living in Oxnard, California, she was the half sister of Ryan's born in October 1943 as the Hell's Angels were heading up the line. It was Jane's daughter Blair, with her fair complexion and short red hair resembling Ryan's, who had coincidentally been telling a friend about her uncle's exploits in early September, prompting him to hop on the Internet, where he came across the newspaper article about the search for lost pilots in New Guinea that mentioned Ryan—just as the JPAC lab was nearing an ID of the remains.

Jane McCown McKinney never knew her older brother, but when she talked about him, it sounded as if she had. Her father, Ryan senior, had spoken often about his oldest child and namesake—in the early years at least, with a hint of hope that he might still be alive. But more often than from Dad, she heard about Ryan from her other brother, Vance. He had idolized him ever since visiting Ryan during flight training in Florida in 1941. Vance repeated over and over again his last memory of Ryan, when he visited the family in North Carolina to say good-bye before leaving for the South Pacific. The image was seared in the eight-year-old Vance's brain of his older brother zipping up his leather flight jacket and pulling away from the house in Tryon on a motorcycle before disappearing around the bend forever. Vance had longed for answers to what happened to his older brother. Decades later, on a trip to Washington in the 1980s, he made his way to the Washington Navy Yard to see what more he could learn about Ryan's fate. It was disappointingly little. Vance, who died in 1977, spent his final years in a wheelchair suffering from an ailment that required him to struggle to keep his joints limber. One way he did it was by constructing model airplanes—mostly Corsairs like his beloved brother's.

Now the final preparations were under way to return Ryan to his family. On November 8, Ms. Johnson traveled to North Carolina to meet with Almeida and deliver JPAC's final report on his uncle's identification along with some paperwork for him to sign. Before leaving Quantico, she had contacted JPAC with a request: Could they send her the dog tag that was stored in the lab? She'd like to bring it with her to give to McCown's nephew.

"Please make it happen," JPAC's scientific director, Thomas Holland, instructed Ben Soria, the lab's evidence manager, when he received the request. "Believe me, you don't want to make Hattie mad."

Johnson arrived at the Almeida household on a Sunday. Jane McCown's daughter Blair was also there on her mother's behalf. Johnson presented them with the ID tag printed with the name Marion Ryan McCown Jr. that had originally been recovered at the crash site in 1991. She also gave them a bound copy of the final recovery report, including photographs of the excavation in New Guinea and the remains that were recovered, and the lab reports.

"It was absolutely fascinating," Blair told her mother later that week. "It turns out that the dental records were such an exact match that they were what was used for the identification."

The U.S. military, Johnson informed them, would also cover the travel expenses for three family members to attend the funeral, which Almeida decided would be in Ryan's beloved Charleston.

"She has already booked the honor guard from Camp Lejeune to perform the full military honor ceremony," Blair reported.

———

In January 2009, eighty-seven-year-old Helen Schiller was sitting in her sunlit kitchen in Summerville, South Carolina, reading the Charleston News & Courier. An article caught her eye. One of Charleston's favorite sons, a World War II pilot who had been lost in New Guinea, would finally be coming home. She read on. The former Helen Miller then gasped.

"Oh, my heavens. It's Ryan. They found Ryan!"

At the end of the article was a request for anyone who knew Major Marion Ryan McCown to contact the paper. Virtually none of the McCown relatives who had known him were still alive. The community was desperate to locate a living link to Ryan.

Helen slowly stood up, went to the phone, and started to dial.

CHAPTER TEN

COMING HOME

A chilly drizzle fell on Charleston on the morning of Sunday, January 18, 2009. Under a gray sky, aging military veterans, fresh-faced cadets from the Citadel, and kinfolk from across the Low Country and beyond lined Archdale Street. Some who had come were members of Rolling Thunder, the national veterans' organization committed to the memory of POWs and MIAs, known by their telltale motorcycles. They had come to stand at attention before the wrought-iron gates of the Unitarian Church, clutching American flags and black-and-white POW/MIA flags imprinted with the slogan "You are not forgotten."

As family members and congregants filed into the church in a stream of umbrellas, they were handed programs for the memorial service, with the words from "The Young Dead Soldiers," by Archibald MacLeish, printed on the cover.

We were young. We have died. Remember us. . . .

Every pew in the cavernous sanctuary was filled, while more onlookers stood along the outer aisles in between the television cameras from local news crews. Still more people crowded in the rear of the church, which was silent save for the steady sound of the rain on the stained-glass windows etched with inscriptions from the Hebrew Bible. They had all come to bid a final farewell to a man most of them never knew—Major Marion Ryan McCown Jr., U.S. Marine Corps Reserve.

Escorted by a cadet from the Citadel military academy to her seat in the front row was Helen Schiller, the former Helen Miller, wearing a black raincoat, her hair elegantly coiffed to reveal a solemn but somehow thankful expression.

She had never forgotten Ryan, the evenings they spent together at the Fort Sumter Hotel, or when they saw *Gone With the Wind.* She remembered it all as if it were yesterday. She could still picture him in his Marine Corps uniform, leaning forward in a formal bow and with that infectious grin of his asking for another dance. "He was a true Charlestonian and a gentleman," she had been saying all morning. For a time after he left for the war, she believed they would be married when it was all over. It didn't turn out that way. She went on with her life, fell in love, got married, had children and now grandchildren. Ryan would forever remain twenty-seven.

Clutched between her fingers was the small box in which he had given her the pair of wings on the balcony of the Fort Sumter Hotel. She also held the humorous little handwritten note that had come with them: "Helen, you were always such a swell guy. Love, Ryan."

Sitting almost unnoticed in the back of the church was Rosemary Hutto, a friend of Ryan's from Sunday school. The two elderly women were among the few in attendance who had seen him alive and lived long enough to witness this day.

The Reverend Peter Lanzillotta, standing near the altar set that Uranie had donated in Ryan's memory after the war, gazed down at the small mahogany box that held the remains recovered from the village of Vunakaur. He intoned: "You served your country with a full measure of your devotion. We shall salute you and say hail and farewell, good and noble Marine."

The mourners read from scripture while the retired Navy captain John Almeida, who knew his uncle Ryan only through the stories of his mother, Claudia, and his hazy childhood memories of his heartbroken grandmother, Grace, looked out at the hundreds of faces packing the pews. "My uncle is much more than my imagination and much greater than my fantasies."

Having gone off to fight in Vietnam in part due to Uncle Ryan's example, Almeida now revered him even more, knowing that he had died fulfilling his duty that fateful day over Rabaul.

His uncle Ryan also managed to accomplish one last mission, bestowing a final gift from the grave. He reunited the McCown clan.

"He is the bond in the family that brought us all together."

The last of Ryan's siblings, who traveled from California to bid a final farewell to the half brother she never met, then spoke of what the family had lost in the jungles of New Guinea.

"At the time of his death," Jane McCown McKinney said, struggling to steady her voice, "there were many that grieved for him."

> I was not one of them. Well, I was only three months old at the time. Our brother Vance had just turned ten, so he had very few memories of him. But as we grew older, we observed the grief of our father, Ryan senior, and that of our sister Claudia. And through their grief we came to a sense of the enormity of our loss. Neither Vance, Claudia, nor Daddy is here to honor Ryan or to lay him to rest. Most of the family that knew Ryan is gone, and most of us here today never knew him at all. But we do remember him and celebrate his life. We stand here for those who died before they could have the comfort of knowing that Ryan would be found and would be brought home to rest beside his mother, grandparents, and sister.

The funeral service for Ryan concluded with the reading of the "Navy Hymn," with its appeal to the Almighty from the defenders not to safeguard their own lives but to protect loved ones back home:

> God, Who dost still the restless foam,
> Protect the ones we love at home.
> Provide that they should always be
> By thine own grace both safe and free.
> O Father, hear us when we pray
> For those we love so far away.

As a Marine honor guard stood at attention outside, a procession of Marine pallbearers carefully carried the small box with Ryan's remains to the adjacent cemetery, where the wildflowers and grasses grew just as thick as on the evening when Ryan and Helen danced in the upstairs ballroom of Hibernian Hall around the corner.

Ryan's half sister, Jane, his nephew John, and their families and friends gathered solemnly under a tent around a headstone engraved with the names Grace and Claudia, where a small patch of earth had been dug for Ryan. The reverend whispered a few final prayers. Two lines of Marines, wearing their dress blue uniforms, held an American flag taut between them before deftly folding it and presenting it to Jane. The honor guard, lined up on Archdale Street in front of the churchyard, lifted their rifles skyward and commenced a three-volley salute. Each shot, fired on command, rang out in the still morning, the sound ricocheting off the imposing eighteenth-century structure of the church. A bugler slowly played taps.

Finally, as the sound of the horn faded, a deep rumble built in the distance, faint at first. Within moments the churchyard was filled with the deafening sound of three Marine Corps Harrier jets roaring across the rain-soaked sky.

As the mourners gazed heavenward, their cheeks streaked with rain and some with tears, the pilots dipped their wings in one final salute.

EPILOGUE

Khost Province, Afghanistan, July 2010. George was hunched over the controls of a Kiowa Warrior, flying just above the treetops looking for signs of the Taliban smuggling weapons and reinforcements from Pakistan, just over the horizon. As he traced the crude network of roads and goat trails through the mountains, he was also keeping an eye out for the dreaded ZPU-1s and their 14.5- and 23-millimeter rounds. The Haqqani network, one of the most ruthless of the Pakistani terrorist groups allied with the Taliban, liked to fire the outdated Soviet anti-aircraft guns, usually mounted on the back of a pickup truck, at U.S. helicopters. The "technicals," as the armed Toyotas were called, were exceedingly difficult to spot from the air in the thick forests below; they could usually be seen only after they opened up, at a velocity of up to a thousand meters per second. One of the armor-piercing rounds could blow a gaping hole through his chopper and out the other side.

George was back at the "tip of the spear," as the Army called the front line, chasing bad guys and swooping in to aid American ground troops when they got into trouble. This time it was in Regional Command East, an area of eastern Afghanistan about the size of Pennsylvania that was once home to Osama bin Laden, whom George presumed might still be hiding somewhere in the vast wasteland he could see out the cockpit. His unit was part of the surge in American forces begun in 2009 that was designed to beat back the Taliban's advance after nearly eight years of war.

"Greetings from Afghanistan!" he wrote to friends back in Florida from his new assignment, after receiving a boxful of cookies and brownies for his soldiers. "It is truly a morale booster to know that we are in the thoughts of so many back home."

Afghanistan was the last place on earth he thought he'd be when he left Iraq at the end of 2005. But George believed in what he was doing, perhaps more than he ever had. At JPAC he finally understood why he wore the uniform. As his assignment there wound down, he was also determined to keep wearing it.

Before he left the island, however, he had some unfinished business. With Rick Huston as his sponsor, George became a fellow "traveling man." He was inducted into Freemasonry, taking his rightful place in another family tradition that dated to before the American Revolution. Huston even bought him his Mason ring.

But what George cherished most of all from his time at JPAC was his relationship with Sandra Patricia, whom he first met via e-mail when he was working in Germany. Their first date was in the Hard Rock Cafe in Panama City, Panama—can't get much cheesier, or more American, than that, he thought. But it was there they began a budding romance. Sandra Pa visited George in Hawaii, where he introduced her to some of his military buddies. He went to meet her parents in Bogotá and brought her home to Tallahassee to meet Ann.

By the time he left for a yearlong tour of Afghanistan in late 2009, they were deeply in love. Both Ann and Sandra Pa came to see him off at Hunter Army Airfield near Savannah, Georgia, when he deployed. They were also there—holding a big "Welcome Home, George" sign and a bouquet of red roses—when he returned. Just in time for Thanksgiving—and to ask Sandra Pa to marry him.

ACKNOWLEDGMENTS

Virtually no human endeavor can succeed without the help and guidance of others. This book was no exception. Foremost I want to thank my parents, Linda Rubin and Norman Bender, and my three brothers, Adam, Joshua, and Aron, for their unstinting love, guidance, and encouragement. To my blessed daughters, Leila Carolina and Joanna Isabel, who like their mom endured a lot of absent days and nights during the writing: you are forever my inspiration, and I love you more than words can do justice. But a book idea is one thing. Finding the right publisher is another. The vision and wisdom of my literary agents, Sascha Alper and Larry Weissman, helped bring the project to life. My editor at Doubleday, William Thomas, believed in the story from the start and his passion and deft hand come through on nearly every page. Likewise, to his gifted team, including Coralie Hunter, Ingrid Sterner, and Bette Alexander: this book is as much yours as mine.

I am deeply grateful to my editors and colleagues at the *Boston Globe*, especially the former editor-in-chief, Martin Baron, who is now the top editor at the *Washington Post*, and throughout this endeavor provided more support than I probably deserved. Peter Canellos, the *Globe*'s deputy managing editor and former Washington bureau chief, encouraged me every step of the way, beginning with greenlighting my seemingly harebrained idea to make a reporting trip to Papua New Guinea in 2008, in search of lost Americans and the men and women looking for them. Christopher Rowland, the paper's Washington bureau chief, let me disappear for the better part of a year to write the book, and I am lucky to count him and my colleagues in the Washington bureau among my personal friends. Special thanks are reserved for Michael Kranish, the deputy Washington bureau chief, who was a nearly endless source of advice, and my former *Globe* colleague Sasha Issenberg, who gave generously of his time and knowledge. My friend filmmaker Sigmund Libowitz provided invaluable feedback and helped me visualize the story from fresh angles. Others whose assistance was crucial with records research and expert perspective were Tim Brown, John Pike, Colonel Rick Kiernan, Glenn Solomon, Wofford Stribling, Cynthia Keiser, and forensic historian David Berry. I will forever be grateful to the late Dr. Jose A. Fuentes, my grandfather-in-law, for his sage advice on the original book proposal and for helping me decipher detailed dental records. The love and support of my in-laws, Jose Fuentes-Agostini and Crissy Fuentes-Gonzalez, were also there from the start. I also want to thank the leadership of the Joint POW/MIA Accounting Command for giving me the honor to be a part of their work, and for virtually never saying no to my requests for information. Especially helpful were Johnnie Webb, Major Raymond Osorio, Lee Tucker, Major Brian Desantis, and Christopher McDermott. This book also benefited enormously from the keen eye for detail and grasp of history of my colleague and dear friend Kevin Baron, who traipsed through the New Guinea jungle with me. Yoon Byun, the *Globe* photographer who was with us every step of the way, captured the scene in ways virtually no one else could.

As I was researching and writing the book I also benefited enormously from Dr. Gil Thorpe, whose brother Bob is still unaccounted for as of this writing. He helped me understand, even just a little, the sense of loss experienced by the families of the missing who have waited a lifetime for closure that has never come. I am likewise indebted to Navy Commander Brian Danielson, who never met his father, Ben, before he disappeared over Laos, but never let him go. Other families of the missing held my hand along the way. A special thanks to Hazel Nelson, who lost her brother Robert Marshall on the same mission as Ryan McCown, and to her daughter Betty Montgomery. I am grateful to call Donna Phillips Dunning my friend; she keeps her cousin, Lieutenant Allan S. Harrison III, alive despite frustratingly few answers about his ultimate fate at Rabaul. Others who generously shared their experiences in the South Pacific were Arthur May, Fred Tuxworth, and "The Professor" Russell Johnson. I consider myself among the luckiest to also call some of the few surviving members of the Hell's Angels my friends, especially Vic Smith and Cosmo Marsh. I will be forever grateful for the trust they have shown in helping me to tell the story of their squadron.

If you asked me where this journey really began, I would say Les Nicholas's tenth-grade journalism class at Wyoming Valley West High School in Plymouth, Pennsylvania. I was also blessed with many mentors who nurtured my potential, afforded me new opportunities, and showed me—with their sleeves rolled up and their patience in check—how to cover the military in all its complexity, both human and machine. Primary among them were Richard Lardner, Dan Dupont, John Robinson, Barbara Starr, and Richard Parker. I am especially grateful to Pittsburgh *Post-Gazette* editor-in-chief and former *Boston Globe* Washington bureau chief David Shribman for his confidence in letting me cover the wars in Afghanistan and Iraq for one of the best newspapers in the country. I wish I could thank two of my former colleagues at the *Globe* in person for all their help and encouragement: Elizabeth Neuffer and Anthony Shadid both gave their lives giving a voice to the voiceless. They are deeply missed.

But there are two men—and their families—to whom I owe the most. I met George S. Eyster V on April 12, 2008, when he came to collect me at the small, ramshackle airport on the shores of Blanche Bay on the northern tip of New Britain Island. George was my escort those weeks I embedded with the JPAC recovery teams. I had expected to be telling ghost stories of fighting men swallowed by the jungle long ago, but through George I came to appreciate that the young men and women searching for them—most of them veterans of America's post-9/11 wars—were in their own way lost, or at least overlooked and underappreciated by society. I am deeply grateful to George and his beautiful bride, Sandra Patricia, for taking this journey with me. The two of them, as well as George's mother, Ann Eyster Whittaker, and his grandmother, Harriet Eyster Linnell, spent many hours answering my questions—often more than once—and permitted me to pick apart family scrapbooks and photo albums, and to scout hard drives.

Then, of course, there are the McCowns. They welcomed me into their lives and homes with open arms and entrusted me with the honor of recounting the life, the death, and the homecoming of their beloved Ryan. I am especially grateful for all the help and support from Captain John Almeida and his wife, Christine Duffey; Jane McCown McKinney, her husband, John McKinney, and their daughter, Blair McKinney; and Mrs. Vance McCown and her children, Ellen McCown Schwab, Katherine McCown Wall, and Bill McCown. To Helen Miller Schiller, you'll always be a "swell guy" in my book, and I couldn't have done it without you. Last but not least, to you, Ryan: Thank you for what you did for me. And for the rest of us.

Bryan David Bender
Wilkes-Barre, Pennsylvania
January 2013

NOTES AND SOURCES

The story of George S. Eyster V and Marion Ryan McCown Jr. could not have been told without the participation of numerous people and primary-source material. All quotations in the book were from interviews conducted by the author; recorded in personal diaries, letters, or official government reports; or related by at least one person who was there. The following notes are not a comprehensive list of every source used in the book but describe the most significant and unique documents, books, articles, and personal interviews. A number of sources were relied upon throughout the narrative, but they have not been cited in every instance for brevity. They include the author's multiple interviews with Eyster in Papua New Guinea and the United States and his family's letters, records, and personal recollections. Other material widely used includes Ryan McCown's personal diary and letters; his official military records; interviews with his surviving family members and fellow pilots; and the official reports from the Hell's Angels of Marine Fighter Squadron 321 between 1943 and 1945. A significant amount of material was obtained from the National Archives and Records Administration in College Park, Maryland; the National Military Personnel Records Center in St. Louis, Missouri; the Library of Congress; and several other public and private libraries and archives. The Joint POW/MIA Accounting Command permitted the author to travel to Papua New Guinea in April 2008 with Eyster and his recovery teams and, with the permission of the next of kin, also made available hundreds of pages of official government case files, investigation notes, maps, and other information on several individual MIA cases from Southeast Asia and World War II. Justin Taylan, the world's most knowledgeable person about American pilots and crews reported missing in the Pacific during World War II, and his database at PacificWrecks.com were invaluable.

PROLOGUE

The main sources were interviews with Eugene V. Smith and Richard Marsh and the official after-action reports of Marine Fighter Squadron 321. Also consulted was *The Siege of Rabaul* by Henry Sakaida, who interviewed many of the surviving American and Japanese fighter pilots who fought in the skies over Rabaul.

CHAPTER ONE: THE LEGACY

The main sources were interviews with Major George S. Eyster V; Ann Eyster Whittaker; Harriet LaRoche Eyster; and the family's voluminous collection of scrapbooks, albums, military records, and personal letters. Other first-person reflections were drawn from Peter Arnett's *Live from the Battlefield*, his dispatches from Vietnam for the Associated Press, as well as interviews and writings of the late photojournalist Horst Faas. Key details of the 1966 episode in Vietnam were also drawn from Tom Mangold and John Penycate, *The Tunnels of Cu Chi*. The history of the Society of the Cincinnati and its rules of membership were derived from an interview with the society's librarian, Ellen Clark, as well as Markus Hünemörder, *The Society of the Cincinnati: Conspiracy and Distrust in Early America.*

Biographical information and details about the wartime service of Captain Wilhelm Heyser were drawn from multiple primary sources at the David Library of the American Revolution in Washington Crossing, Pennsylvania, including pay and muster rolls, company reports, and Continental Army General Orders. The writings of William Heyser III were contained in his personal diaries, published by the Kittochtinny Historical Society in Chambersburg, Pennsylvania. The biographical information on J. Allison Eyster and his relatives was drawn from the *Pennsylvania Scrap Book Necrology*, vol. 44; Anita L. Eyster, "The Pioneering Ancestor of the Oyster-Eyster Family," *Historical Review of Berks County*, April 1941; and the obituary of the Honorable George Eyster, *Lutheran Observer*, January 7, 1887. Details on the maternal Pate family history were contained in John Ben Pate, *The American Genealogy of the Pate Family.*

Other books and articles consulted include Thomas J. Scharf, *History of Western Maryland*, vol. 2; Charles Francis Stein, *The German Battalion of the American Revolution*; Henry C. Peden Jr., *Revolutionary Patriots of Washington County, Maryland, 1776–1783*; Henry J. Retzer, *The German Regiment of Maryland and Pennsylvania in the Continental Army, 1776–1781*; Philip S. Foner, ed., *The Complete Writings of Thomas Paine*; William M. Dwyer, *The Day Is Ours! An Inside View of the Battles of Trenton and Princeton*; the personal letters of General George Washington; and *Cumberland Valley Sentinel*, June 23, 1851.

CHAPTER TWO: A TRUE CHARLESTONIAN

The chief sources were Ryan McCown, *Five Year Diary: A Comparative Record of Events*, a daily personal record kept between December 25, 1938, and January 1, 1943; and interviews with Helen Miller Schiller. Wartime Charleston was re-created from Fritz P. Hamer, *Charleston Reborn: A Southern City, Its Naval Yard, and World War II*; William J. Fraser, *Charleston! Charleston! The History of a Southern City*; Walter Edgar, *The South Carolina Encyclopedia*; and "The South's Charleston," *Review of Reviews*, December 1929. McCown's personal attributes also came from interviews with his nephew Captain John L. Almeida; half sister Jane McCown McKinney; sister-in-law Mrs. William Vance McCown; and cousin Robert Maxcy McCown. The McCown family history was also derived from Louise McCown Clement, *The McCown Family of the Peedee Section of South Carolina*. The history of the maternal Aimar branch was recounted in William Turner Durban Jr., *La Connexion Française: A Reflection on Three French Families, Durban, Aimar, and Me'Nard*. Also consulted were records of the Unitarian Church of Charleston, on file at the South Carolina Historical Society.

Details of Washington, D.C., and the National Mall were gleaned from photographs taken by the U.S. Office of War Information between March and May 1942, courtesy of the Library of Congress Prints and Photographs Division. Also consulted were David Brinkley, *Washington Goes to War*; and Scott Hart, *Washington at War, 1941–1945*. The Marine Corps Base at Quantico during World War II is recounted in Paolo E. Coletta and K. Jack Bauer, *United States Navy and Marine Corps Bases, Domestic*; Charles A. Fleming, *Quantico: Crossroads of the Marine Corps*; and Mark Blumenthal, *Quantico: Images of America*. Further details were obtained in an interview in the New Way Café with the former Quantico mayor Mitchell Raftelis.

CHAPTER THREE: HEEDING THE CALL

The main sources were interviews with Major George S. Eyster V and Ann Eyster Whittaker and their personal and family archives, including letters, e-mails, cards, funeral programs, and eulogies. Details about Army Ranger School were obtained from J. D. Lock, *The Coveted Black and Gold: A Daily Journey Through the U.S. Army Ranger School Experience*; and Mona D. Sizer, *The Glory Guys: The Story of the U.S. Army Rangers*. Additional information about the suicide of Specialist Wayne Gajadhar came from "Soldier, 20, Kills Himself," *Fayetteville Observer*, March 17, 1999. The technical characteristics of the Kiowa Warrior helicopter were derived from M. M. Kawa and J. M. Kirk, *Program and Operational Highlights of the Armed OH-58D Kiowa Warrior*.

CHAPTER FOUR: PREPARING FOR WAR

The main sources were McCown's Aviator's Flight Log and interviews with VMF-321's Richard Marsh; Eugene V. Smith; Grover Cleveland Doster and his wife, Eloise; Robert Whiting; and the ground crew members James L. Kalleward and Gordon Renshaw. Additional personal recollections came from a December

22, 1943, letter from McCown to his mother, courtesy of the Charleston Military Museum; a letter dated April 23, 1944, from Major Edmund F. Overend to Mrs. E. W. Marshall, courtesy of Betty S. Montgomery; an essay published by Overend in 1946 titled "I Fight for Tomorrow"; and interviews with Hazel Marshall Nelson and the late Leroy Wilkinson. The activities of VMF-321 were also outlined in Peter B. Mersky, *A History of Marine Fighter Squadron 321*, and in the squadron's official Daily War Diary; a letter from Gordon Knott preserved by the Marine Corps History Division in Quantico, Virginia; and the official deck logs of the USS *Nassau* and USS *Pocomoke*.

The history and features of the F4U-1 Corsair were derived from a series of books, including Fred Blechman, *Bent Wings: F4U Corsair Action and Accidents: True Tales of Trial and Terror*; William Green, *Famous Fighters of the Second World War*; Boone T. Guyton, *Whistling Death: The Test Pilot's Story of the F4U Corsair*; Mark Styling, *Corsair Aces of World War II*; Barrett Tillman and Kenneth A. Walsh, *Corsair: The F4U in World War II and Korea*; John A. DeChant, *Devilbirds: The Story of United States Marine Corps Aviation in World War II*; Robert F. Dorr, *Marine Air: The History of Flying Leathernecks in Words and Photos*; Corwin Meyer, *Corky Meyer's Flight Journal: Dodging Disasters—Just in Time*; Frederick A. Johnsen, *F4U Corsair*; and Pilot's Flight Instructions for the F4U-1, F3A-1, and FG-1 Airplanes, March 1, 1944.

Additional information about American and Japanese fighter tactics was drawn from Robert C. Mikesh, *Zero*; Gregory "Pappy" Boyington, *Baa Baa Black Sheep*; and a series of official intelligence assessments during World War II, including the undated "Quality of Japanese Pilots," on file at the Marine Corps History Division in Quantico, Virginia. Also consulted for background was Alan J. Levine, *The Pacific War*; Bruce D. Gamble, *Black Sheep One: The Life of Gregory "Pappy" Boyington*; and Daniel Ford, *Flying Tigers: Claire Chennault and His American Volunteers, 1941–1942*. Additional details of Tutuila in American Samoa were contained in John J. Carey's memoir, *A Marine from Boston*; Gordon L. Rottman, *The WWII Pacific Island Guide: A Geo-military Study*; *History of U.S. Marine Corps Operations in World War II*, vol. 1; and J. A. C. Gray, *Amerika Samoa*.

CHAPTER FIVE: A LOSS OF FAITH

The chief sources were a personal war diary, in the form of scores of Internet chats between George S. Eyster V, Ann Eyster Whittaker, and Scott Eyster from December 2004 to July 2005, preserved by Whittaker on her home computer. The communications were supplemented by interviews with the participants and a series of personal letters to and from several generations of Eysters. The episode involving George S. Eyster IV—Big George—at the outset of the 1990–91 war was recounted by Chaplain Gordon Terpstra and a letter he wrote to Whittaker dated August 17, 2000. The high-speed chase and firefight in Mosul in August 2005 were recounted in detail in an eighteen-page, first-person dispatch on the incident published by the war correspondent Michael Yon on August 31, 2005. Background on the Forty-Second Infantry Division was drawn from Hugh C. Daly, *42nd "Rainbow" Infantry Division*; and an article by Kirk Semple in the *New York Times*, February 13, 2005. Information on overall military operations and demographics in Iraq during Eyster's tour was drawn from *On Point II: The United States Army in Operation Iraqi Freedom*; *Helicopter News* 42, no. 15; Michael Hastings, "America's New Cavalry," *Men's Journal*, September 2010; Michael Gordon and Bernard E. Trainor, *Cobra II: The Inside Story of the Invasion and Occupation of Iraq*; Loretta Napoleoni, *Insurgent Iraq*; and the military database maintained by GlobalSecurity .org. Additional information on Warrant Officer Matt Lourey was provided by his mother, Becky Lourey, as well as a letter she received from a soldier whose life was saved by Lourey's final act. Growing public opposition to the war was recounted in Peter Laufer, *Mission Rejected*; interviews with Senator Chuck Hagel aired on ABC's *This Week* on August 21, 2005; and a September 28, 2005, press conference in North Carolina featuring General William Odom. The history of the ancient city of Nineveh was recounted in Brian M. Fagan, *Return to Babylon: Travelers, Archaeologists, and Monuments in Mesopotamia*; and the Old Testament.

CHAPTER SIX: MOVING UP THE LINE

The New Guinea and Solomon Islands campaigns in World War II were recounted in *The United States Army in World War II*, vol. 8; *History of U.S. Marine Corps Operations in World War II*, vol. 2; William B. Hopkins, *The Pacific War: The Strategy, Politics, and Players That Won the War*; William Manchester, *Goodbye, Darkness: A Memoir of the Pacific War*; Edwin P. Hoyt, *Japan's War: The Great Pacific Conflict*; Donald M. Goldstein and Katherine V. Dillon, eds., *The Pacific War Papers: Japanese Documents of World War II*; Fletcher Pratt, *The Marines' War: An Account of the Struggle for the Pacific from Both American and Japanese Sources*; Douglas Oliver, *Bougainville: A Personal History*; James Campbell, *The Ghost Mountain Boys*; Ritchie Garrison, *Task Force 9156 and III Island Command: A Story of a South Pacific Advanced Base During World War II*; Robert Sherrod, *History of Marine Corps Aviation in World War II*; and Gordon L. Rottman, *The World War II Pacific Island Guide: A Geo-military Study*.

Information on Allied reconnaissance missions over Rabaul was contained in reports of the U.S. Army Air Corps's Seventeenth Photographic Reconnaissance Squadron. Operations at Torokina, on Bougainville Island, were also recounted in Donald Jackson, *Torokina: A Memoir*; *Building the Navy's Bases in World War II: History of the Bureau of Yards and Docks and the Civil Engineer Corps, 1940–1946*; Henry Sakaida, *The Siege of Rabaul*; and *Yank*, February 18, 1944. Additional Japanese perspective was drawn from Masatake Okumiya and Jiro Horikoshi, *Zero: The Story of Japan's Air War in the Pacific*.

CHAPTER SEVEN: A NEW PATH

The chief sources were interviews with Major George S. Eyster V; Major Grover Harms; Lieutenant Colonel James Hanson IV; General Michael Flowers; JPAC deputy commander Johnnie Webb; JPAC anthropologists Dr. Thomas Sprague, Dr. Owen Luck O'Leary, Dr. Paul Emanovsky, and Dr. Derek Benedix; Commander Brian Danielson; Robert Maves; Rick Huston; Alvin Teel; Major

Brian DeSantis; Major Jeremy Taylor; Sergeant Kili Baldeagle; Davy Baldeagle; Colonel Ines White; Kenny Scabby Robe; Sergeant Sengchanh "Sammy" Vilay-sane; and Dr. Andy Baldwin. Crucial details were also contained in dozens of case files and mission reports made available by the Joint POW/MIA Account-ing Command. Publications consulted included *POW-MIA Fact Book*; official reports to Congress by the Defense POW/MIA Office; Hoang Khoi, *The Ho Chi Minh Trail*; Susan Sheehan, *A Missing Plane*; Michael John Claringbould, *Black Sunday: When Weather Claimed the Fifth Air Force*; and Robert Utley, *The Lance and the Shield: The Life and Times of Sitting Bull*. Biographical details and the wartime service of Major Nam Thuan were drawn from Tom Mangold and John Penycate, *The Tunnels of Cu Chi*.

CHAPTER EIGHT: MISSING

The chief sources were official records and after-action reports from Marine Fighter Squadron 321 and the Army Air Corps's Forty-Second Bombardment Group, as well as McCown's voluminous Individual Deceased Personnel File con-taining reports and correspondence on his MIA case from 1944 to 2008. Grace McCown's neighbor Meri Roberts Dame provided first-person recollections, and McCown's nephew John L. Almeida also shared family history and personal letters. More details about McCown's final mission were drawn from written testimony by the former VMF-321 pilot Leo Harmon, courtesy of the Charleston Military Museum. Information about wartime shortages and bond drives was gleaned from the series the Week in America, American News File.

CHAPTER NINE: REDISCOVERY

The chief sources were interviews with Major George S. Eyster V; Rick Hus-ton; Alvin Teel; Johnnie Webb; JPAC's chief historian, Chris McDermott; Major Raymond Osorio; Bernd Henkelmann; Sandra Patricia Eyster; Dr. Peter S. Miller; Enis Wartovo; Gil Thorpe; Ken Dooley; John L. Almeida; Hattie Johnson; Jane McCown McKinney; Mrs. Vance McCown; Blair McKinney; Ellen McCown Schwab; Bill McCown; Katherine McCown Wall; and Helen Schiller; additionally, an ABC interview with Rick Huston on February 25, 2008.

Modern-day political and tribal problems in Papua New Guinea were recounted in the *Europa World Year Book*, vol. 2, 2004, while key details of the island's history and topography were gleaned from Gordon L. Rottman, *The WWII Pacific Island Guide: A Geo-military Study*; and Herman Boyek, *Kairiru: Island of Legends*. The MIA recovery mission data was based on the official case histories compiled by JPAC's history section; mission reports and after-action reviews on file at JPAC's Detachment 4; and interviews with multiple officials at JPAC's Central Identification Laboratory. Information on the recovery and identification process was also drawn from the author's personal notes from the crash site and recovery effort; McCown's MIA case file at JPAC; Eyster's daily reports from New Guinea in January and April–May 2008; the field notes of Dr. Owen Luck O'Leary; and the laboratory's final forensic report on McCown. Additional background information was drawn from Thomas Holland, John Byrd, and Vincent Sava, "Joint POW/ MIA Accounting Command's Central Identification Laboratory," in *The Forensic Anthropology Laboratory*, edited by Michael W. Warren, Heather A. Walsh-Haney, and Laurel E. Freas.

CHAPTER TEN: COMING HOME

The main sources were the author's personal notes and interviews from the funeral of Marion Ryan McCown Jr.

EPILOGUE

The main sources were interviews with Major George S. Eyster V; Sandra Patricia Eyster; and Ann Eyster Whittaker.

•

ABOUT THE AUTHOR

Bryan Bender is the national security reporter for the *Boston Globe*. He has covered U.S. military operations in the Middle East, Asia, Latin America, and the Balkans. He also writes about terrorism, the international arms trade, and government secrecy. He is currently president of the Military Reporters and Editors Association.